S0-AXJ-158

TESTIFYING IN COURT
A GUIDE FOR MENTAL HEALTH PROFESSIONALS

TESTIFYING IN COURT
A GUIDE FOR MENTAL
HEALTH PROFESSIONALS

Richard A. Gardner, M.D.

Clinical Professor of Child Psychiatry
Columbia University
College of Physicians and Surgeons

Creative Therapeutics, Inc.
155 County Road, Cresskill, New Jersey 07626-0317

© 1995 by Creative Therapeutics, Inc.

All rights reserved.
No part of this book may be reproduced in any form
or by any means without permission in writing from the publisher.

Library of Congress Cataloging-in-Publication Data

Gardner, Richard A.
    Testifying in court : a guide for mental health professionals
/ Richard A. Gardner
        p.   cm
    Includes bibliographical references and index.
    ISBN 0-933812-39-6 : $30.00
    1. Forensic psychiatry—United States.   2. Evidence, Expert—
United States.   I. Title
KF8965.G37   1995
347.73'67—dc20
[347.30767]   95-11203
                                                                          CIP

PRINTED IN THE UNITED STATES OF AMERICA
10   9   8   7   6   5   4   3   2   1

To those who have been enthusiastic and receptive
   to my contributions:

   Your commitment has served as an impetus to my
productivity.

   It has also served as a welcome antidote to the
frustrations and misrepresentations one need be
willing to tolerate while testifying in a court of law.

CR

Other Books by Richard A. Gardner, M.D.

The Boys and Girls Book About Divorce
Therapeutic Communication with Children:
The Mutual Storytelling Technique
Dr. Gardner's Stories About the Real World, Volume I
Dr. Gardner's Stories About the Real World, Volume II
Dr. Gardner's Fairy Tales for Today's Children
Understanding Children: A Parents Guide to Child Rearing
MBD: The Family Book About Minimal Brain Dysfunction
Psychotherapeutic Approaches to the Resistant Child
Psychotherapy with Children of Divorce
Dr. Gardner's Modern Fairy Tales
The Parents Book About Divorce
The Boys and Girls Book About One-Parent Families
The Objective Diagnosis of Minimal Brain Dysfunction
Dorothy and the Lizard of Oz
Dr. Gardner's Fables for Our Times
The Boys and Girls Book About Stepfamilies
Family Evaluation in Child Custody Litigation
Separation Anxiety Disorder: Psychodynamics and Psychotherapy
Child Custody Litigation: A Guide for Parents
  and Mental Health Professionals
The Psychotherapeutic Techniques of Richard A. Gardner
Hyperactivity, The So-Called Attention-Deficit Disorder,
  and the Group of MBD Syndromes
The Parental Alienation Syndrome and the Differentiation
  Between Fabricated and Genuine Child Sex Abuse
Psychotherapy with Adolescents
Family Evaluation in Child Custody Mediation, Arbitration,
  and Litigation
The Girls and Boys Book About Good and Bad Behavior
Sex Abuse Hysteria: Salem Witch Trials Revisited
The Parents Book About Divorce—Second Edition
The Psychotherapeutic Techniques of Richard A. Gardner—Revised
The Parental Alienation Syndrome: A Guide
  for Mental Health and Legal Professionals
Self-Esteem Problems of Children: Psychodynamics
  and Psychotherapy
True and False Accusations of Child Sex Abuse
Conduct Disorders of Childhood: Psychodynamics and Psychotherapy
Protocols for the Sex-Abuse Evaluation
Psychotherapy with Children Alleging Sexual Abuse
Psychogenic Learning Disabilities: Psychodynamics
  and Psychotherapy
Dream Analysis in Psychotherapy

Equal Justice Under Law
　　　　　　　　The alleged foundation of our legal system

Unequal Injustice Under Cunning Manipulation of the Law
The More Money You Have, the More Injustice You Can Buy
　　　　　　　　The actual foundation of our legal system
　　　　　　　　　　　　　Richard A. Gardner

CONTENTS

ACKNOWLEDGMENTS

I deeply appreciate the dedication of my assistants, Donna La Tourette, Carol Gibbon, and Linda Gould for typing the manuscript of this book in its various renditions. I am especially grateful to Donna La Tourette for her additional work on this book, her role in its production and indexing and, even more importantly, her valuable contributions to its content. Special thanks are due to Danny Angel, who installed our new desktop publishing system, and whose expertise with this technology helped make the successful composition of this book possible. I am also grateful to Muriel Jorgensen for her diligence in copyediting the manuscript. She provided useful suggestions and, at the same time, exhibited respect for my wishes regarding style and format. In addition, she also provided extremely valuable contributions to the book's production. I am grateful to Susan Cox for her diligence in the proofreading of the page proofs.

My next acknowledgment will come as a surprise to the reader, especially because it is not a common acknowledgment for an academic. Specifically, I wish to express my deep gratitude to my commanding officers at the U.S. Army Hospital in Frankfurt-am-Main, Germany, who from 1960 to 1962 assigned me my first patients in the realm of forensic psychiatry. During this period I had the opportunity to testify on numerous occasions in military courts as well as German civilian courts. Because military dependents were not under the jurisdiction of military courts (one cannot court martial a dependent wife or husband, no matter how much one might want to), crimes committed by such individuals were adjudicated in German courts. These experiences served as the foundation for all my subsequent work in the field of forensic psychiatry. In fact, if not for them this book might never have been written.

I also wish to express my gratitude to the hundreds of attorneys whom I have encountered during the more than 35 years I have been involved in providing courtroom testimony. I am not referring here only to those whose positions I have supported, but to those who viewed me as their adversary. Although I have much more benevolent feelings for the former than for the latter, both categories of attorneys have contributed to my growth as a psychiatrist, especially because of the objectivity required in a court of law—an objectivity often ignored in the mental health professions.

Last, I wish to express my deepest gratitude to the thousands of children and parents in whose cases I have provided testimony. All (and I use the word without hesitation) have suffered because of their embroilment in adversarial proceedings. All of you are testament to Voltaire's wisdom: "I have been ruined but twice in my life: once when I lost a lawsuit and once when I won one." At every point in my involvement I have always made every attempt to lessen your suffering—especially by trying to serve as an impartial examiner, rather than as an advocate—in adversarial proceedings. I believe that I have thereby reduced your grief in many cases. And this book, in a sense, is designed to provide other mental health professionals with better tools for testifying in court and thereby reduce the suffering for those unfortunate enough to have become embroiled in adversarial proceedings.

INTRODUCTION

HOW I GOT INVOLVED IN
CUSTODY LITIGATION

For most, life provides many surprises and unexpected experiences. We often get caught up in events in which we never anticipated we would become embroiled. I first began testifying in court in 1960. I was fulfilling a two-year military obligation as a psychiatrist at the United States Army Hospital in Frankfurt am Main, Germany. Early in my tour of duty, it became apparent that my commanding officer had no great affection for me; nor did I have significant love for him. I viewed him as having a "military mentality," and he viewed me as having an "Ivy League mentality." (I believe that these were quite accurate conclusions about one another.) But he was a colonel, and I a captain. This difference in rank provided him with an excellent opportunity for expressing his animosity toward me, which he did by selecting me for the less desirable assignments. And I had no option but to accept them. (As they say in the military, "Orders is orders.") He considered providing court testimony to be the most repugnant of the many detestable jobs that one could have and so, not surprisingly, he assigned me these cases.

Considering his motivations, I initially assumed that the work would indeed be odious. Much to my surprise, I found legal work fascinating.

Fundamental issues of human behavior were being dealt with and questions that have plagued the greatest thinkers over the span of history had to be addressed. One had to learn very quickly in order to appear as an "expert," only a few months out of residency. (The military has a way of making "experts" out of people quite quickly.) I evaluated soldiers who were being court-martialed and learned much of interest about military law. Furthermore, I had the unique experience of giving testimony in German civilian courts. Because military courts have no jurisdiction over wives and children, such dependents could only be tried in German civilian courts. However, these people were still entitled to military medical care, including psychiatric consultation and treatment. Included in such consultations were court evaluations. I thereby found myself testifying in German courts, where I learned some fascinating things about European systems of adjudication. In order to save time, I was often flown by helicopter to the various cities in Germany where I testified. As a fringe "benefit" en route, I would hang out the side hatch (supported well, of course, by safety belts) and take photos that I could not have otherwise obtained. I never let on to my commanding officer how thankful I was to him for having provided me with these experiences; had I done so, I am certain he would have assigned me elsewhere (like winter maneuvers on the Czechoslovakian border).

In the mid-1960s (now out of the Army and in private practice), when the divorce rates started to climb, I once again became involved in lawsuits—primarily custody litigation. During that period, no-fault divorce laws were being introduced. In most states they replaced the system whereby one had to prove that one's spouse was guilty of a marital crime such as infidelity or mental cruelty. In many states this had had the effect of requiring people to involve themselves in adulterous behavior (or at least stage or claim "adultery") even if they had no desire whatsoever to do so. The new laws, though, only required the spouses to agree that they were incompatible and to live apart a prescribed period (usually one to two years, depending upon the state). Although the new no-fault laws or the easier grounds for divorce reduced the likelihood that people would have to litigate in order to get divorced, they did not reduce the frequency of litigating for money, property, and/or children.

In the 1970s things began to "steam up" in the field of custody litigation. Prior to that time women were generally viewed as the preferable parents under the *tender years presumption*. When men claimed that this presumption was intrinsically sexist, courts were sympathetic, thereby ushering in a new era of egalitarianism in custody disputes. Under the *best interests of the child philosophy*, courts were required to make custody decisions on the assessment of parenting capacity, ignoring the sex of the parent. Presumably such "sex-blind" decisions served the best interests of children. In fact, children then became open prey to both parents, each of whom claimed equal right to their custody. In the late 1970s and early 1980s the joint custodial concept became increasingly popular. The notion that one parent should have sole or primary custody and the other should be designated the visitor was also considered inegalitarian, especially by fathers who generally felt that the mothers were rewarded "most of the pie" and they, on weekends, only picked up the crumbs. Accordingly, fathers clamored for a greater "piece of the pie." In line with with this new spirit of egalitarianism, terms like "shared parenting" and "parenting plan" became increasingly popular. This too resulted in further custody litigation as fathers now had more hope for greater time with their children. The result of all these developments has been an epidemic of custody litigation unlike that which has ever existed in the history of humankind. I too, over the years, became progressively more involved in such lawsuits.

My experience with divorcing families enabled me to write a series of books, the first of which was *The Boys and Girls Book About Divorce* (hardcover, 1970; paperback, 1971), which is now in its 20th printing and has been translated into Spanish, French, Dutch, Hebrew, and Japanese. It is, I believe, the most widely utilized divorce book for children. Its companion volume, *The Parents Book About Divorce* (hardcover, 1977; paperback, 1979), deals extensively with legal issues, especially child custody litigation. It was reprinted eight times and was translated into French and Czech. Its updated and expanded second edition (hardcover, 1991a; paperback, 1991b) deals even more than its predecessor with legal issues and includes much material on sex abuse, especially sex-abuse allegations that arise in the context of child custody disputes. In the 1970s I began, as well, to publish articles on child-custody litigation in both legal and mental health journals. *Psychotherapy of Children of Divorce* (1976; update, 1990) also deals extensively with legal issues. *The Boys and Girls Book About One-Parent Families* (hardcover, 1978;

paperback, 1983) was translated into Japanese. *Boys and Girls Book About Stepfamilies* was published in 1981.

My first book on custody litigation, *Family Evaluation in Child Custody Litigation*, was published in 1982. It was around that time that I began seeing a new psychiatric disorder, primarily in children embroiled in child-custody litigation. The child is obsessed with deprecation of a parent (usually the father). On detailed investigation, I concluded that the campaign of denigration was not simply the result of parental programming ("brainwashing") but that there were significant contributions provided by the children. Accordingly, I did not consider the terms *brainwashing* and *programming* proper and introduced the term *parental alienation syndrome* to describe this disorder. My first article on this disorder appeared in 1985, and my first book describing the syndrome, *Child Custody Litigation: A Guide for Parents and Mental Health Professionals*, appeared in 1986. This book describes a wide variety of psychiatric disturbances seen in children and parents who become embroiled in highly contested child-custody litigation. It also discusses alternative modes of child-custody dispute resolution, especially mediation. The most comprehensive statement of the disorder is to be found in my 1992 publication, *The Parental Alienation Syndrome: A Guide for Mental Health and Legal Professionals*.

In the early 1980s I became increasingly involved in sex-abuse evaluations, especially sex-abuse allegations that arose in the context of child-custody disputes. I was convinced that some of these were false, even though I fully appreciate that genuine child sex abuse is widespread. Accordingly, I began working on criteria for differentiating between true and false sex-abuse accusations. This culminated in my first book on the subject, *The Parental Alienation Syndrome and the Differentiation Between Fabricated and Genuine Sex Abuse Allegations*, published in 1987. In 1989 *Family Evaluation in Child Custody Mediation, Arbitration, and Litigation* was published, a book that was an update and significant expansion of *Family Evaluation in Child Custody Litigation* (1982).

My involvement in sex-abuse evaluations in association with child-custody disputes led to my involvement in such assessments in the context of nursery school and day-care centers. Since the late 1980s I have been involved in other types of sex-abuse cases, especially cases in which adult women belatedly accuse their fathers and other relatives of having sexually abused them in childhood. In addition, I have been asked to conduct sex-abuse evaluations in cases involving accusations against clergymen, scout masters, teachers, and neighbors. Accordingly, I was (and still am) involved in some nationally known cases in this category. These experiences resulted in my *Sex Abuse Hysteria: Salem Witch Trials Revisited* (1991c), *The Parental Alienation Syndrome: A Guide for Mental Health and Legal Professionals* (1992a), and *True and False Accusations of Child Sex Abuse: A Guide for Legal and Mental Health Professionals* (1992b). The latter books represented a vast update and expansion of my 1987 volume on these subjects. In 1995, my *Protocols for the Sex-Abuse Evaluation* was published. This book is generally considered to provide the most comprehensive and detailed protocols for systematically conducting sex-abuse evaluations.

In addition to the aforementioned books, numerous articles of mine on the subject of child-custody litigation and sex abuse have appeared in both legal and mental health journals. To date, I estimate that I have provided court testimony in about 300 cases (testimony lasting as long as three days in some cases). Most often, I have testified in child-custody disputes, and more recently in sex-abuse cases (child-custody disputes, nursery school and day-care centers, and incestuous families). On occasion I have testified in other areas, e.g., competence, liability, and sanity. Whereas my testimony in child-custody cases has taken place in civil courts, my testimony in sex-abuse cases has been in both civil and criminal courts. Furthermore, for a variety of reasons, I have done many legal evaluations that were never brought to the point of my providing court testimony. In *all* of my court appearances, I have always been recognized as an expert by the court in the areas in which I was providing testimony. Such areas include child custody, sex abuse, child development, learning disabilities, competence, and child psychotherapy. At this point (mid-1995), to the best of my recollection, I have testified in 25 states. I have also provided testimony in Canada (Hamilton and Thunder Bay).

Since the 1960s I have lectured to psychiatrists, psychologists, social workers, and other mental health professionals in major medical schools, teaching hospitals, and universities throughout the United States. I have lectured to lawyers at bar association meetings, judges' colleges, and law schools. I have provided presentations in 48 states (including Alaska and Hawaii) on child-custody litigation and sex abuse. I have lectured in many foreign countries: Mexico (Mexico City, Cancun), Canada (Vancouver, Edmonton, Winnipeg, Sudbury, Hamilton, Toronto, Montreal), Bermuda, England (Oxford), Belgium (Louvain), Holland (Amsterdam, Utrecht), West Germany (Frankfurt am Main, Goettingen), Austria (Vienna), Sweden (Stockholm, Malmo), Norway (Oslo), Russia (St. Petersburg, Moscow), Italy (Varese), and Japan (Tokyo, Kobe, Kyoto, Hiroshima).

WHY I GOT INVOLVED
IN CUSTODY LITIGATION

As I look back, I ask myself the question: "How come, and why?" (We psychoanalysts are always asking questions like these.) There were other child psychiatrists who were not getting involved. When they smelled litigation (even over the telephone), they ran the other way. In fact, that was the usual reaction. I couldn't run the other way in the military, but I certainly had the freedom to refuse such referrals in my private practice. One factor related to my recognition that such involvement enhanced my expertise as a psychiatrist. Psychodynamic psychiatry (and, to an even greater extent, psychoanalysis) is probably the most speculative of all the allegedly scientific disciplines. In fact, it is reasonable to say that it is much more an art than a science. We spin off the most fantastic explanations for human behavior and often come to believe our own delusions. I learned in the military that courtroom experience could be a wonderful antidote to such professional morbidity. Good lawyers are schooled in separating fact from fantasy, evidence from speculation. In cross-examination one must "stick with the facts." Observations and direct quotations carry weight. Speculations, fantasies, theories, and hearsay have no place in good testimony. Although such involvement has often been very demanding and emotionally draining, I will always consider this aspect of the experience to have been an extremely beneficial one for me (with regard to my professional competence, not my mental health).

Whereas in the early days I was somewhat fearful about testifying in court, as the years progressed and as my expertise grew I gradually reached the point where I found it an enjoyable game (as strange as that may seem).

I have often compared it to a fencing match. I learned the rules and I played rather well. I didn't even view it as a fencing match between equals; rather it was a match between a person with a longer sword and more protection (the lawyer) and a person with a shorter sword and less protection (the individual on the witness stand). The rules of cross-examination put the witness (even the so-called expert) in the weaker position. The witness is competing with an intrinsic handicap, built into the rules of the sport—which is what adversary litigation basically is (at least for the lawyers). Accordingly, when the witness wins it is an even greater victory. The cross-examining attorney was allowed to confine me to yes-no responses, select and focus on out-of-context material, and pose questions in a way that distorted and misrepresented my opinions. Getting across one's point under such circumstances was indeed a challenge, and I often felt that I was successful in accomplishing this. And this brought an ego-enhancing gratification to many of my court appearances.

As my knowledge and expertise grew, I became ever more relaxed and confident on the stand and realized that I was often providing impressive performances. (The courtroom scene is also a "spectator sport.") Furthermore, my books on custody litigation were becoming increasingly popular and were often referred to as the "standards" and "classics" in the field. Throughout the country they were being quoted by lawyers and judges. Decisions derived from my publications and testimony occasionally cited these works as legal precedents. Although, as mentioned, my experiences have primarily been in the areas of child custody and sex abuse, I believe that the principles provided in this book should prove useful to mental health professionals who may be asked to provide testimony in other realms. It is basically a book that will help prepare them for going into battle and will hopefully enhance the likelihood that they will prevail. Its aim is to help others avoid some of the problems I have dealt with, and sometimes the traps I have fallen into. I believe that those who are willing to take the trouble to read it carefully and implement its advice will find it useful, and may even be grateful for what is contained herein.

AN IMPORTANT CAVEAT

Mental health professionals who plan to involve themselves in forensic psychiatry should recognize that they are subjecting themselves to confrontations and criticisms above and beyond what they may be exposed to in the course of therapeutic work. In therapy, we certainly expect patients to be angry at us sometimes, and most mental health professionals deal with this adequately. We recognize that most often (but certainly not always) anger directed toward us is a product of patient psychopathology and we tend not to personalize it. In the courtroom, however, it is an entirely different situation. There are serious consequences to the outcome of the confrontations, e.g., in custody cases the future lives of the children and in sex-abuse cases whether or not a person is imprisoned.

Mental health professionals involving themselves in such cases should recognize that they are *not* dealing with *patients* or *clients* but *litigants*. The lawyers, with rare exception, are generally *hired guns*, by every good definition of the word. The courtroom is generally a war zone and the evaluator, when on the witness stand, is very much in the middle of the battlefield. One must appreciate that even before entering the case one of the litigants, and often both, are going to be angry at the evaluator for the conclusions. And the lawyers, whose roles are to zealously fight for their clients' positions, will often use every bit of ammunition known in order to knock down, compromise, humiliate, and even destroy the evaluator. Accordingly, one needs a thick skin for this kind of work.

I am not claiming that my skin has become so thick over 35 years that such involvement never bothers me. The years of involvement on the witness stand have had their psychological toll, but it is the price I have been willing to pay for the benefits to be derived from such involvement, especially the contributions I have made to the people who have come to me for help. I believe that my work in custody cases has resulted in more judicious placement for the children I have evaluated and that my involvement in sex-abuse cases has protected many innocent people from being incarcerated and many of those who were guilty to be dealt with properly.

ONE
A BRIEF REVIEW OF THE HISTORICAL DEVELOPMENT OF THE ADVERSARY SYSTEM

INTRODUCTION

Throughout this chapter, when I use the term *adversary system*, I am referring to a legal procedure that prevails in the United States, England, and its former colonies. It is a system based on the principle that the best way of learning the "truth," when two parties have diametrically opposed positions, is for each to present his or her case before an impartial decision maker(s) (a judge and/or a jury). Each side is permitted to withhold (within certain guidelines and procedures) facts that might compromise its position and to present those that support it. The theory is that these opposing presentations provide the impartial evaluators with the best opportunity for ascertaining the truth. In the adversary system, this method of data (evidence) collection is used primarily as a method of dispute resolution. The fact finder (whether it be a judge or jury) serves primarily in a neutral position. Although it originated in criminal proceedings, where the dispute is between a prosecutor and an accused person, it is used in civil proceedings as well, where the dispute is between a plaintiff and a defendant.

When I use the term *European* legal system I am not including the English legal procedure (from which the American is more directly derived) but the European *continental* procedure, which is generally referred to as the *inquisitorial* system. In this system the judge is less neutral and more active in the cross-examination process than the judge in the adversary system. It has been used more extensively for criminal than for civil proceedings. Later in this chapter I will discuss these two systems in greater detail. The adversary system is also the predominant one in countries that were formerly English colonies. Furthermore, countries on the European continent have utilized varying degrees of adversarial procedures within the inquisitorial structure. For example, Spain, Italy, and France utilize systems that are direct derivatives of the inquisitorial procedures from the 15th century, whereas in Germany, the inquisitorial system is fused with a number of traditional adversarial procedures. And the Soviet system, although modeled after the inquisitorial system, has been modified by Marxist principles and restrictions on certain freedoms taken for granted in the West.

It is not my purpose to present here a detailed history of the adversary system. Not only do I not consider myself knowledgeable enough to do this, but it goes beyond the purposes of this book. Rather, I will outline the system's development, with particular emphasis on issues that are relevant to modern-day practices in divorce law and especially custody litigation. My main purpose here will be to demonstrate that we are still using techniques that have their origins in the ritualistic practices of primitive tribes, ancient societies, and the "Dark Ages" (literally) and that these techniques are used in only a small fraction of present societies, namely England (and its former colonies) and the United States. As I trace the historical development of the adversary system, I will point out how some of these early practices have served as the basis for many of our present-day procedures in divorce and custody litigation.

In the preparation of this material, I first sought references from attorneys, friends, and colleagues—many of whom I hold in high regard. I was surprised how little they knew about the historical development of the system, and I was even more surprised to learn that it is rarely taught as a formal course (or even part of a course) in the majority of law schools in the United States. Law students are presented with the adversary system as *the* system for resolving various kinds of disputes. Most are not even told about alternative methods of dispute resolution traditionally used in many other societies. Many, at the time of graduation, automatically assume that the adversary system is the best and the most efficient. And many maintain this unquestioned allegiance to the system until the end of their professional careers.

The material on the history of the adversary system presented in this chapter was obtained primarily from the comprehensive articles by Neef and Nagel (1974), Landsman (1983), and Alexander (1984). In addition, some material was obtained from the sections on the legal profession and the law of evidence in the *Encyclopaedia Britannica* (1982). These thorough and extensive articles provide numerous references to the primary source material from which this chapter has been derived. I would strongly recommend these articles to those readers who wish more detailed information on this subject. In addition to these sources, I present information that has become part of my general knowledge and experience, the sources of which are no longer known to me. The reader will soon note that my comments on the adversary system are quite critical. This is the result, I believe, of the fact that my experiences with it have primarily been in its utilization in divorce/custody proceedings. I recognize that its utilization in other kinds of cases may be less psychologically damaging to the clients. Accordingly, the reader does well to keep this in mind when reading this book and to recognize that the reforms I will recommend at the end relate primarily to its utilization in custody/visitation disputes. I suspect, however, that its utilization in other areas may also be psychologically traumatic and that the criticisms I present here may very well be applicable to these areas of utilization as well.

PRIMITIVE SOCIETIES

Our knowledge of the kinds of dispute-settling mechanisms utilized by primitive societies is largely speculative. There are, however, some general principles subscribed to by those who have investigated this area. One cannot put a particular date on this phase. What is described here is a *developmental theory* that ascribes a sequence of procedures utilized for dispute resolution. The sequence began at different times in different places, and there are some societies today still operating in accordance with these primitive principles.

In the earliest primitive societies, wherein the whole society lived in a small cluster in which everyone knew one another, the general method for dispute resolution was through compromise. The purpose was to reach a solution that would enable the individuals to live as harmoniously as possible with one another after the settlement of the dispute. Such groups avoided any system that might result in residual animosity between the disputants. This was especially important because the extended families of the disputants might harbor residual animosity toward one another, which could be even more detrimental to the survival of the small group. Accordingly, compromise techniques were utilized rather than the winner-take-all principle that the modern adversary system employs. Although many judges attempt to get the disputants to compromise, if they are unsuccessful and the dispute goes to trial there is often a winner-take-all victory for the party that prevails. Present-day compromise analogies are labor management disputes and disputes between businessmen and customers, wherein both parties recognize that, following the dispute, they may still have to have a relationship with one another. It is only when communities become larger and individuals are able to remove themselves entirely from one another that a more adversarial and permanently divisive arrangement comes to prevail.

Another method of primitive dispute resolution that could insure cohesiveness was one in which leaders imposed punishments in accordance with speculations regarding what ghosts, dead ancestors, and other spirits considered to be justifiable punishments. In this way, the punishers were not viewed as being personally responsible for implementing the punishment, but were merely considered to be the vehicles through which these higher powers operated. As a result, the system still allowed for a certain amount of cooperation between the accusers and the accused, between the punishers and the punished. The system was also a reflection of the ignorance of tribal leaders. By ascribing wisdom to spirits and other unseen powers, tribal leaders compensated for their own lack of understanding of the complex and even unknown issues that were involved.

As societies became larger and more complex, the likelihood increased that the disputants would not subsequently have to live with one another. Under these circumstances, other methods of dispute resolution evolved. However, the aforementioned method by which supernatural powers were brought into play served in later phases as well. Invoking these unseen powers served to protect the accusers and the punishers from the acrimony of the guilty party and thereby allowed for ongoing cooperation between the parties.

I believe it was unfortunate that more complex and recent societies developed systems that did not take into proper consideration the factor of ongoing cooperation between the disputants. Had they done so, we might not have gone so far afield regarding our methods of dispute resolution; we might have maintained the systems of compromise first utilized by the earliest societies. In a sense, these most primitive methods were the most advanced in that they were the methods most likely to insure resolutions that promised ongoing conciliation.

In many Asian societies the mediation/conciliation notion is very much present to this day. In Japan, for example, people who are unable to resolve their disputes themselves generally take them to mutually respected elders who attempt to resolve the dispute privately. People who are unable to resolve their disputes by themselves or with the help of elders are generally viewed as socially atypical and may be stigmatized. The fear of such social stigma deters them from carrying the dispute further. When, however, a situation does warrant intervention by third parties, they may resort to neighborhood dispute-resolution centers. It is rare that individuals must go further and use attorneys to resolve their disputes. This is one of the reasons why there is now only one attorney for every 10,000 people in Japan; in the United States there is one attorney for every 320 people.

In recent years we have witnessed evidence of increasing appreciation of conciliatory procedures in the United States. Alternative methods of dispute resolution are now being taught in some law schools, and divorce mediation has also gained some limited popularity recently (Coogler, 1978; Folberg and Taylor, 1984).

GREEK SOCIETY

The ancient Greeks, as the first step toward the resolution of a dispute, submitted the conflict to an arbitrator. This was the earliest form of dispute resolution used by the ancient Greeks. The arbitrator was often paid a small fee and his goal was to try to reconcile the parties. One could not go to court before one had gone through the arbitration process. As is the case with the inquisitorial system, all the information from both the disputants and the witnesses was submitted to the court in written form before the trial began. This information was sealed in a special box and opened when the court was ready to hear the case. These documents were read by a panel who decided the case on the basis of this written material. It is of note here that at that point in Greek history the disputants did not confront one another. Residua of this absence of confrontation are to be found in the inquisitorial system used in the Middle Ages. And it may be that some residua of this are present in our present-day adversary system, where there is still some restriction on the disputants confronting one another, although they are certainly in the courtroom together.

As the Greek society became more complex, the disputants were permitted to be represented by orators or rhetors (people who used rhetoric). It was in this setting that there developed the practice of dramatic presentations, a practice that probably has its counterpart in modern-day courtroom lawyers, especially those who pride themselves on their oratorical skills. When used in moderation, this residuum of the Greek system is probably of benefit to the client; however, when the dramatizations reach the point of bombast, then the courtroom becomes the stage for melodrama, hyperbole, and even a circus-like atmosphere.

It is important for the reader to note that I am referring here only to free men of ancient Greece, not to slaves. Slaves could not hope to get redress in court or bring suit against another person unless they could find a citizen to represent them. On occasion, however, a slave could be a witness. The assumption was generally made that slaves lied. Accordingly, their testimony was often accompanied by torture in order to extract the "truth." This practice discouraged masters from allowing their slaves to testify because they might be worthless as workers following their testimony. (It would seem to me that if it were indeed true that all slaves automatically lied, then a more judicious and humane way of dealing with their testimony would be to assume that the *opposite* of what they said was true. This would save both the tortured and the torturer much time and trouble.) Sometimes an ordeal (see below) was utilized when the judges were unable to arrive at a decision.

Juries were used in the Greek courts, but they voted secretly (as they do today in the United States). Following the jury's decision, the accused and the accuser together were permitted to suggest to the court a reasonable punishment, suggestions that were given serious consideration. This practice is often seen in courtrooms today when both sides are given the opportunity for input to the judge before sentencing.

Among the ancient Greeks, trial by ordeal was commonly used as a method of ascertaining whether a party was guilty or innocent of a crime. It generally involved subjecting the accused to a wide variety of pains and tortures. Guilt or innocence was established on the basis of the accused's reactions to the ordeal. Ordeal by water was especially popular among the ancient Greeks. This system operated in a world that was viewed as anthropomorphized, i.e., inanimate objects were considered to contain spirits and to have wills, thoughts, and feelings. The Greeks assumed that if the accused were to float in the river, then it indicated that the river found the accused objectionable and did not wish to embrace him or her. If the accused sank, this indicated that the individual was innocent and good and that the river thereby wanted to embrace him or her. Attempts were usually made to pull the sinking innocent to safety. In contrast, the person who floated would be punished for the crime, often by being put to death.

Trial by fire was also common among the ancient Greeks. The accused might prove innocence by walking on fire, swallowing fire, or passing through flames unharmed. Boiling liquids and hot irons were also used to determine guilt or innocence, based on the extent of the injuries sustained after exposure. Other ordeals involved the use of snakes, swords, and poisons. Girls whose virginity was questioned were compelled to descend into a cavern in which a poisonous snake had been placed. If they were bitten by the snake, it indicated that they were no longer virgins. Among the ancient Greeks, male nonvirgins were not considered to have committed a crime. This more liberal attitude toward male nonvirginity persists in many societies to this day, and there are many societies today that basically do not deal with *female* nonvirgins any differently than the ancient Greeks did.

ROMAN SOCIETY

In *early* Rome a priest was generally considered crucial when dealing with legal matters. Priests were considered to be the ones most knowledgeable about how to deal with the problems of finding out which of the disputants was telling the truth. The priests kept their laws and techniques in personal secret books. Gradually, however, lawyers did evolve, replacing the priests. They advised their clients and pleaded for them in court. The parties rarely engaged in direct confrontation with each other in the courtroom. As was true in Greek society, slaves, as a matter of course, were tortured on the witness stand. Juries were used, but only in cases involving senators and equites (horse-mounted warriors with status halfway between senators and common men). Either the defendant or the plaintiff could object to the selection of certain jurors at his trial (a practice still in operation today).

Like the Greeks, the Roman lawyers enjoyed their orations. Sometimes a client would have many lawyers representing him, each of whom would provide elaborate speeches to the magistrate and jury. Histrionics were accepted and even considered desirable. It was not uncommon to display the wounds of a client and bring injured children before the court. Lawyers were in oversupply and they often competed with one another to obtain clients. They were allowed to hawk their wares in the streets and often hired "clappers" to applaud their orations in the courtroom. They hoped thereby to enhance their reputations and obtain more clients. Although the judge and jury might decide that a defendant was guilty, it was the accuser's responsibility to impose the punishment, and sometimes he did not have the means to do so.

In the early fourth century *A.D.* a new development took place in Roman law. Whereas previously trials were open and public, they now became secret. This was rationalized by the argument that members of the judicial hierarchy were beyond criticism, were dedicated to work honestly and efficiently, and could be trusted to make judicious decisions. They also rationalized secret judicial decisions as necessary for the stability of the empire. Accordingly, prior to the downfall of the empire, the Romans abandoned a very complex and sophisticated courtroom system for a somewhat totalitarian one. It regressed thereby from a more democratic and egalitarian legal system to one that infringed much more on the freedom of individuals. However, certain aspects of the Roman system persisted and can be found in the legal profession today, e.g., lawyers representing their clients, juries and jury selection, and lawyers advertising.

TRIAL BY ORDEAL

Trial by ordeal was one of the three commonly used methods of trial used in the Middle Ages. Reference was made to it in my discussion of ancient Greek society. However, in the Middle Ages it became much more commonly used. Trial by ordeal is based on the belief that God will intervene and by a miraculous sign indicate whether the litigant undergoing the ordeal was in the right. It has appeared in many countries and at different times. Ordeal by fire is an ancient tradition. The accused might establish innocence by walking on fire, swallowing fire, or passing through the flames unharmed. In many societies the ordeal was only used after the judge or jury found itself unable to arrive at a decision. Trial by ordeal was especially popular during the Middle Ages in Europe and England. A priest usually administered an oath before the ordeal, and quite frequently the ordeal was conducted on Church grounds. Of the three forms of trial used in the Middle Ages (trial by battle and trial by wager being the others), trial by ordeal was the most likely to be under church auspices. In England common forms of ordeal required the litigant to carry a red-hot iron bar a certain distance or place an arm in boiling water for a prescribed period. If the litigant's burns did not fester after a prescribed period (usually three days), he or she was considered to be in the right. A typical example of trial by ordeal was to place the litigant's arm in a seething cauldron. Afterward, it was carefully enveloped in cloth, sealed with the signet of the judge, and three days later was unwrapped. The guilt or innocence of the party was ascertained by the condition of the hand or arm. The theory was that the guilty individual's arm would be infected or seriously scarred and the innocent person would remain unhurt.

Immersion in deep water was another common form of ordeal. The person was considered to be in the right if he or she sank rather than floated. Ordeal was used for women who were charged with witchcraft. In the Middle Ages (and subsequently) women charged with witchcraft were often assumed to have had sexual intercourse with Satan. In the course of such sexual relations, part of his spirit was considered to have entered into and invested them. Their human attributes were considered to be altered by his spirit, which, because it is lighter than air, lightens the body. The woman charged with witchcraft was dropped into a river with her hands and feet tied. If she sank she was considered innocent, because the presumption was made that the devil had not invested her. If she floated she was considered guilty and punished, sometimes by being burned to death. The Salem Witchcraft water-dunking ordeal is an example of the utilization of trial by ordeal in America.

Trial by ordeal is basically a statement of mankind's feelings of impotency and appreciation of ignorance regarding dispute resolution and the determination of whether or not an alleged perpetrator did indeed commit a crime. In trial by ordeal the assistance of supernatural powers is brought into play. There is a certain grandiosity in trial by ordeal in that it is based on the assumption that the deity, the Great Judge, is paying attention to the particular ordeal and manipulating the events in the service of helping the good or the innocent survive the ordeal.

Trial by ordeal was generally an earlier phenomenon than trial by battle (to be discussed below). In trial by ordeal the individual is helpless in playing a role in his or her fate, and it is left entirely in the hands of higher powers. In trial by combat, which generally came later, some power was placed in the hands of the combatants in the decision regarding guilt and/or innocence.

Trial by ordeal in English society was traditionally for the lower classes, whereas trial by combat was for the upper classes. This was especially the case because trial by combat required the ownership or utilization of horses and often involved disputes concerning land ownership (which poor people, obviously, did not have). Trial by ordeal was declared unacceptable in England and on the Continent in 1215 by the

Fourth Lateran Council (to be discussed below). Once the Church removed priest participation, the practice quickly fell into disuse. However, residua of the method, I believe, exist today in adversary proceedings. Many attorneys, by design, will subject witnesses to ordeals of exhausting and painstaking interrogation. The individual is brought to the point where he or she may not even realize what is being said. Such tactics could also be viewed as a method of extracting a confession by subjecting the individual to such an ordeal. Here, verbal whips are used as the method of torture.

TRIAL BY COMBAT (TRIAL BY BATTLE)

Trial by combat (or trial by battle) was a common form of trial utilized in the Middle Ages, especially on the Continent. In trial by battle the disputants or their representatives (sometimes referred to as *champions*) engaged in physical combat until one side yielded or was subdued. The party who prevailed was considered to be telling the truth. The defeated party could admit defeat by speaking the word "Craven" (*Middle English, cravant:* overthrown, coward) or by stopping the battle when it was obvious that that party was defeated. Or the battle continued until one party no longer had the capacity to go on or was slain. In certain serious criminal matters, it was understood from the outset that the fight would continue until one party was indeed killed. The fight was overseen by judicial officers, and the combat began only after each of the combatants had taken a solemn oath that his cause was just. Each party would invoke the judgment of God and declare that he did not use sorcery or enchantment. A fundamental assumption of trial by combat is the notion that being right is expected to be productive of the just result. This is related to the belief that justice will prevail and that God will see to it that good will win out over evil.

In this form of trial, as in trial by wager (to be discussed below) and trial by ordeal, Divine intervention was considered to be the important determinant as to who would prevail. There was no presentation of evidence. The individual was often permitted to be represented by a substitute, called a champion. Accordingly, trial by combat has also been called trial by champion. Because women and children were considered unable to fend for themselves, they were almost routinely provided with champions. Professional champions were available to fight for anyone who paid them. The battle would begin when the challenger threw down a glove and the person who accepted the challenge picked it up. Sometimes the weapons used were not designed to be lethal; rather they were made of wood, bone, or a horn. In criminal cases, however, the loser was hanged or mutilated. In civil cases the loser would cry "Craven," which meant that he had perjured himself, was a liar, and was guilty. He then paid a fine and came to be known as a liar. On occasion the two combatants would continue to fight until nightfall ("before the stars appeared"), at which point the battle would be discontinued and the person who appeared to be prevailing was considered the innocent party. This practice protected people from being killed. Sometimes champions were individuals who had proven themselves successful in previous trials by battle. Trial by battle clearly favored the rich, who either had better martial skills or could afford to hire those with such skills. Trial by battle was common throughout most of northern Europe in the early Middle Ages and was introduced into England from France after the Norman Conquest in 1066. It was never a very popular or influential form of adjudication in England.

In one form of trial by combat the accuser might have been a public prosecutor. He would then battle the accused, the defendant. Accordingly, the accuser was not only a prosecutor, but in many cases also served as the executioner. This was especially the case when champions were not used. Although champions were probably used earliest for women or children because women and children were less capable of "fighting their own battles" and thereby less capable of proving their innocence, champions later came to be used by men as well. The use of champions came after the realization that it didn't seem reasonable that the taller, stronger, and more powerful defendants would almost invariably be innocent.

An interesting tradition evolved in trial by battle. In criminal proceedings between an accuser and an accused, the men themselves would fight. However, if the dispute was about ownership of land, then the battle was fought by champions who represented the disputants. This was done because, if the participants themselves fought and both died in battle, there would be no owner for the land in dispute.

It was not until 1819 that trial by combat was abolished in England, but it had fallen into disrepute long before that time. The last recorded trial by champion took place in England in 1571. Many critics of the adversary system (including the author) claim that it is a direct extension of trial by battle. Those who defend the system claim that this is not the case, for the following reasons: (1) trial by battle was basically outlawed in England by the 13th century, (2) there is no evidence for its use beyond the 16th century, and (3) adversarial proceedings in their present form did not emerge until about the 18th century. However, the tradition in trial by battle of the litigants being represented by another party has its equivalent in the adversary system. I believe that we have not moved as far from trial by combat as many proponents of the adversary system profess. In many cases it is still very much a "bloody battle." Peoples' lives have literally been destroyed by the system. Many have been drained completely of all financial resources. Many have suffered irreparable psychological damage over the course of protracted litigation. The practice of ending the battle at sunset, and making a decision then, is in a sense more humane than the system today, where litigation can go on for years.

TRIAL BY WAGER

Wager of law and ordeal were more common in England than trial by battle. Wager of law required each of the litigants to take an oath that his claims were true and to produce other persons, usually referred to as *compurgators*, to support the litigant's oath by making their own oaths. It was also called *trial by compurgation*. It was basically a "character test" in which the oath taker established his or her case by demonstrating good standing in the community. The compurgators were not asked to provide testimony about the facts of the case, but only served to guarantee that the oath taker was an honest person. The more compurgators who would swear on behalf of a litigant, the greater the chances of acquittal.

In trial by wager the person took an oath. Such an oath involved invoking supernatural powers, who were allegedly listening to the oath, operating at the time of the trial, and who would intervene on behalf of the person who was innocent or right. There was an appeal here to a supernatural power, with the implication that if one was not telling the truth, God would somehow punish the individual. The participants did not expect that God would rule immediately; instead the perjurer would be punished at some future date. Such oaths were taken seriously by primitive peoples. They were also taken seriously by people in the Middle Ages, who genuinely believed that if they lied, there might be some punishment in the hereafter.

Residua of trial by wager exist today. The oath that we take in court with our hand on the Bible is a derivative of this system, as is the use of character witnesses. There is little reason to believe that the vast majority of people who take such oaths today under the European/American system take them seriously and can be relied upon not to perjure themselves from the fear that they will be punished by God. They might fear punishment by the court for perjury, but not punishment by a supernatural power. Perjuring oneself before a court of law is routine nowadays and most often promulgated by the attorneys (the champions). Recent examples of this are the Watergate hearings and the more recent Iran-contra congressional hearings. On the basis of my own experiences with divorce/custody litigation, I would say that 80 to 90 percent of all the clients I have seen will lie in court without any hesitation or guilt. Although attorneys profess publicly that it is unethical for them to encourage their clients to perjure themselves, this is routinely done. One method is to foster lies of omission. Because there may be some readers who are not familiar with the difference between lies of omission and lies of commission, I will define this important distinction here. A lie of omission is simply a kind of deceit in which an individual knowingly omits data in the service of misleading the listener. In a lie of commission the individual adds fabrications toward the same goal, namely, that of misleading the listener. Lies of commission are not permitted by the adversary system, but lies of omission are not only permitted but are actively encouraged. As I see it, a lie of omission is no less a lie than a lie of commission; it is a form of deceit. A man who does not tell a woman with whom he is amorously involved that he has a sexually transmitted disease is lying by omission. A woman who does not tell her husband that he is not the biological father of the child she is bearing is also lying by omission. Obviously, the consequences of such silences may be grave. Although the system will not uniformly condone all such egregious examples of lies of omission, its principle of sanctioning such withholding of vital data often produces similar grievous results. But clients and their attorneys often go further and actively support lies of commission as well. Even character witnesses are generally not uncomfortable perjuring themselves. Accordingly, the residua of trial by wager are primarily ritualistic. They exist in the oath taken on the Bible and in the character witnesses. And, like most rituals, their original purposes have long since passed into oblivion.

In recent years, some states have changed their courtroom procedure and no longer require a witness to take an oath on the Bible and/or may omit the word "God" from the oath taken before testifying. In some European countries witnesses are allowed to object to taking an oath and are permitted to substitute a solemn affirmation. In Denmark, oaths in legal procedures have been abolished. In the Soviet Union, consistent with the antireligious position of the government, oaths and solemn affirmations are prohibited in the courtroom.

FOURTH LATERAN COUNCIL—1215

The three methods of trial used in the Middle Ages were not mutually exclusive and often coexisted in the same area. Often the accused could choose the method of trial. All three methods were based on the premise of Divine intervention. Direct heavenly intercession was postulated for ordeal and battle, and eternal damnation was supposed to enforce trial by wager. The emphasis was on the judgment of God rather than on the judgment of man. Very little use of evidence was considered necessary, nor were fact-finding procedures considered important. Because of the heavy reliance on Divine intervention, there was little concern with the appellate process. Active participation by both the accused and the accuser was central to the three medieval methods, as it is to the adversary system. Such participation is not central to the inquisitorial system (to be discussed below).

In the year 1215, the Fourth Lateran Council prohibited Church participation in trial by ordeal. The Lateran Councils were ecumenical councils held in the pope's palace in Rome (the Lateran Palace) between 1123 and 1517. Pope Innocent III's 1215 edict against trial by ordeal ended the practice, because priestly participation had been one of its fundamental components. At the same time, both ecclesiastical and secular critics began a series of sustained attacks on trial by wager and trial by battle, but these were not prohibited. These systems of determining guilt or innocence did, however, become far less frequently utilized. As a result, a partial vacuum was created that permitted the development of alternative systems for ascertaining whether an accused did indeed commit a crime. On the Continent the inquisitorial system emerged as the predominant system, as is the situation today. In England, however, other systems evolved, culminating in the adversary system, which took its present form in the 18th and 19th centuries. I will first discuss briefly the inquisitorial system and then discuss in greater detail the evolution of the adversary system, first in England and then in the United States.

THE INQUISITORIAL SYSTEM

As mentioned, in 1215 the Fourth Lateran Council banned Church participation in ordeals. In addition, wager of law and trial by battle were also on the wane. On the Continent the inquisitorial system evolved. This procedure was the product of combining certain aspects of the laws of ancient Rome (Roman law) with judicial principles developed in European ecclesiastical circles (canonical law). By the 16th century this amalgam of Roman and canonical approaches was dominant throughout Continental Europe. A central element in this approach was active inquiry by the judge in order to uncover the truth. He wielded great power, so much so that it became prudent to limit his authority by means of strict evidentiary requirements. Generally, the judge could only convict a criminal defendant under two circumstances: (1) when two eyewitnesses were produced who observed the crime or (2) when the defendant confessed. Circumstantial evidence was generally not considered sufficient to warrant conviction. However, under these same laws, judges were authorized to use torture to extract the necessary confessions. Torture came to be viewed as an excellent and reliable method of finding out "the truth." Thus, torture became a tool of judicial inquiry and was used to generate the evidence upon which the defendant would be condemned.

At this point I will discuss some of the reasons why the inquisitorial system developed on the Continent and why the adversary system evolved in England. In 1215, the same year that the Fourth Lateran Council convened, the English barons forced King John to sign the Magna Carta, which guaranteed certain rights and liberties to Englishmen (men, not women; nobility, not lower classes). Certain rights of individuals (upper class) were thereby established, and a precedent was set for the democracy that ultimately evolved in England. In contrast, on the Continent, derivatives of Roman law still prevailed—especially the notion of the centralized authority of the state. Another factor that contributed to the expansion of the inquisitorial method on the Continent was the Catholic church's fear of the spread of anti-Catholic movements.

One of the earliest and most powerful of the anti-Church groups was the Albigenses (a name derived from the city of Albi in southern France), who spread anti-Church doctrines throughout Europe (especially southern Europe) in the 11th and 12th centuries. They posed such a threat to the Church that a special crusade, the Albigensian Crusade (1208-1213) was organized in the attempt to exterminate them. In addition, the earliest papal inquisition, the medieval Inquisition, was set up to bring to trial and execute these and related groups of heretics. These proved successful in obliterating almost completely the Albigensians and related movements.

However, in the late 15th century the Spanish Inquisition was established in Spain to extinguish Jews and Muslims, who were then considered to be a threat to the Church. And in the 16th century the Roman Inquisition was set up, this time to stem the rising tide of Protestantism. The methods utilized by the medieval and Spanish Inquisitions were much more brutal and sadistic than those used by the later Roman Inquisition. The methods described below were more typical of the two earlier inquisitions than the third. All three, however, served in part as models for the secular inquisitorial systems that developed on the Continent.

The Church did not consider the relatively primitive judicial systems operative at that time to be sufficient to handle the widening threat of the anti-Catholic movements. The key word here is *heresy*, and the inquisitions were constantly searching for heretics, who were then brought before them. Heretics were rounded up, persecuted, and tried for their heresy. There was little concern for evidence and veracity of witnesses. Accused individuals did not know the names of the witnesses against them, for fear of retaliation. Witnesses in support of the accused were not permitted to appear. There was no confrontation (cross-examination) of witnesses. Death by fire was made the official punishment for heretics, and they were usually burned at the stake. If they warranted special clemency, they were sentenced to life imprisonment. However, because life imprisonment was a much more expensive proposition, it was rarely utilized. Torture was used to elicit confessions. The Church and the State worked together, with the Church authorizing the torture and the State being the arm of enforcement. The inquisitors could excommunicate and label as heretic any civil magistrate who refused to inflict the punishment the inquisitors prescribed. The methods of torture commonly used to elicit confessions included the rack, thumbscrew, and flogging. There was an extremely high rate of conviction; acquittal was rare. Archbishops traveled throughout the Continent and would force people to denounce one another. Those who refused risked being considered heretics themselves. Often the cases were judged without the names of the accused or witnesses. The inquisitions were not universally embraced. It was not utilized in Scandinavian countries, nor did it take root in England. This is partly related to the fact that these countries were geographically isolated from the Continent. Also, the Albigenses and related sects did not spread as far north as Scandinavia or across into England. Thus, there was little need for the utilization of the medieval Inquisition in these areas. In addition, as mentioned, a parallel system of adjudication was developing in England, one based more on individual rights.

Whereas the adversary system is based on the premise that truth will emerge as an outgrowth of a clash between adversaries, the inquisitorial system is based on the assumption that truth is most likely to emerge as a result of an inquiry by neutral persons, such as judges. The judge in the inquisitorial system is a fact finder, but a very active fact finder. It is he who controls the mechanisms of inquiry. In the American and English adversarial system, the lawyers collect and present the facts and the judge is a more neutral hearer of the facts, although he does have some power of inquiry.

In the European system, both sides generally provide all pertinent information to the court and to one another prior to the onset of the proceedings. In the adversary system, each side tries to keep "aces up its sleeve" in order to catch the other side off guard and limit opportunity for response. In the adversary system, the attorneys call in the witnesses. In the European system, the judge calls in the witnesses and interviews them in the presence of the attorneys and the clients. Whereas in the adversary system the witnesses are generally selected because they are likely to support a particular side's position, in the European system the witnesses are more neutral and are generally called in by the judge.

In the inquisitorial system the judge is an active fact finder. The European trial is more an investigation rather than a battle of two opposing sides. The judge collects all the information before the trial and is given information by both attorneys. Witnesses are not interviewed by the attorneys for either side before the trial begins. Rather, they are interviewed by the judge. They do not belong to either side; rather, they belong to the judge. The witnesses testify in an uninterrupted narrative. The judge is the one who questions the witnesses. After the judge interrogates the witnesses, the lawyers can do so but not in the restrictive cross-examination type of inquiry used in the United States and England.

As a person who has appeared as a court-appointed expert on many occasions, I am sympathetic to the inquisitorial system's practice of giving witnesses (expert and nonexpert) free rein to present their testimony. The argument given by proponents of the adversary system that such restriction ultimately balances out and that all the facts are ultimately presented to the judge is a myth. I have never been involved in a case where this has proven to be true. What usually happens is that only a fraction of opposing arguments is presented to the court. But even those arguments that are brought forth are usually presented at some other date, long after the judge (no matter how brilliant and no matter his or her memory) has forgotten the initial points.

THE DEVELOPMENT OF THE ADVERSARY SYSTEM FROM THE 13TH TO THE 17TH CENTURIES

The foundations of our present-day adversary system in England and the United States were laid down primarily between the 13th and the 17th centuries. As mentioned, the Fourth Lateran Council created a partial vacuum with regard to methods of dispute resolution and determination of guilt or innocence. On the Continent conditions prevailed that led to the development of the inquisitorial system. In England, for reasons already stated, the climate was one in which the adversary system gradually evolved. Four institutions developed that served as foundations for the system: juries, witnesses, judges, and lawyers. I will discuss each of these separately and then describe how they coalesced into the adversary system, first in England and then in the United States. Of course, discussing them separately is somewhat artificial in that each influenced the others.

Juries

The Normans probably brought the jury system to England at the time of the Norman Conquest in 1066. The jury has served many different functions over the years. In the 11th century juries served to inform the court of cases it should try because jurors, as friends and neighbors of the parties involved in the litigation, were more likely to know what was going on in the community. The early jurors, however, were not really peers of the litigants because they were generally freeholders (landowners and titled individuals). They were free men, and they were often higher on the social ladder than those on trial.

Originally jurors were not the neutral fact finders they are today, listening to others present the facts; rather, they were actively involved in collecting evidence. Traditionally, they were individuals who lived in the same community as the litigants and were thereby more likely to have information about the events to be dealt with at the trial. In fact, not to have such knowledge was considered reason for disqualification. In addition, there was often a time gap between the assignment of the jury members and the beginning of the trial, during which time the jurors were expected to collect facts relevant to the dispute. They were empowered to make investigations, to ask questions, and to acquaint themselves with the details of the case. Accordingly, Divine guidance was replaced by collection of pertinent data. Jurors could be punished if the judge decided that their decision was the "wrong" one. This check on the jury system enhanced dedication and honesty and was probably a factor in its survival. The growth of the jury system as a method of fact-finding reduced and obviated the utilization of torture, another method of fact-finding. The jury, then, was the adversary system's means of fact-finding, in contrast to torture, which was the inquisitorial system's method of obtaining information.

From the 13th to 15th centuries, the practice evolved that the litigants could challenge the jurors; if the jurors were found to be biased, they could be removed. From the 15th century onward, jurors generally became less involved in out-of-court investigations and began to rely upon facts presented in court as the basis for their decision. The use of a considerable volume of evidence had the effect of shifting the function of the jury from active inquiry to passive review and analysis. Juries also evolved from being the king's representatives to being independent entities, unconnected with the objectives and influences of the government. It was not until 1705 in civil cases and 1826 in criminal cases that jurors could be drawn from places other than the immediate locality in which the dispute arose. This was done to reduce the likelihood that jurors would enter the courtroom with preliminary, and possibly prejudicial, information. Our present-day grand jury is similar in its function to the earlier juries (prior to 1705); it is primarily an inquisitorial body that seeks evidence in order to determine whether a trial should be held.

In the late 1300s and early 1400s contact between the litigants and the jurors after the submission of a case was significantly curtailed to reduce the possibility of prejudice and influence. Separation of the litigants from the jury is a central element in the adversary process and is one of the ways in which the jury system laid the foundation for the development of the adversary system.

By the 18th century the jury was not only viewed as a neutral and passive fact-finding group but as a check on judicial despotism. The Constitution of the United States, fashioned in the 1780s, specifically incorporated the right to jury trial as a check on other institutions of government, not only the judiciary, but those who chose the judges and wrote the laws. The juries served as monitors of the laws by having the power to control the judges empowered to implement them.

Witnesses

Up through the 15th century the testimony of witnesses was held in low esteem. In fact, witnesses were not generally used in English trials until about 1500. Voluntary testimony was viewed with suspicion, and witnesses could not be compelled to testify against their will. However, in the 16th century the presentation of testimonial evidence grew dramatically. The information provided by witnesses came to replace private juror inquiry as the basis for decisions in criminal cases. Prior to 1555 witnesses were not compelled to testify, but after that year witnesses were compelled to do so. This change more deeply entrenched the role of the jury as a passive fact-finding group, and the witnesses became primary sources of information for the court. Attention shifted away from the juror's private knowledge toward witnesses' testimony as a primary source of evidence.

In the mid-1500s, we see the beginnings of the development of rules governing the presentation of evidence, especially by witnesses. During that period rules were developed that prohibited the use of data from untrustworthy informants, such as proven perjurers. In addition, wives were not permitted to testify against their husbands. Other rules that came into being were the *best-evidence rule* (the court must only consider evidence that has high credibility and must deem as inadmissible evidence of low credibility), the *opinion rule* (the court has the power to give priority to the opinions of experts over those who have no expertise in a particular area), and the *hearsay rule* (the court has the power to give priority to testimony based on direct observations of the witness as opposed to information transmitted indirectly and/or via second and third parties). The opinion rule defined the kinds of testimony lay people could provide and the kinds experts could provide—with strict definitions for each. It was not until the 18th and 19th centuries, however, that the rules of evidence became more formalized and stringent.

Judges

During the 12th and 13th centuries the offender was generally forced to pay the family or his victim compensation for causing the victim's death or injury. However, it gradually evolved that the state became viewed as the wronged party, because offenses were viewed as breaches of the "king's peace." Judges then became viewed as representatives of the king. By the 13th century English law and procedure had become sufficiently technical to warrant the designation of full-time judges. Before 1300, judges were civil servants, often appointed by the king. After 1300, judges were appointed *only* from among the ranks of the serjeants (*sic*), a small group that constituted the elite of the bar.

The aforementioned changes notwithstanding, judicial procedures between 1300 and 1700 were not truly adversarial. In the typical trial of the 1500s and 1600s, the judge served as an active inquisitor, whereas the jury was passive. The judge would directly question the defendant and the witnesses. Following these inquiries there was a kind of freewheeling discussion among the witnesses, defendant, and judge. When the judge was satisfied that he had heard enough, he would summarize the case to the jury, charge them to decide it, and they were generally not allowed to eat or drink until a decision had been rendered. Lawyers were not involved in the judicial process to an active degree. The defendant was not usually represented by counsel and was often prohibited from having legal representation. The defendant was not allowed to call witnesses, conduct any real cross-examination, or develop an affirmative case. The judge wielded great power over the jury and was free to urge a verdict upon the jury. Up until 1670, jurors who refused to follow the judge's directions could be jailed or fined. There was no appellate procedure by which the litigants could secure review of the decision. These procedures did, however, have certain precursors of the adversarial system: they were orally contentious, were decided upon by the evidence of witnesses, and were judged by a neutral and passive jury. However, the emphasis was not upon adversarial presentation of evidence. The judge was a very active participant, the protection against misleading prejudicial evidence was minimal, and appellate review was not available.

The focus was not so much on accurate data collection and evidence, but on the development of legal principles of procedure.

In the latter part of the 17th century, judges became less active fact finders and took a more passive role in the courtroom. They devoted themselves more to serving as umpires. Judges today in the English and American adversarial system are neutral. Their duties are to interpret the laws by which the contestants are operating and to enforce the rules of procedure during the trial. They do, however, have great power in that they can manipulate the court procedures in a manner prejudicial to the party he or she believes to have the better case.

In the United States, since the beginning of the 19th century, further developments insured that judges would remain neutral and passive fact finders. They were required to adopt a neutral political stance, could not run for office, and were discouraged from supporting political candidates. They were also required to adhere strictly to rules of evidence and were limited as to the kinds of remarks that they could make in the course of a trial.

In the 19th century the appellate courts developed. They were designed to be the guardians of the adversary system, insuring that judges complied with the rules of evidence and procedure. If not, the appellate courts could reverse a decision in order to insure compliance with the new principles. In addition, appellate courts could reverse what they considered to be the trial court's misinterpretation or misapplication of the law.

Lawyers

About the beginning of the 14th century, requirements were established regulating the education and conduct of those who would be allowed to argue cases in the king's courts. In time, the advocates formed special organizations, called Inns of Court, for training members of the bar. In the 15th and 16th centuries, as the jury's investigative role diminished and juries became more passive, the responsibilities of the advocates increased. Lawyers undertook the job of supplying the jury with the evidence upon which the decisions would be based. By 1600, lawyers had established for themselves their special status as masters of the evidence-gathering process.

It was around 1577 that an important change occurred that became central to the development of our present-day adversary system. It was at this time that the concept of attorney-client privilege came into being. It granted lawyers special exemption from the obligation to provide evidence that had been provided by clients, if divulgence of such evidence might compromise the client's position. Lawyers then developed a special status of immunity from certain courtroom obligations. I consider this to be a mixed blessing. On the one hand, it increased the likelihood that the client would be honest with the attorney in a manner similar to the confidential relationship that patients have with their doctors. On the other hand, it gave sanction to lies of omission, a practice that reflects a basic weakness in the system that has produced grief for many over the centuries.

During the 15th through 17th centuries lawyers were generally less concerned with gathering accurate evidence than they were with narrowly defining various legal principles. The lawyers involved themselves in endless nitpicking about formal legal rules and procedure. They wasted incredible amounts of time arguing fine points of law rather than the substance of their cases.

Codes governing lawyers' behavior are basically products of the 18th and 19th centuries. One of the central ethical conflicts was this: On the one hand, attorneys were expected to be officers of the court and speak the truth. On the other hand, they were expected to be loyal advocates on behalf of their clients. This problem has been resolved, primarily, by allowing attorneys to withhold from the court any information that might compromise their client's position. This is basically a lie of omission. It is justified on the grounds that the adversary is also permitted to engage in lying by omission. At the same time, both sides are encouraged to present before the court those arguments that support their clients' positions. Presumably, such evidence will also include what each side has attempted to withhold. The assumption, then, is that all the data and evidence will ultimately be brought before the court. In practice, this assumption is rarely realized because of the complexity of the process and the fact that very few can afford the indulgence of a trial in which all pertinent evidence is brought before the court. Furthermore, lies of commission are frequent. If one sanctions lies of omission, one cannot be surprised if lies of commission soon follow. The result of all of this, I believe, is that attorneys are trained in law school to be liars. In Chapters Seven and Eight I will discuss in detail further views of mine on lawyers' role in adversary proceedings, especially with regard to their participation in bringing about stress and psychopathology in their clients.

THE DEVELOPMENT OF THE PRESENT-DAY ADVERSARY SYSTEM IN ENGLAND

The development of the adversary system, which prides itself on giving the accused and the accuser the opportunity to confront one another directly in an open courtroom, was retarded significantly in 1487 by Parliament, when it established the judicial proceedings that came to be known as the Star Chamber proceedings. The Star Chamber proceedings were established at the instigation of King Henry VII in order to curb the power of feudal nobles. The council met in the royal palace of Westminster in a room decorated with stars on the ceiling, thus the name *Star Chamber*. Initially, Parliament defined the Star Chamber's jurisdiction over riots, unlawful assembly, and other events beyond the power of ordinary courts to control. Subsequently it widened its jurisdiction to include any other issues with which its judges or the king wished to deal. Juries were not used, the meetings were often secret, rumor was accepted as evidence, and torture was often utilized to obtain testimony. Rising resentment resulted in Parliament abolishing the Star Chamber in 1641. On the one hand, the Star Chamber's dictatorial and repressive habits played a role in suppressing the development of the adversary system. On the other hand, when the Star Chamber was finally discontinued, memory of its repressive tactics encouraged reforms that resulted in the guarantees of openness central to adversary proceedings.

The present-day adversary system dates its origins to the mid-17th century, the time of the abolishment of the Star Chamber. By the end of the 18th century the adversary system, as we know it today, was established in both the United States and England. It was during this 150-year period that both judge and jury came to conform closely to the ideals of neutrality and passivity. By 1700 decisions could be reversed and a new trial ordered if the judge believed that evidence was insufficient to warrant a verdict. By 1756 the retrial mechanism was effectively extended to all cases. After 1705, in civil cases, there was an abolishment of the requirement that juries be drawn from the exact neighborhood in which the case arose. This reduced the likelihood that jurors would have any private information to rely on when making their decisions.

In the 19th century we see the development of cross-examination. The lawyer's obligation to provide zealous representation and loyalty to his or her client's cause was the product of the 18th and 19th centuries. However, lawyers were restricted from harassing or intimidating an opponent. As proceedings became more adversarial, however, conflicting ethical demands were exerted upon lawyers. On the one hand, attorneys were expected to be officers of the court and to seek the truth; on the other hand, they were expected to be keen advocates on behalf of their clients. In the mid-19th century the emphasis shifted to zeal and loyalty (denials notwithstanding), and this is the present state of affairs. In the 19th century we see the development of courts set up for the sole purpose of deciding appeals. They reviewed trial records and determined whether errors warranting reversal had occurred. They did not conduct open hearings with clients or witnesses.

Over the last 300 years, three sets of rules have evolved that are generally considered crucial for the successful utilization of the adversary system. First, there are the *rules of procedure*, which are designed to produce in an orderly fashion a climactic confrontation between the parties in the trial. The *rules of evidence* protect the integrity of the evidence. They prohibit the use of evidence that is likely to be unreliable and might bring about misleading information to the judge and jury. These rules also prohibit the use of evidence that poses a threat of unfair prejudice against one of the parties. Last, there are certain *ethical rules* designed to serve as guidelines and controls for the attorneys. They require, for the clients' protection, that counsels zealously protect the clients' interests at all times. They require the attorney to be loyal to the client. Because of the danger that attorneys will become excessively swept up in the battle, they are not permitted to harass or intimidate an opponent. Courts of appeal insure that litigants and judges will comply with these mandated procedures.

THE ADVERSARY SYSTEM
IN THE UNITED STATES

In the early days of colonization the legal systems were very much like those of primitive societies, because there were few individuals in any particular setting and the need for compromise was very great. Because of the separation of the various colonies and their colonization by different countries, there was little uniformity in their legal procedures. However, arbitration was commonly used. Many of the emerging middle class who came to America had been abused by the aristocratic government in England. Because many colonists came to America with a feeling of antagonism toward the status quo and the entrenched establishment, there was resistance against the incorporation of English law into the colonies. The colonists were intent on preventing the formation of another aristocracy. This reluctance predictably became even more pronounced at the time of the American Revolution. The American system of government is based heavily on the concepts of self-reliance and individualism. Accordingly, there was great distrust of a central authority, and the judiciary was the target of such distrust. Any move toward centralization was resisted, and individuals were viewed as capable of defending themselves in courts. However, in time the English adversary system came to be viewed favorably because the judge, as umpire, exerted far less authority than the magistrates under Continental law. The adversary system came to be viewed as the best protection of the middle class against the aristocracy. It was viewed as excellent protection against judges becoming arms of the state. The framers of the Constitution, then, included such revisions as due process, the right to a trial by jury, habeas corpus, the right to counsel, the right to bail, and the privilege against self-incrimination. It would be an error to conclude that the founding fathers were particularly interested in the protection of the lower classes of society; they were interested in protecting the middle class's commercial and entrepreneurial interests.

During the pre-revolutionary period judges and juries became increasingly independent of political and governmental influence. This was one of the cornerstones of the American Constitution. The founding fathers were adamant in their belief that trial by jury was a central protection for the freedom of individuals. But juries had to be established that were independent of government control (while still complying with the law). Prior to the 1800s, judges were likely to have been political partisans who openly advertised their opinions in court. After Thomas Jefferson was elected, his supporters removed a number of incompetent or partisan Federalist judges from office. Supreme Court Chief Justice John Marshall became the standard by which the propriety of judicial behavior came to be measured. He was the first of the truly impartial chief justices. Since the early 1800s, judicial conduct was controlled by applying strict rules of evidence and by placing exacting limits on the types of remarks that could be made at the close of a case.

The adversary system has flourished in the United States, so much so that it is reasonable to say that there is no other country in the world in which it has enjoyed such widespread utilization. It is also reasonable to say that the United States, at this time, is the most litigious country on earth. Lieberman (1983) devotes significant sections of his book to a description of the reasons why litigation has burgeoned in the United States. He states that the further one goes back in history, the more individuals have considered themselves to be at the mercy of nature and the less likely they were to view calamities that befell them to be related to indignities they suffered at the hands of other human beings. As man gained more control over the environment, other individuals came to be blamed more frequently for the traumas and catastrophes that inevitably befell humans. If one views botulism, for example, to be God-sent, then one cannot blame fellow human beings for one's suffering. However, if one considers the disease to be caused by food contamination, which was the result of negligence on the part of those who packaged the food, then the blame is easily traced back to some human agent. In such situations the sufferer is likely to want retribution, or at least to prevent the recurrence of the event. Because the United States has been one of the countries at the forefront of modern scientific advances and its associated environmental control, this shift of blame from God to mankind has been particularly evident here, especially in the last century.

Another factor that has contributed to the litigiousness of the American people relates to the fact that we are a "melting pot." In the countries from which our immigrants came, there was generally a greater degree of homogeneity among the population than exists in the United States. Accordingly, there was general unanimity with regard to what customs and traditions should be adhered to. In the United States, however, we have a potpourri of traditions that are often in conflict with one another. Thus there has been a greater need to utilize higher powers to enforce uniformity of behavior. In a democratic country, the imposition of rules by a dictator, monarch, aristocrat, or group of oligarchs is not a permissible form of regulation. Rather, the rule of law, equally applied to all, has been the guiding principle for bringing about compliance with social standards.

With an ever-enlarging body of laws, there has been an ever-growing number of methods for challenging and altering the legal structure. This is an intrinsic concomitant to the growth of a democratic system governed by laws. Accordingly, since the earliest days of our government, litigation has been ubiquitous. Although the democratic countries of Europe have also witnessed a significant growth in the body of their laws, there has been an important difference with regard to the growth of litigation. Specifically, in the past, only those highest in the social hierarchy enjoyed the protection of the laws, and it was only they who were significantly involved in litigation. In America, however, every person, no matter how low on the social scale, has the right to the protection of the law and can litigate. Although poorer people were (and still are) less likely to enjoy the services of the most skilled attorneys, the route to litigation was (and is) very much available to them—a situation that did not prevail in Europe, where the litigation potential was enjoyed primarily by the aristocracy.

Another factor that has contributed to the litigiousness of Americans is our individualism, which lessens the likelihood that people will submit to more community types of dispute settlement. Our spirit of individualism has gone so far that people are increasingly representing themselves in court and refusing the assistance and guidance of attorneys. Part of this practice relates to the expense of engaging professional counselors, but part relates to a system that allows individuals to represent themselves, referred to as *pro se* (Latin: for oneself). Although there is some general recognition that one is likely to do better in litigation when one is represented by an attorney, the court systems provide ready vehicles for *pro se* representation.

Since World War II, litigation has expanded in other ways in the United States. Whereas in the past it was generally considered unethical for attorneys to solicit litigants (this is generally referred to as *ambulance chasing*), this is no longer the case. In December 1994 (the last available figures) there was approximately one practicing lawyer for every 302 people in the United States. At that time there were 866,000 practicing lawyers (American Bar Association, 1995) in a population of 261,647,395 (U.S. Census Bureau, 1995). Obviously, competition is keen, and under these circumstances it is not surprising that soliciting litigants has become an acceptable practice. For example, a well-known American litigator recently instituted a suit against the Union Carbide Company for the death of thousands of Indians in Bhopal as the result of a leakage of lethal chemical gases from one of its plants there. He is asking for 15 billion dollars. If successful, he can conceivably retain as his fee one-third of this amount. Although it is not clear from newspaper accounts whether this lawyer solicited clients in India, with incentives such as this it is no surprise that other attorneys quickly found their way to India to sign up clients in the streets, hospitals, and their homes. Of course, personal monetary gain is denied as the primary motivating factor for these "Samaritans"; rather, they self-righteously proclaim that innocents must be protected from the negligence of giant corporations and that they are thereby serving in justice's cause.

At one time in the United States there was an adage, "You can't fight City Hall." This is no longer the case. One cannot only sue City Hall; one can sue local governments, states, civic officials, and even the federal government. People who are only tangentially and remotely involved in a case may be sued. People can be liable for acts undertaken by others. For example, the National Broadcasting Company (NBC) was sued by a girl's family because her rape followed a film depicting a similar assault from which they claim the assailant obtained his ideas. Law suits may be initiated on mere suspicion, the extent of the injury may remain unknown, and the plaintiff's lawyer may hope that a discovery procedure may force the defendant to prove the case against himself (herself). Recently, I saw a magazine cartoon depicting a man watching a salesman giving his pitch on television. The caption read: "Having trouble with your next-door neighbor? Sue; it's less trouble than you may think." A court may impose a liability on an entire industry because the wrongdoer could not be identified. In such a setting it is no surprise that litigation is ubiquitous and that most of the best law schools are flooded with applicants.

The adversary courtroom battle is often viewed as a sport similar to that of a traditional sporting event. Each side has its attorney(s), client(s), and witness(es). The court's rules of procedure, evidence, and lawyer ethics have their analogies in the rules of the various sports. People cheer for their side, especially if brought to public attention. Attorneys get swept up in their clients' battles, and the name of the game is to win. The game or sport theory becomes even more apparent when a trial is brought to public attention and gets significant coverage in the public media. The litigants, however, may not view the adversary trial as a game; rather, they might justifiably view themselves as the pawns in the game.

One could argue that the adversary system is indeed a blessing and that it is a manifestation of the most powerful and effective way that individuals in a democratic society can protect themselves from indignities, whether they be inflicted by other individuals or by the government. If a government is oppressive, then should we not have a means of fighting back? If someone breaks a contract, should we not have the means of enforcing commitment?

One cannot deny that individuals should have a means of fighting back, and it may very well be the case that the adversary system provides us with the best method for protecting ourselves. However, it is not well designed to deal with situations in which there was no intrinsic opposition at the outset. When the doctor's intent is to help and he errs, should one make him or her an adversary? Should two parents who have differences regarding who is the better parent utilize the adversary system to make this decision? In our conflictual society we create conflicts when there may initially not have been any. Courts working within this system are not permitted to decide disputes that are not brought to them by genuinely adverse parties. A controversy *must* be created—even if there was none before—if the courts are to consider hearing the case. For example, courts decide whether to remove life-sustaining machinery from terminally ill comatose patients. Adversaries are created in order to function within the structure of the adversary system. The courts thereby manufacture an adversarial situation out of one that is not intrinsically adversarial for the purposes of fitting individuals into the Procrustean bed of the adversary courtroom proceeding.

As mentioned, the adversary system is based on the assumption that the truth can best be discovered if each side strives as hard as it can to bring to the court's attention the evidence favorable to its own side. It is based on the assumption that the fairest decision can be obtained when the two parties argue in open court according to carefully prescribed rules and procedures. They face each other as adversaries in a kind of constrained battle procedure. Criticism of this method of dispute resolution dates back to ancient times:

Both Plato and Aristotle condemned the method. They considered the advocate as one who was paid to make the better cause appear the worse, or endeavor by sophisticated tricks of argument to establish as true what any man of common sense could see was false. The feeling against advocacy in the criminal law was so strong that, at least in the case of the more serious kinds of crime, a right to representation by a trained advocate was nowhere generally recognized until the 18th century *A.D.* (Encyclopaedia Britannica, 1982).

CONCLUDING COMMENTS

At the time of this writing (mid-1995) I have been involved in adversarial proceedings for 35 years. There are few in the mental health professions who have spent more time on the witness stand as an expert. I have not simply been involved as a participant in the proceedings. In addition to providing testimony, I have observed the system at work, admittedly from the vantage point of the witness stand. I am convinced that the system has far less to do with the administration of justice than it has to do with the acquisition of money for lawyers. It allows for endless bickering, hairsplitting, and spin-off litigation. I have been involved in very complex cases in which the same lawyers are working together as part of the defendant's team and yet are involved in spin-off lawsuits in which they are one another's adversaries. In such cases I have been warned by one member of the team to be careful of what I say to the other, lest I compromise that attorney's position in one of the derivative lawsuits. Attempts to change the system by the introduction of such procedures as mediation and arbitration are generally met with enormous resistance by members of the legal profession, and a wide variety of rationalizations are utilized, the most common one being that it is the best system we have for learning "the truth" and for resolving disputes. Those who, like myself, consider it one of the worst for learning "the truth" are not likely to get very far with our attempts to bring about change. The main reason for this is that legislators, who are in the best position to effect such changes, are for the most part lawyers themselves. Many work part-time in the very firms that keep generating a flow of money into their coffers. And judges themselves, who one would think would be the first to be fed up with the system, are not likely to do very much about changing it. First, the system ensures them a steady flow of cases. If there were fewer cases reaching their courthouses, there might be fewer judges needed. And they, too, come from law firms and go back into law firms after retirement. Accordingly, if the expert on the witness stand wonders why there is all this nitpicking, he (she) does well to remember that it has less to do with the commitment that "justice prevail" and more to do with the fact that the more nitpicking, the longer the litigation, the more spin-off lawsuits, the more money the lawyers will make. Even the seemingly ethical position that it is the obligation of lawyers to zealously support the client's position is quickly ignored when the client runs out of money. Although the lawyer may be required by professional ethics to continue representing the client, the zealousness with which such representation is conducted evaporates rapidly.

It is not surprising, then, that adversarial proceedings are primarily for those who can afford to pay for them. There is a direct correlation between the length of the trial and the amount of money the parties have. Basically, the system is not available to the poor and even those of medium income (unless they are prepared to be wiped out in a short time). It operates in "full bloom" for the very wealthy, those who can afford to pay high-priced lawyers to involve themselves in the endless nitpicking that the system generates. At the time I write this, the O. J. Simpson trial is attracting worldwide (I repeat, *worldwide*) attention. Simpson, a well-known black celebrity, is being accused of murdering his former wife and a male friend of hers (both white). I do not know whether O. J. Simpson committed these crimes. I do know that if he were a poor black man, he would not be getting the same trial. In fact, within a few weeks (or at worst a few months) he probably would have been found guilty of murdering two white people, and in all probability sentenced to death by lethal injection. O. J. Simpson, however, who has millions of dollars at his disposal, is able to afford many high-priced lawyers (commonly referred to as a "dream team") who, presumably, are "the best that money can buy."

Furthermore, going back to the question of "justice," which is what the system is allegedly supposed to ensure, I am convinced that in the vast majority of cases considerations of justice are less important than other factors having nothing to do with that lofty goal. There are laws that will support anyone's position, and it is just a matter of a lawyer's finding those that support a particular client's position. The law works similarly to the Bible. A religion will find statements therein that will support its beliefs and selectively ignore those that do not. A recent well-known example: A woman named Lorena Bobbit cut off her husband's penis. Obviously, this is an act that engenders enormous emotions, which are generally divided along gender lines. For obvious reasons, this trial also enjoyed worldwide attention. Long before the trial I made the following statement:

> I am convinced that even before all the facts are known, the vast majority of people on the jury know exactly how they are going to vote. And after all the "facts" are in, most will still hold to their original positions. But even if some do change their positions, the next step will be to learn from the lawyers what laws can be invoked to support one's position. If one wants to find Lorena Bobbit innocent, then the most convenient one would be "temporary insanity." If one wants to find her guilty, then one should merely learn what the legal name is for the criminal act that had been perpetrated. The system basically provides the rationalizations to do what judges and juries want to do in the first place.

For the reader who does not already know: Lorena Bobbit was found not guilty, on the basis of "temporary insanity."

Mental health professionals who provide courtroom testimony should appreciate these important factors that are operating when they provide testimony. They should appreciate, also, that their testimonies, as brilliant as they may be, may be entirely ignored because of factors having absolutely nothing to do with the facts of the case, the justification for their conclusions, and even "justice." Accordingly, they should not take it too personally when their recommendations are ignored by the court or are modified in such ways that their contributions are of little value. Nevertheless, this is the system that we have at this point. And this is the system within which one must work if one is to be of help to the people who are its victims (I use that word without hesitation). One can operate on a parallel track, as have I, and try to bring about changes in the system through public statements and articles about its depravities. At the end of this book I will devote a chapter to changes that might be effected that could improve the system, but the main focus of this book will be on providing testimony within the system and, hopefully, enabling the evaluator to be of help to clients and patients, the enormous drawbacks of the method notwithstanding.

TWO
CONDUCTING THE
FORENSIC EVALUATION

INTRODUCTION

In this chapter I focus on the kinds of forensic examinations mental health professionals are asked to conduct in the context of child-custody and sex-abuse litigation. I believe, however, that most of the principles presented herein are applicable, with minor modifications, to other types of forensic evaluations such as sanity and competence cases. Furthermore, my purpose here is to provide only general principles with regard to conducting such evaluations. Elsewhere (Gardner, 1989, 1992a, 1992b, 1995) I have provided specific details regarding conducting such evaluations in the context of child-custody disputes and sex-abuse litigation.

When a forensic examination is being conducted under a court order (often the case in a child-custody and/or sex-abuse dispute), it is crucial that the examiner require that the exact assignment be spelled out. For example, if the order only indicates a sex-abuse evaluation, the evaluator may find himself (herself) restricted from making comments on custody—which obviously is going to be affected by the outcome of the sex-abuse evaluation. Although the parties may not pay particular attention to this point throughout the course of the evaluation, once the examiner has presented his (her) conclusions, the nonsupported party and/or attorney is likely to pick up the fact that the examiner was only asked to conduct a sex-abuse evaluation and was not requested to do a custody evaluation.

Also, the examiner should make sure that the order has been signed by the presiding judge prior to proceeding. Such orders are generally prepared by one attorney, with or without the approval of the other, before being submitted to the presiding judge. Many years ago, I did not look carefully enough at the alleged court order and, at the end of my evaluation, the nonsupported attorney brought to my attention that there was no bona fide order. My position in the courtroom was significantly weakened in that case and I learned well from that bitter experience. Forewarned is forearmed.

Examiners do well to make every reasonable attempt to evaluate all the primary parties involved in the lawsuit. Generally, the two sides have very different opinions regarding the issues involved, and obtaining input from both sides (especially with joint interviews) puts the evaluator in the best position to assess the situation. Such an approach is exactly the opposite of the method used by the adversary system wherein each side utilizes its expert to argue its position before a judge and/or a jury. This system deprives itself of the free-flowing and open interchange of information that is often the best way to learn what is really going on. In a child-custody dispute the mother and father invariably have very different opinions regarding each other's assets and liabilities regarding child rearing. Interviewing only one of the parents places the evaluator in a significantly compromised position for conducting a proper assessment of parental capacity. When there is a sex-abuse accusation in the context of such lawsuits, it is usually the mother who is accusing the father of having sexually abused the child. Accordingly, we have three parties involved: the accuser, the alleged perpetrator, and the alleged child victim. Without interviewing all three parties, the evaluator is seriously compromised in his (her) ability to provide a proper assessment of the situation—especially with regard to whether the alleged molestation actually occurred.

Accordingly, before examining anyone, the examiner should take every reasonable step to involve the participation of all concerned parties. I recognize that this is much more easily accomplished in civil than in criminal cases, but this impedance should not preclude the examiner's making an attempt anyway. Sometimes lawyers will say that it is unconstitutional for the plaintiff's examiner to interview the defendant because this would deprive him (her) of the right to remain silent, as guaranteed by the Fifth Amendment of the United States Constitution. Although the Fifth Amendment guarantees defendants the right to remain silent, it does not require them to do so. Nor does it restrict them from speaking to anyone and everyone they wish to. I have seen many sex-abuse cases in which the defendant has been very eager to speak to the plaintiff's experts but was prevented from doing so by his (her) attorney. Lawyers, especially in criminal trials, often take the position that it is best for the defendant to remain silent. Even if innocent, they fear that the client may become so tense on the witness stand that there will be inconsistencies in the testimony that may lessen the client's credibility. My own opinion is that this is a serious error and that any negative effects of occasional errors are more than outweighed by the client's deep-seated conviction of innocence. Furthermore, juries are likely to conclude that the person who does not testify had "something to hide" and that what is being hidden relates to the defendant's guilt. My experience has been that defendants who are truly innocent are generally eager to speak with responsible evaluators and feel frustrated that their attorneys prohibit them from doing so. In many such cases I am convinced that such restriction resulted in the defendant's position being weakened, especially because had I had the opportunity to interview that party, I might have supported the plea of not guilty. My experience has also been that those who refused to see me were more likely to have been guilty of the crime.

When conducting the evaluation, examiners do well to appreciate that *anything* they may say or do during the course of the evaluation may be focused on in the course of testimony. Accordingly, evaluators should be ever aware of this possibility and conduct themselves accordingly. Examiners themselves do well not to say or do anything that they would be ashamed of admitting or repeating on a witness stand or find embarrassing when revealed by another party. In circumstances in which the examiner has something to cover up—some improper statement or injudicious act—he (she) is likely to be defensive and embarrassed on the witness stand, and this cannot but compromise the credibility of one's testimony.

THE PROVISIONS DOCUMENT

Addendum I is an outline of the provisions document I send to attorneys and/or clients who invite me to conduct a forensic evaluation in the context of a child-custody/sex-abuse lawsuit. The reader does well to review at this point the three steps necessary to involve me in the case. Simply put, the first step involves attempts to have me appointed the court's independent examiner. This usually involves the caller's side asking the other side to join together and ask the court to designate me its independent examiner. If this fails, an attempt is made to obtain a court order in which I am recognized as the expert of the inviting party, but the reluctant side is required to participate in my evaluation. When the court agrees to appoint me in this capacity, it generally allows the other side to engage a parallel expert, and both parents are ordered to cooperate with both experts. When I function in this way, I make it clear to all concerned that, even though recognized by the court as the inviting party's expert, I will still conduct the evaluation as if I were indeed the court's independent examiner. If attempts to conduct the evaluation under these circumstances also fail, I am willing to interview the inviting party, without any promises beforehand that I will support his (her) position. If I do so, I am willing to come to court to testify on his (her) behalf. However, at the outset, I make it clear to all concerned that I took steps to serve as the court's independent expert examiner. If, after interviewing the inviting party, I conclude that I cannot with conviction support his (her) position, we generally part ways.

The full provisions document (Addendum II) describes in detail all the provisos for my involvement. It includes, among other stipulations, information about my fees as well as a request for the security deposit. It is to be noted that this is not an advance retainer against which fees are drawn. Rather, the money is placed in a nearby bank and is only drawn against if there has been a failure to pay. Examiners who do not require such a security deposit are inviting predictable frustration. Such examiners should remember that we are *not* dealing here with patients but *litigants*. Inevitably, one of the sides is going to be angry. And if that party happens to be the payer, the likelihood of receiving payment is extremely small—especially if such payment is for services involving testifying against the payer in a court of law. The document specifically requires the inviting party(ies) to sign a statement that my fees will be paid even if I do not support the payer's position. One of the important fringe benefits of this contract is that it protects against evaluator bias, in that no examiner is so "holy" that he (she) will not be affected by the prospect of not being paid if the conclusions do not support the paying party. This provision also provides assurance for the nonpaying party that the examiner's objectivity will not be compromised by this concern.

CONDUCTING THE FORENSIC EVALUATION

Audiotapes and Videotapes

In many cases—especially sex-abuse evaluations—it is highly desirable to make audiotapes and even videotapes of the interviews. Courts are becoming increasingly appreciative of the value of videotapes because of the recognition that they can be extremely useful sources of information. Videotapes are especially useful for comparing original statements with subsequent ones—in order to pick up alterations and discrepancies that are valuable for differentiating between true and false sex-abuse allegations. An important further benefit of the videotape is that it can protect the child from the psychological trauma of multiple interviews. If the court will permit the videotape to be shown in the courtroom, it will protect the child from direct interviews with the judge, jury, attorneys, mental health professionals, and others. It may even be used in lieu of the child's giving testimony directly. Courts vary with regard to their receptivity to the use of such taped interviews. I believe, however, that courts are becoming increasingly appreciative of their value and are thereby becoming more receptive to their utilization.

The argument that a tape can be tampered with (and therefore risky evidence) is not a good one. Although this may have been the case for audiotapes, it is not the case for videotapes. If one suspects tampering, one can have the tape examined by an expert qualified to detect the presence of such. But even a nonprofessional can often detect an unnatural interruption or break in the smooth flow of a videotaped interview. The fear of such tampering is a throwback to the times when only audiotapes were available. Tampering with them was much less likely to be recognized easily by the average person, and even experts might have difficulty if the tampering was done by an extremely skilled technician.

When I videotape interviews in the course of a sex-abuse evaluation, I generally make three tapes simultaneously, an original and two copies. I keep one in my office and I give one to each of the clients. They, in turn, may reproduce them for their attorneys or other pertinent parties. If I am serving as an impartial examiner, and I am certain that I am going to submit copies of the tape to the court, I will make another copy for the judge. Because each of the parties takes a copy of the tape at the time it is made, each has the assurance that the other is not likely to tamper with the tape. In fact, this is the best protection against tampering. One problem with videotapes is that they are extremely time-consuming to review, edit, and transcribe. This drawback notwithstanding, their advantages far outweigh their disadvantages.

Generally, I videotape the interviews of children when I conduct a sex-abuse evaluation that is confined by circumstances. For example, when I travel outside the greater New York City area to conduct an evaluation, I make every reasonable attempt to have all of the evaluation videotaped. I send in advance a detailed description of the kind of arrangement I find optimum; this is described in detail in Addendum III (the reader does well to review that document at this point). Typically, I do not have any discussions with the clients before or during breaks in the course of the videotaping. Both at the outset and at the termination of the interview, both the client and I reiterate that the videotape includes all substantive interchanges. Typically, I will begin at 8:30 or 9:00 *a.m.* and continue interviewing until 2:30 to 3:00 *p.m.,* with only short breaks. We send out for lunch and continue interviewing while eating sandwiches. During this time frame I am generally able to collect the data necessary for a sex-abuse evaluation. I try to see the child at the outset and then once or twice more during the course of the interviewing. Although this is less than the ideal arrangement possible in my office (two or three separate interviews), it suffices in most cases. At the point when I believe I have enough information to make a reasonable decision, I meet with the parents and attorneys and discuss with them my findings and recommendations. This gives them the opportunity for input prior to the preparation of my final report. It saves them from the feeling of helplessness associated with receiving a report into which they have had absolutely no input and which they feel is not properly reflective of their position. This conference, then, provides them with some sense of power. It also protects the parties from the unnecessary tensions and anxieties associated with waiting to find out what my findings and recommendations will be. In some cases, however, especially complex and vicious child-custody disputes, I cannot complete my evaluation in a six- or seven-hour time frame and may require a longer time, even staying on until the next day. (This eventuality is discussed beforehand.)

When I do evaluations in my office in New Jersey, I generally videotape those that are well circumscribed, i.e., evaluations in which only two to four hours are necessary. Under such circumstances the descriptive material described in Addendum IV is applicable. When I conduct a more extended child-custody/sex-abuse evaluation in my office, an evaluation in which the child-custody issue is the primary consideration, I may require 10 or 12 interviews. Under such circumstances I do not routinely videotape the child's interviews, although I may. The determinant as to whether I do this is the sex-abuse issue. I will generally tape-record interviews in which I anticipate that it is likely that it will include material that would be important to demonstrate while testifying.

One could argue that I should videotape *all* my sessions when I am conducting an extended evaluation. The problem with this is that there are few people who are going to take the trouble to scrutinize 12 or more hours of videotaping. Furthermore, if the people being asked to view this are attorneys, it could cost the client an enormous amount of money. One does not have this problem for well-circumscribed interviews in which the duration of the videotaping does not go beyond a few hours. In closing, I wish to emphasize that a selected video segment can be a powerful part of an expert witness's testimony. Such a segment may provide compelling evidence to support the examiner's position, evidence that may be far more powerful than anything he (she) might say directly.

Last, one fringe benefit of videotaping with the presence of the clients' lawyer present throughout, is that it makes it extremely difficult, if not impossible, for the client to sue the examiner for malpractice, or even to make complaints to the examiner's professional ethics panel. As mentioned, examiners who conduct forensic evaluations must be ever aware of the fact that they are not dealing with patients but *litigants*. And when litigants are angry, they are likely to sue. They already have lawyers at hand and have already proven themselves to be litigious. Under such circumstances, they may reflexively consider suing an examiner who has come forth with a recommendation that is not to their liking. One of the best defenses against such a lawsuit is a videotape made with the client's lawyer observing through a video monitor, especially a videotape in which *all* substantive interchanges have been recorded. If the examiner has indeed been innocent of the charges, the videotape is the best proof of his (her) innocence. Furthermore, if the examiner was acting improperly, then he (she) could argue that even the client's lawyer did not consider there to be any improprieties at the time the evaluation was being conducted.

A Suggested File Arrangement

I find it useful, when conducting a forensic evaluation, to divide my materials into six categories, each of which has a separate folder or pile of documents:

> (1) Administrative File. This includes all preliminary documents and correspondence prior to the first interview as well as all other letters and communications of an administrative nature, even up to the day of testimony.
> (2) Gardner. Clinical Notes. Here I place my own notes taken during my interviews.
> (3) Gardner. Clinical Report(s). Here I place not only my original report but updated reports.
> (4) Reports of Other Examiners. Here I place the reports of other examiners, attached to which may be my own notes and commentaries.
> (5) Legal Documents. Here I place motions, depositions, affidavits, certifications, etc. Again, I generally attach to each of these documents my comments.
> (6) Additional Documents. Here I place assorted materials not reviewed (because they have been considered to be of little probative value

or of low yield in the present lawsuit), e.g., nonrelevant documents such as pediatric medical notes (unrelated to sex abuse), hospital administrative notes, insurance forms, etc. Documents deemed worthy of review are placed in file #4 or #5. In a sense, file #6 is a "dead file."

Within each category the examiner does well to keep the documents in chronological order. As will be elaborated upon in Chapter Five, this method of organization can be particularly useful at the time one is providing testimony.

Dealing with Clients' Lying

Patients recognize that it behooves them to tell the truth if they are to be helped by their therapists. Accordingly, they are usually willing to overcome the embarrassment they may suffer in the course of shameful disclosures. In contrast, *litigants* are likely to lie, especially in a situation in which the specter of a prison sentence may be hanging over the head of the interviewee. Commonly, lawyers brief their clients prior to the forensic evaluation and advise them specifically regarding what they should and/or should not say. In child-custody disputes, each party's lawyer may warn the client about disclosures in the course of the evaluation that may compromise him (her) in the courtroom. When I recognize or suspect that this is going on, I will often say to the reluctant party something along these lines:

> I fully appreciate that you have a dilemma here. If you comply with your lawyer's suggestions that you not reveal certain information to me, you may very well strengthen your legal position. However, the more information you withhold from me, the more compromised I will be with regard to providing you with a meaningful evaluation and judicious recommendations with regard to the custody of your child(ren). I leave it to you to decide what you want to do.

I refer to this as "The-ball-is-in-your-court" principle. It is not my child who might be injudiciously placed by withholding information from me. It is their child. If they wish to lie and thereby compromise my evaluation, then they will only have themselves to blame if my well-thought-out conclusions ultimately do not serve the child's best interests.

My experience has been, however, that in the heat of the evaluation, especially during joint interviews, the pressure to present me with all pertinent information is so strong that the lawyers' briefings tend to be forgotten.

In certain respects mental health professionals are more naive than lawyers with regard to believing a patient's statements. Generally, the therapist expects the patient to be truthful. We are certainly trained to be dubious about what our patients tell us, and our antennae are ever out sensing for deceptions. But the kinds of deceits that most mental health professionals are trained to detect are self-deceptions: things that our patients are trying to hide from themselves. We are trained to be sensitive to such forms of self-deception as reaction formation, rationalization, and denial. We are also sensitive to the kinds of self-deceptions involved in the formation of many psychopathological symptoms such as phobias, obsessions, compulsions, and paranoia. In all of these symptoms there is the factor of an attempt, usually unconscious, to suppress and repress consciously unacceptable thoughts and feelings. But patients most often do not consciously and deliberately deceive us. They recognize that it behooves them to reveal things that may be difficult and even embarrassing to talk about, because they appreciate that such revelations are vital if the therapy is to be successful.

Lawyers, however, more frequently deal with clients who are consciously untruthful with them, and they routinely assume that their adversaries' clients will be so as well. Having some experience with duplicity, they may be more astute than therapists in detecting it. Police officers, judges, and those who work in penal institutions are also more sensitive to conscious duplicity than we are. Accordingly, therapists are handicapped somewhat in the ability to evaluate patients involved in legal proceedings. For example, when we examine a parent in a custody evaluation, the individual generally (either consciously or unconsciously) withholds information that might weaken or be detrimental to his (her) position. And, in sex-abuse evaluations, there is an even greater likelihood of lying, especially in criminal cases when admitting sex abuse might very well result in a prison sentence. Furthermore, parents litigating for custody of their children are bound to distort the truth to a significant degree. Each is likely to exaggerate the other's deficits and downplay the other's assets. Traditionally, each parent will make "mountains out of mole-hills" with regard to the spouse's alleged liabilities. And this is another kind of duplicity with which custody evaluators inevitably have to deal.

joint interview can be extremely valuable for "smoking out" fabrications. Proponents of the adversary system consider it one of the best (if not the best) methods for finding out who is telling "the truth." They claim that the kinds of confrontations provided in the open court-room allow the two sides to directly confront one another in the presence of a judge and jury. They believe that from this presentation of opposing views "the truth" is most likely to emerge. Although the method is certainly an advance over the previous inquisitorial system in which ac-cused persons often did not have the opportunity to confront their accusers, it has certain obvious deficiencies that limit the system's ca-pacity to find out what is "the truth." One of its deficiencies is that the confrontation is not a natural one, but rather one in which the two par-ties confront one another through their intermediaries: the attorneys. In addition, courtroom procedures do not allow for the free flow of in-formation and the back and forth discussions that are more likely to provide meaningful information. The restrictions to direct communica-tion with one another, especially via cross-examination (with its constraining and frustrating yes/no questions), are likely to suppress a significant amount of material that could be useful for ascertaining what is "the truth." Although lawyers claim that ultimately all the important information is likely to come out, this has not been my experience.

Accordingly, adversarial procedures interfere significantly with the acquisition of the kinds of data that mental health evaluators can obtain in their offices, especially in joint interviews, data that can be more important than the actual statements made by the parties. For example, one mother claimed that one of the reasons her husband spent so little time with the children was that he was out gallivanting with a whole string of women. He would often not come home until two or three in the morning and claimed that he was in business meetings that were held under such circumstances that no telephones were available. (It is only the most naive and gullible examiner who would not sense duplicity at this point.) In response to this allegation the father denied infidelity and responded:

> Doctor, she doesn't know what she's talking about. She just keeps imagining things. Business requires me to stay out very late, sometimes till 2:00 or 3:00 in the morning, at meetings where I can't get in touch with her.

To this the wife responded:

> Doctor, I've lived with that man for 18 years and I know him inside out. When he's lying he has that shit-eating grin on his face, just the expression you're seeing right now.

In response to this confrontation the husband began to blush, stutter, and ramble. Although such responses might be obtained on the witness stand, they are far less likely to be elicited because of the time lag between the confrontation and the response, the opportunity to formally prepare a response, and the transmission of many of the communications through intermediaries. This loss of spontaneity reduces the likelihood that one will obtain "the truth" in the courtroom.

In another case a wife complained that her husband had been unfaithful to her on numerous occasions. He flatly denied that this was the case and stated:

> She's always looking for trouble. She's just got a vivid imagination.

The woman then asked her husband to explain the presence of a condom in her car, after she had let her husband use it during a weekend when she was away on a business trip. His reply was:

> I lent the car to my brother, and you know he sells condoms.

The wife replied:

> Oh, your brother sells *used* condoms?

The husband said:

> There you are, just trying to make trouble again. I don't know how it got there. Maybe he took a girlfriend in the car.

The wife then replied:

> And how do you explain the used condom I found behind the couch in our living room? Was that your brother's too?

The husband's reply was:

> Doctor, she's always trying to make trouble. As I told you, she's got a vivid imagination.

I leave it to the reader to decide which person's version here sounds more credible. What is important to my discussion is the value of face-to-face interchanges in "smoking out" the truth, interchanges that are not possible in adversarial courtroom proceedings.

Furthermore, the adversary system strictly prohibits the accuser from directly cross-examining the accused. When one is dealing with domestic situations, in which the accuser and the accused are spouses, their knowledge of one another is far superior to that of any attorney and/or judge—no matter how brilliant and no matter how skilled in the law. Letting the spouses "have it out with one another" is more likely to bring about responses that will enable the evaluator to more accurately assess the situation than is possible in a court of law. Even though there are situations in which the individuals may become emotional, angry, and even agitated, these unpleasant and often painful concomitants of the interchange do not warrant examiners' depriving themselves of this valuable source of information. There may even be situations in which one might have to protect the individuals from one another, but this should not preclude routinely conducting such interviews in the course of one's evaluations.

In joint interviews one has the immediate opportunity to telephone, without any delay, other individuals who might be able to provide important information regarding which parent is telling the truth. The judge cannot do this; an impartial evaluator can do so readily. It might take weeks or months to bring in this third party to provide testimony, and even then one might not be successful because of the reluctance on the part of the third party to "get involved." In addition, during the delay, one or both parties will generally have the opportunity to speak with the third party and try to influence his (her) response. A quick telephone call—made at the time of the conflict of opinions—circumvents this problem. A telephone call made, then, is much more likely to elicit the third party's spontaneous and honest comments. It is very different from appearing on a witness stand in a courtroom weeks or months later. And the spouse who lies and is being potentially "smoked out" by such a call is not likely to resist it strongly because of the knowledge that such resistance implies guilt, shame, or some kind of cover-up that will compromise that party's position in the custody evaluation. There is no lawyer involved to "protect" the client's rights and to justify, via the utilization of some legal technicality, a cover-up and the perpetuation of the fabrication.

I recall one situation in which a mother claimed that her husband had a problem with petty thievery and described in detail how he prided himself on how much food he could steal from supermarkets and other items from a wide variety of stores, especially department stores. I asked the mother how many times, to the best of her knowledge, her husband had involved himself in such thievery. (The reader will note here the importance of trying to get numbers and frequency when conducting forensic evaluations.) The mother replied, "I really don't know how many times, but I'm sure it's been in the hundreds." The father denied any such behavior. The mother then stated that her husband would often steal with a certain friend, George. Again, the father denied that this was the case.

I then asked them if they would have any objections to our calling George. Both agreed that I could do so immediately; however, the father did so with a slight but definite tone of hesitation. (We already have some information here regarding who is more likely to be telling the truth.) I asked them who they preferred to make the call and the father agreed that he would let his wife do so. I suspected again that this related to some reluctance on his part to put through the call, but I was pleased to have the mother make it in that there would be less chance of her communicating any messages to George regarding cover-up of the father's activities. The reader will note that I asked the parents to make the call rather than call George myself. This is an important point. One does not want to be in the position of calling a stranger who has not had any previous relationship at all with the evaluator. It is far better to have the interviewee bridge that gap. It not only facilitates the inquiry but protects the evaluator from the criticism of being too aggressive when conducting the evaluation.

I instructed the mother to call George and merely tell him that she was in my office and that a custody evaluation was being conducted. I asked her to ask George to speak with me, without giving him any further information. Once on the phone I told George who I was and informed him that I was conducting the evaluation under court order and that he should understand that any information he provided me could be transmitted to any of the involved parties and used in any way whatsoever in the course of the litigation. I also informed him that what he said to me might have to be repeated on a witness stand in a court of law. (Obviously, it is crucial that one impart this information to an interviewee when one is conducting a forensic examination.)

George agreed to speak with me. I then simply asked him if he had any information about any possible stealing habits on the part of either of the parents. George immediately described the same pattern of stealing presented by the mother: in supermarkets, department stores, etc. I then asked George how many times he himself had actually observed the father to be engaged in thievery. His responses: "I'm ashamed to admit it, but I myself must have gone with him 20 or 30 times. He told me that he had done it hundreds of times, but I never saw him do it other than the times I was with him. But he was proud of what he was doing and I believed him when he said he had done it hundreds of times." I asked George if he would be willing to come to a court of law and state under oath what he had just told me. He responded that he would, although he was most reluctant to get involved. The father suddenly "remembered" that perhaps on one or two occasions he had stolen items, but denied that the problem was as serious as George and his wife had described.

Family interviews, i.e., interviews that include the children, can also be extremely valuable for finding out who is telling "the truth." After all, the children live in the home and are direct observers to what is going on there. Although they may initially express some reluctance to involve themselves in such confrontational interviews, my experience has been that they generally do so, and as the interview moves along they eventually become more relaxed. Such interviews also help the evaluator learn something about the reality behind exaggerations. The children's input is likely to give the examiner a more accurate picture of exaggerated criticisms.

Some Comments About Data Collection

As mentioned, it is not the purpose of this book to provide examiners with specific details regarding how to conduct forensic evaluations. Even though I focus on child-custody and sex-abuse disputes, even in those realms I am not providing details of the data-collection process. (As mentioned, these have been published elsewhere [Gardner, 1989, 1992a, 1992b, 1995]). My primary purpose here is to focus on testifying in court, regardless of the type of forensic evaluation being conducted. There are, however, some general comments relevant to the data-collection process that are important for mental health professionals to appreciate when conducting a forensic evaluation. Psychologists somewhat reflexively administer tests. Typically, they will utilize the old standbys: the *Rorschach* (Rorschach, 1921), the *Thematic Apperception Test* (TAT) (Murray, 1936), the *Millon Clinical Multiaxial Inventory-II* (Millon, 1987), the *Minnesota Multiphasic Personality Inventory-2* (MMPI-2) (Hathaway and McKinley, 1989), and sometimes even intelligence tests. None of these were specifically designed to provide information for forensic evaluations. Generally, one must squeeze data out of them in order to find something of probative value in a court of law. Take the sex-abuse examination, for example. None of these instruments was designed to ascertain whether a child was sexually abused, an accuser is telling the truth, or a defendant sexually abused a child. These instruments might give information about manifestations of impulsivity, psychopathic trends, or psychosis, but they are of very little probative value in a sex-abuse evaluation. Of course, sex abusers may be impulsive, psychopathic, or even psychotic. But the vast majority of people who have any of these qualities are *not* sex abusers. Accordingly, these instruments are not specific enough to be of much value in such an evaluation.

Similarly, psychiatrists reflexively get background history, do a mental status examination, and consider it important to come up with a diagnosis. This procedure may be very useful for deciding what kind of treatment is necessary, but it generally gives little information in many kinds of forensic evaluations—especially sex-abuse evaluations and child-custody disputes. And social workers are even less equipped to conduct a sex-abuse evaluation. They are not trained to administer psychological tests, which would do them very little good in a sex-abuse evaluation anyway. They are trained to get family background and to utilize this information for therapeutic purposes. But all of this is of little value in a sex-abuse evaluation, although it may be of some value in a child-custody evaluation. Accordingly, most sex-abuse evaluations conducted in the three major mental health disciplines waste significant time collecting data that is of no probative value in ascertaining whether the sex act has been perpetrated. Accordingly, examiners who conduct forensic examinations should "stick to the point" and focus primarily on questions that are going to give them useful information with regard to the particular lawsuit.

But this may not be a simple thing to do. For example, leading questions and anatomical dolls are often utilized in sex-abuse evaluations because they ostensibly focus the child on the sex-abuse issue. However, these techniques introduce so many contaminants that one may not know whether the child has been genuinely abused or whether what the child says and does is a result of the contaminating influences of these approaches. Fortunately, one can still learn an enormous amount about sex abuse by utilizing more open-ended procedures that enable the examiner to learn exactly what is spinning around in the child's mind without leading the child in any particular direction. Among the 62 differentiating criteria described in my own protocol (Gardner, 1995), there are no leading questions or coercive interview techniques, yet each criterion has the potential for providing specific information regarding whether the child has been sexually abused. Similarly, my protocols for the evaluation of the alleged perpetrator and the accuser, although specific enough to focus on issues relevant to the sex-abuse evaluation, do not include leading questions that are likely to contaminate the inquiry. And the same principles hold in the custody evaluation, the evaluation for incompetence, and sanity evaluations.

Reports from Other Examiners

In most of the evaluations in which I have been involved, there have been previous examiners. Accordingly, I often have reports of their findings and recommendations. There have been examinations, however, that I have conducted in which there have been previous examinations but the reports have not been prepared. Under such circumstances, I generally request that the previous examiners provide me with a written report. Some examiners are loathe to provide such reports, especially when they appreciate that what they have written will be utilized in a court of law. The patient, however, is entitled to such a report, and an examiner's failure to provide one is at best unethical and may subject the examiner to justifiable criticisms and possibly reprimand by his (her) professional organization. Sometimes the previous examiner will inform the patient that he (she) prefers to speak with me on the telephone rather than prepare a written report. I have *never* complied with this request. It is an error for an evaluator to do so. Invariably, there will be differences of opinion regarding what has been said, and this is especially the case in lawsuits where there are often such high emotions and formidable concerns about courtroom revelations that misperceptions, misconceptions, and even conscious falsification are common. Accordingly, I insist upon a written report and advise the patient that he (she) is entitled to one. Under such circumstances, there is absolutely no question about what the previous examiner has reported.

Reports from Hospitals

I routinely get permission to request reports from hospitals. In fact, it is a proviso of my involvement that the parties agree in advance to sign releases that facilitate my obtaining such material. Hospital reports are often useful to confirm allegations of suicidal attempts, drug overdoses, and child abuse. They also provide useful information about the depth of pathology when hospitalization was required. Hospital documents can be very powerful sources of information, and it is not likely that an opposing attorney will try to refute them. Nevertheless, such information is still, strictly speaking, hearsay in that the examiner has not observed directly the difficulties described therein. Corroborating statements by the parties concerned can strengthen the value of these already important and convincing documents.

It is also important for the evaluator to make a sharp differentiation between commitments to psychiatric hospitals and voluntary admissions. If a person has been committed, it usually indicates serious psychopathology. In contrast, voluntary hospitalizations need not necessarily reflect serious psychiatric disturbance. Evaluators must appreciate that private hospitals are often lucrative businesses and the doctors working therein (sometimes part owners of the hospital) encourage hospitalization because of the money to be made from such patients. But even those admitting doctors who are employees recognize that the more "business" the hospital has, the more stable their position. Under these circumstances, such doctors will often utilize what I consider frivolous and superficial criteria for recommending hospitalization. Not surprisingly, patients so admitted generally get "cured" at around the time their insurance runs out. Elsewhere (Gardner, 1988) I have discussed in detail my views on hospitalization, with particular focus on the private psychiatric hospital.

Reports from Attorneys

I usually ask the parties to ask their attorneys to forward to me any material that they and/or their attorneys think will be of interest or value to me. Generally, these include motions, pleadings, affidavits, depositions, certifications, etc. I have sometimes found that the party with the stronger case is very quick to respond to this request, whereas the party in the weaker position responds slowly or not at all. In short, the party with the stronger arguments is very happy to send me all kinds of supporting evidence. The party in the weaker position senses this and recognizes that there is not much to be gained by my reading his (her) complaints or refutations.

The ideal way to review these documents is to read them along with both parties involved in the lawsuit. Of course, this may not always be possible. In child-custody disputes and sex-abuse accusations in the context of such disputes, this generally is easily accomplished. Under such circumstances one has the opportunity for immediate comment on the part of both parties, and in this way distortions, misrepresentations, and exaggerations can be addressed immediately. This method is also far less costly than one in which the examiner reads these documents in privacy and then brings up the pertinent issues to each of the parties. And, if the parties have to be interviewed separately, this becomes even more cumbersome, time-consuming, and expensive. Usually, when reviewing the document with the concerned parties, I utilize a special notational system that I have found particularly useful. Specifically, I will identify the particular issue with a marginal notation regarding the item under consideration, starting with the number 1, for example. Then, on a separate sheet of paper, I will record what each of the parties has to say about item #1. And this same procedure is utilized with item #2, etc. The comments are then attached to the original report, and this material serves as a point of departure for dictation when I prepare my final report.

Videotapes of Previous Examinations

I have found review of videotapes of the interviews of previous examiners to be a valuable source of information, especially in sex-abuse evaluations. Generally, I prefer that I be given a written transcript along with the videotape. This facilitates the viewing, especially if the tape is of poor quality and/or any of the parties is not speaking coherently. Much that I have learned about how "validators" work has been via painstaking review of their videotapes as well as detailed analyses of the transcripts made from such tapes. And such information has provided powerful testimony in court.

I recall one case in which the "validator" was interviewing a two-year-old girl. The evaluator was stroking the penis of the anatomical doll in a clearly masturbatory fashion. While doing so she was talking to the child about whether the alleged perpetrator had asked her to play with his penis in the manner being demonstrated by the validator. The child, not surprisingly, then began to imitate the therapist and began stroking the doll's penis in an identical way. The validator concluded by this maneuver that this child (who didn't have the faintest idea what the validator was talking about) had been sexually molested by the accused. It is important to note that the written transcript gave no hint of all these manipulations that were taking place: thus the importance of viewing the videotape directly. In the courtroom, I had the opportunity to play that segment of the tape and said to the judge, while pointing to what the evaluator was doing:

> Your honor, if you want to know about sexual molestation in this case, you are viewing it with your own eyes. This child is being sexually abused here by this validator. If a teacher or a neighbor did this, that person would be brought up on charges and probably reported to the child protection services. Yet this mother is voluntarily subjecting her child to this kind of sexual and emotional abuse.

The tapes of previous examiners can provide valuable information. One should look for leading questions. Many evaluators claim that they don't use leading questions; yet it is obvious that they not only use many leading questions, but don't even appreciate that they are doing so. They have little if any appreciation of the basic concept of leading questions, specifically, that they introduce notions that might not have otherwise entered the mind of the person being questioned. Written transcripts will generally not provide information about leading gestures. An examiner who utilizes leading gestures serves as a model for the patient (especially the child) to behave similarly. If this involves touching, stroking, and manipulating anatomical dolls, it is likely that the patient will act similarly. As mentioned, the written transcript accompanying the videotape of the aforementioned interview, in which the validator was stroking the doll's penis, made absolutely no reference to the leading gestures so dramatically depicted therein.

Videotapes (and less predictably audiotapes) also provide information about whether the child's affect was appropriate to the ideation. When conducting a sex-abuse evaluation, one wants to know whether the child's emotional tone was appropriate to cognition when describing the sexual abuse. Overzealous examiners typically describe the child's affect as being appropriate, providing confirmation thereby that the abuse took place. The appropriate-affect ploy is utilized by many "validators" to provide credibility to their statements. Because other parties were not present, they may think they can "get away" with this rationalization. Even the written transcript may not "smoke out" this maneuver. The videotape, however, will provide definite evidence, one way or the other, as to whether this was indeed the case. One can observe there the child's facial expressions and also hear directly the vocal intonations of the child's voice—the true indicators of affect. One can also see the movement of the child's head in answer to yes/no questions. Transcribers generally use the term *nod* to refer to an affirmative response and the term *shakes* to indicate negative responses. Also, transcribers traditionally utilize *uh-huh* to refer to positive responses and *uh-uh* to refer to negative responses. However, I have seen transcripts in which these traditional notations are not utilized and the notation does not clearly indicate to the reader whether the child has said yes or no. By looking at the facial expressions associated with the child's responses, the evaluator can usually determine whether the child has indeed given an affirmative or negative response to the yes/no question. Of course, such evaluators are not appreciative of the extreme drawbacks of the yes/no question, especially when interviewing young children.

CONCLUDING COMMENTS

It has not been my purpose in this chapter to describe in detail the methods by which one conducts a forensic evaluation. Rather, my purpose has been to focus on certain elements in the structure of the evaluation that are important to consider when one is preparing to testify in court.

When the data-collection process has been completed, the examiner does well to prepare a preliminary report for presentation to the clients and their attorneys. This gives them the opportunity for input prior to the preparation of the final report and significantly reduces tensions associated with wondering what the examiner's findings will be. Because this preliminary report serves as the foundation for the final report, I will discuss this at the beginning of the next chapter, the chapter devoted to the preparation of the final report.

☐ THREE
THE FINAL WRITTEN REPORT

PRESENTATION OF THE
PRELIMINARY FINDINGS

After all the data has been collected from the interviewees, and after I have reviewed all pertinent documents, I generally prepare a report. This report is not my final report; rather it is a first-draft preliminary report. The procedure I generally use is to set up important categories for my secretary to enter into the computer file devoted to the case. In a custody case these would generally include: background of my involvement (including attempts to serve as an impartial examiner), basic data ("name, rank, and serial number" information about the various parties), the dates the various parties were seen, documents reviewed, the mother's parental capacity, the father's parental capacity, interviews with the children, comments on the reports of other examiners, and conclusions and recommendations. Then I review all the material in my files and dictate specific data to be incorporated into each of the categories entered into the computer file. My secretary accomplishes this by scrolling up and down through the file and inserting the items into the proper categories. This can be subsequently reviewed and reorganized into subcategories within each category. It is this document that serves as the point of departure for my presentation to the attorneys. The provisions document, which I require signed before involvement in child-custody and sex-abuse evaluations, makes the following statement regarding this conference:

> Upon completion of my evaluation—and *prior to* the preparation of my final report—I generally meet with both parents together and present to them my findings and recommendations. This gives them the opportunity to correct any distortions they believe I may have and/or alter my opinion before it becomes finalized in my report. In addition, it saves the parents from the unnecessary and prolonged tension associated with wondering what my findings are.
>
> Both attorneys are invited to attend this conference. However, this invitation should be considered withdrawn if only one attorney wishes to attend because the presence of only one attorney would obviously place the nonrepresented parent in a compromised position. When a guardian ad litem has been appointed by the court, he or she will also be invited to attend this conference. Before accepting this invitation attorneys should appreciate that the discussion will be completely free and open. Accordingly, during this conference it would be improper for an attorney in any way whatsoever to restrict or discourage the client from answering questions or participating in the discussion. On occasion, the litigants have used this conference as a forum for resolving their custody/visitation dispute, avoiding thereby the formidable expense and psychological trauma of courtroom litigation. After this conference the final report is prepared and sent simultaneously to the court, the attorneys, and the parents.

Although it is uncommon for me to change completely my position regarding custody during the course of this conference, I have done so on occasion because I have been convinced that my initial position was injudicious. But this is unusual. Most often my data-collection process is so thorough that I have reached the point where the evidence is compelling regarding which party's position I am going to support. Had I not reached that point, I would have lengthened the evaluation. Often the meeting enables me to modify certain errors in my report that could have been a source of embarrassment on the witness stand.

The final written report is an expansion of the preliminary report designed for the initial presentation of the findings and recommendations to the clients and attorneys. It includes the modifications derived from that conference and, obviously, it must be a much more "polished" product than the first draft. In fact, its preparation generally involves two or three steps in order that it be free of poor grammar and typographical errors. A poorly written report compromises its value, no matter how astute the observations and no matter how compelling its conclusions.

THE SHORT VS. LONG REPORT

Whereas in other fields of medicine attorneys generally do not try to influence an expert with regard to the length of the report, attorneys somehow feel freer to do so with mental health professionals. There are two aspects of the final report that are pertinent here: the contents and its length. With regard to the contents, the aforementioned conference with the clients and attorneys invites such input; however, it is done in a setting where both attorneys and both clients are present and so there is nothing secretive about attempts to alter and/or modify my position. With regard to the length of the report, there are some attorneys who hold strongly that the shorter the report, the better. Their reasoning is that a short report still satisfies the requirements of the court and concerned parties that a report be submitted. However, because it is short, it will only contain a fraction of all the material that will be presented in the courtroom. Such a report, then, places the adversary attorney at a disadvantage because he (she) does not know beforehand exactly what the expert is going to say, especially with regard to the particular reasons why the expert has come to certain conclusions. There are some lawyers who rigidly adhere to this principle and will place great pressure upon the mental health professional to submit a very short report.

Under such circumstances, the opposing attorney may require a deposition. The deposition is basically a type of court inquiry, generally conducted by the opposing attorney. Its primary purpose is to enable an attorney to interview an opposition witness prior to trial. It provides this attorney with the opportunity to "size up" the witness and thereby be in a better position to examine the individual in the courtroom. Another benefit of the deposition—not generally advertised—is that it provides yet another opportunity for the attorney to earn more money.

Also not advertised is the fact that the deposition can enable the interviewee to "size up" the examining attorney. I personally have found depositions very valuable in this regard, and they have provided me with "leads" regarding the areas in which the attorney is likely to go in the courtroom. Accordingly, they enable me to strengthen what might otherwise have been weak points in my testimony. All this is consistent with the old saying: "What's good for the goose is good for the gander." The procedures are very similar to those found in the courtroom with the exception that there is no judge present. Typically, there is a court reporter, and objections are placed in the record but not ruled upon because of the absence of a judge. Presumably, the depositions are read by the judge, who will then be alerted to such objections in the course of the hearing or trial. Over the years that I have been involved in forensic psychiatry, I have witnessed a steady progression in the frequency and length of depositions. Although this may serve useful purposes in accordance with the proverbial "forewarned is forearmed," it obviously adds enormous expense for the client.

There are, however, attorneys who are pleased to have a much longer report. They recognize the risks of the long report but consider the advantages to outweigh the disadvantages. One advantage of the long report is that it provides a detailed outline for the direct examination by the attorney whose position is being supported. It is to be hoped that the expert knows more about the subject than the attorney and he (she) therefore is in a good position to provide guidelines for the direct examination. Another advantage of the long report is that it can serve the evaluator well when preparing for trial. It can serve as a comprehensive statement of the examiner's position and provides all the important arguments in support of that position. Basically, it pulls together all the important information necessary for testimony. And when there is a significant time gap between the time of the evaluation and the time of testimony (the usual case), it can serve as an excellent refresher and summary for the evaluator.

Another advantage of the long report is that it places into the written record the most comprehensive statement of the examiner's position. No matter how detailed the direct examination has been, it rarely allows for a full and detailed description of every fact that the examiner may wish to get into the record. And this is especially the case when the opposing attorney is very aggressive, interrupts the direct examination frequently, and makes many objections. A judge who is unsympathetic to the examiner's position may sustain many, if not most, of these objections, no matter how unjustified, and thereby truncate significantly what the examiner can place on the record. The full report, which is generally allowed into evidence if the examiner has been court-appointed (either as an independent or as one side's expert), circumvents this problem. As I write this, I have been testifying in courts of law for 35 years. I have never (I repeat, never) had the opportunity to provide as much testimony as I would have liked. I have never had the opportunity to include in my testimony every single supporting fact that I would have liked to bring to the attention of the court. Accordingly, the comprehensive report, which is generally submitted to the court at the time of the trial, puts in the record all of the examiner's arguments. In addition, if the case is appealed, the report is then available for review by the appeals court. Examiners do not testify in appellate courts. Such courts review records and hear arguments from attorneys only. Accordingly, this is the examiner's only chance to have some input into the appeals process if that takes place.

Obviously, my preference is to submit a comprehensive report. In a custody case, my reports may run anywhere from 30 to 60 pages, and sometimes even longer. There is usually an enormous amount of information to sift through. If the reader concludes here that I include every bit of frivolous and inconsequential information, that would be an error. I usually separate "BBs" from "bombs" and include only bombs in my report. But some of the bombs may require a page or two for proper presentation. My sex-abuse reports are even longer. At the time of this writing (1995) I have 62 criteria for differentiating between true and false sex-abuse accusations in the child, 26 for the alleged perpetrator, and 32 for the accuser. Accordingly, I have a total of 120 differentiating criteria. A typical sex-abuse report, then, generally runs over a hundred pages. One may consider this "overkill," but I believe such a long report is necessary if one is to do justice to this very demanding and difficult type of evaluation. For the interested reader these criteria are detailed in my book *Protocols for the Sex-Abuse Evaluation* (Gardner,

1995). Most lawyers are receptive to my preference to write long reports.

There are times, however, that the lawyer will rigidly hold to the position that long reports do more harm than good and will not give serious consideration to the aforementioned arguments for the longer report. On a few occasions this has resulted in a confrontation, polite but definitely adversarial. I recall, in one such situation, the following interchange taking place:

> *Gardner:* So what you're telling me is that all of the arguments I've given for a long report still haven't convinced you that it might be preferable?
>
> *Attorney:* That's right.
>
> *Gardner:* Let me ask you this. Would you tell a cardiologist how long or short his or her report should be?
>
> *Attorney:* No.
>
> *Gardner:* Would you tell a brain surgeon how long or short his or her report should be?
>
> *Attorney:* No.
>
> *Gardner:* Would you tell a specialist in any other branch of medicine, other than psychiatry, how long or short his or her report should be?
>
> *Attorney:* No.
>
> *Gardner:* So why are you dictating the length of my report to me?
>
> *Attorney:* Well, psychiatry is different.
>
> *Gardner:* How is it different?
>
> *Attorney:* I don't know, it's just different, and I'd like you to write a short report.
>
> *Gardner:* Sorry, I have an obligation to your client as well. Mr. X is *your client*, but he's also *my patient*. And I believe that in this case a short report will do him more harm than good, especially because your adversary has a reputation for being very hard-nosed in the courtroom and, I am certain, will do everything possible to restrict my testimony.

Obviously, it is not a good idea for the expert to have an adversarial relationship with the attorney whose position is being supported. However, in this situation, I felt I had no choice. To avoid that kind of confrontation would have resulted in my doing something that was not in the patient's best interests.

There are some readers who may have wondered why I still refer to the interviewee as a *patient*. One could argue that a patient is only someone whom the evaluator is treating. As a physician I do not refer to the people I see, whether it be as an evaluation or treatment, as *clients*. Attorneys do this and certain mental health professionals do so. Physicians rarely do so. More important than the semantic issue here is the question of malpractice. From the point of view of someone who may sue the evaluator, any party seen by the psychiatrist in his (her) office is a patient—regardless of whether the purpose is therapeutic evaluation, legal evaluation, or treatment. By the same reasoning, our moral and ethical obligations to those being evaluated are identical to those whom we are treating. I believe that submitting an artificially short report, a report that omits crucial details because it may serve some courtroom maneuver, is unethical. It is unethical because I believe, justifiably or not, that a short report is not serving my patient well.

THE FINAL WRITTEN REPORT

Introduction

My general format is to begin with the report's title: PSYCHIATRIC CUSTODY/VISITATION EVALUATION, SEX-ABUSE EVALUATION, COMPETENCY EVALUATION, or SANITY EVALUATION. Because the report might be buried in a pile of complaints, affidavits, certifications, and other documents, this lets the reader know exactly what is contained in the document. Next, I indicate the date on which the full report was sent. Then I indicate the name and address of the party to whom the primary copy was sent. When I serve as an impartial examiner, this party is the judge. When I am formally recognized as one party's expert (even though operating as much as possible as an impartial), I indicate the name and address of the attorney who has enlisted my services. Next I indicate the particular case to which the report related by stating (1) the names of the litigants, e.g., Parker vs. Parker and (2) the docket number or file number, e.g., M-2753-81. It is extremely important that the examiner include this reference number. This is what the court clerk will look at when filing the report. Court calendars are so tight and the number of cases so great that it is unlikely that the judge is going to read the examiner's report immediately. Rather, it will be filed until the time the case comes before the judge, which may be a few months after the report is submitted, or even longer. (This is my experience in the New York-New Jersey area. It may be different elsewhere.) I cannot emphasize strongly enough the importance of placing the docket number in a conspicuous place on the first sheet of the report, as well as on any other correspondence with the court. Without it there is the risk that the report will be unfiled or misfiled. (This happened to one of my earlier reports, so I speak from bitter experience.)

As mentioned in Chapter Two, it is important that examiners clarify beforehand *exactly* what their roles shall be in a forensic evaluation. For example, in a child-custody dispute in which there is a sex-abuse accusation, one wants to have it clearly spelled out whether one is simply going to conduct a sex-abuse evaluation, a child-custody evaluation, or both. Examiners who do not clarify this point at the outset may find themselves seriously compromised in the courtroom as segments of their testimony may be found inadmissible, both with regard to the written report and the opportunity to provide testimony. In situations when I am a court-appointed examiner, my letter is addressed to the judge directly. Under such circumstances, my introductory paragraph usually follows this format:

> This report is submitted in compliance with your court order dated February 28, 1995, requesting that I conduct an evaluation of the Simpson family in order to provide the court with recommendations that would be useful to it in deciding which of the Simpson parents should have primary custody of their children, James and Sarah.

The paragraph indicates that the evaluation is submitted in compliance with a court order—once again affirming my position as an impartial examiner who serves the court. It makes it clear that I am merely providing recommendations that would be useful to the court in helping the *court decide* which of the parents would be the preferable one to assume primary custody. This makes it clear to all concerned that it is the court's final decision. In many cases it is judicious for the examiner to quote exactly what the court order states regarding the request being made of the impartial examiner, for example:

> This report is submitted in compliance with your court order dated April 22, 1986, in which you state: "Doctor Richard A. Gardner shall evaluate the parties in order to advise the court regarding a custody and visitation arrangement that would be in the best interests of the children."

This serves to protect the examiner from legal nit-picking that may take place if the report includes material not specifically requested by the court order.

In situations in which I am recognized as one attorney's expert, the letter is not only addressed to him (her), but the introductory paragraph will describe the attempts that were made for me to serve as an impartial and the exact reasons why such designation was not realized. It is *crucial* that the examiner include these in the report and it is preferable that these steps be delineated in the first paragraph. A typical statement in this regard:

> This report is submitted to you in response to your request, indicated in your letter to me of February 1, 1994, that I conduct a sex-abuse evaluation on your client, Mrs. Mary Jones, and her son, James Jones, Jr. (age 5). As described in the materials I sent you on February 5, 1994, I make every attempt to serve as an impartial examiner rather than as an adversarial expert. In compliance with this request, you asked Mr. James Jones, Sr.'s attorney, Mr. Henry Smith, to request of the court that it appoint me its independent expert. This request was made in your letter to him of February 15, 1994. In his letter to you of February 20, 1994, he declined this invitation. Accordingly, on March 1, 1994, you asked the court to order Mr. James Jones, Sr. to cooperate in my evaluation. On that day the court recognized me as your expert and ordered Mr. James Jones, Sr. to participate in my evaluation. However, it also allowed Mr. James Jones, Sr. to select an expert of his own choosing and required Mrs. Mary Jones and James Jones, Sr. to cooperate in the evaluations with each other's experts.
>
> Subsequently, even though recognized by the court as your expert, I notified all parties, at the outset, that I would be conducting my evaluation in accordance with the same procedures I use when I am formally

recognized as the court's independent expert. In accordance with this policy, my records have been open throughout to both parties, even during the presentation of my findings to both attorneys and both clients on April 15, 1994.

Dates of the Interviews and The People Interviewed

I introduce this section with a statement: "My findings and recommendations are based on interviews conducted as itemized below:" I then list the date of each interview, the person(s) seen, the duration of each interview, and the *total* number of hours of interviewing. I then add the date and duration of the meeting in which the findings and recommendations were discussed with the parents and their attorneys.

Other Documents Reviewed

Here I list other documents that I have reviewed in the course of my evaluation. I generally do not list every single scrap of paper, especially those of an administrative nature. Rather, I list in this section the important documents and their dates. Following the presentation of this list I generally add:

It is important to emphasize that the findings and recommendations described in this report are based on my own findings and observations. The information provided by these documents served as points of departure for my own inquiry. I believe that I would have come to the same conclusions had none of these documents existed.

This is an important statement. One does not want to be on the witness stand and be in the embarrassing position of having to admit that one's findings and conclusions were based on hearsay information. This is not simply a question of admitting a weakness that is embarrassing; it is a matter of conducting a proper evaluation.

Basic Data About Each of the Parties Interviewed

I then provide a mere skeletal description of each of the parties. This includes the age, residence, occupation, and the people with whom the party is living. In this section I list all of the parties interviewed. In child-custody/ visitation evaluations this generally includes each parent, each of the children, and individuals such as stepparents, live-in friends, grandparents, a housekeeper, or anyone else interviewed in the course of the evaluation. In sex-abuse evaluations the list includes the alleged perpetrator, the accuser, and the alleged child victim(s). I also indicate the code initials I will be using for that party throughout the course of the report. This makes reading and writing the report more efficient. I have seen many reports in which the examiner refers to the parents by first name. I consider this improper and some parents, with justification, might consider the practice demeaning. After all, the examiner is probably referred to as Dr. X by the parents, so the parents should be referred to as Mr. Y and Mrs. Y. A typical description at this point would be:

> Mr. Henry Johnson (hereafter referred to as Mr. HJ), age 43 (date of birth April 15, 1951), lives alone in Belmont, N.J. He is an accountant employed by the Star Employment Agency in Rockville, N.J. He is the father of John and Mary.

With regard to the children, I have no problem referring to them by first name in that this practice, in our society, is not generally considered offensive or demeaning. Accordingly, for a child my statement might read:

> Jennifer Smith (hereafter referred to as Jennifer), age six (date of birth September 3, 1987), is in the first grade at St. Mary's School in Graceland, N.J. She lives primarily with her mother but visits with her father in accordance with the temporary court-ordered schedule.

Summary of Conclusions and Recommendations

A short statement then follows in which I summarize my final recommendations. As was the case in the meeting with the clients and attorneys, prior to the preparation of my final report, I begin with a short statement of my conclusions and recommendations. Whereas in the interview with the parents and attorneys its purpose was to lessen parental anxiety and provide the opportunity for input, here it lessens the reader's curiosity and enables the reader to avoid hunting at the end of the report for the final recommendations. A typical statement in a child-custody/visitation evaluation:

> 1. It is my opinion that Mrs. Mary Marino should be granted primary physical and primary legal custody of both children.
> 2. Mr. John Marino should be given a liberal visitation schedule, formulated by the attorneys with the approval of the court.
> 3. My reasons for coming to this conclusion are elaborated upon below. Although much information was obtained in the course of the evaluation, only those items specifically pertinent to the custody consideration will be included in this report.

For a sex-abuse evaluation, a typical statement:

> 1. I see absolutely no evidence that Jane Goldberg was sexually abused by her father or anyone else.
> 2. I see no evidence that Mr. Stanley Goldberg sexually abused his daughter, nor does he show any evidence for pedophilic tendencies.
> 3. I believe that Mrs. Veronica Goldberg's allegation that her former husband sexually abused their daughter is a false accusation. I believe that this allegation began as a conscious and deliberate fabrication and has now progressed to the point where it is a delusion.
> 4. In spite of this false accusation, I believe that Mrs. Goldberg should still remain the primary physical custodial parent of Jane Goldberg. However, if she continues this campaign of sex-abuse accusations, then the court should give serious consideration to transferring primary physical custody to Mr. Stanley Goldberg.
> 5. I recommend that the court order a discontinuation of treatment immediately with Joan Smith, M.S.W. There is compelling evidence that this therapist is inculcating the notion in the child that she was sexually abused when there is absolutely no evidence for such.
> 6. Mr. Stanley Goldberg should have primary legal custody, especially with regard to the appointment of therapists. This is the only way the court can prevent Mrs. Goldberg from finding another therapist who will support her delusion that her child was sexually abused.
> 7. Although much information was obtained in the course of the evaluation, only those items specifically pertinent to the sex-abuse

evaluation will be included in this report.

This final statement covers me for a possible question by a cross-examining attorney as to why a particular bit of information may not have been included. This is easy to do because the most voluminous report will never include *all* the possible data that might be considered relevant. Actually, there are degrees of pertinence and I make it clear that I am presenting only the information that I consider most pertinent. However, because my reports are unusually comprehensive (often 60 to 70 pages), it is not common for this criticism to be directed toward me.

This is only one example of an extremely important consideration for examiners when writing their reports. Specifically, examiners should frequently be thinking about the cross-examining attorney interrogating them on the witness stand. The dedicated attorney will scrupulously examine the report and look for any loophole—even a word—that might represent a weakness. Sometimes a poorly chosen word may be enough to provide the opposing attorney with ammunition in the attempt to discredit the evaluator. It is not that the attorney will expect the examiner's entire testimony to be discredited by pointing out one such defect, but the more such deficiencies, the weaker the valid parts of the report will appear to be. For example, in one report in which I described a mother's extreme ambivalence about her marriage, I wrote, "She has left her house countless times in the last few years, only to return after a few days or weeks." Her lawyer picked up on the word *countless* and asked with incredulity and associated histrionics if that was indeed the case: "You mean to say, Doctor," he asked in utter disbelief, "that she left the house so many times that it would be absolutely impossible to count them?" Actually, the number of such episodes was about ten to fifteen, but I did not consider it important to spend time calculating the specific number. I had to admit it was an ill-chosen word and he managed to get some mileage from this "defect" in my report. Opposing attorneys will find flaws that do not in fact exist; the examiner should not provide them with real ones as well. This experience, which happened many years ago, impressed upon me the importance of getting approximate numbers and frequency for most of the events described by the patients in the course of the evaluation.

Background Information

At this point I present background information. The purpose here is to give the reader fundamental information regarding the development of the issues being litigated and the series of events that led to the conflict. On the one hand, one does not want to be so brief that the reader does not have a basic grasp of the problem(s). On the other hand, one does not want to be so comprehensive that the reader is overwhelmed by a sea of data. Some middle ground must be found.

For the custody/visitation evaluation I indicate the date of the present marriage, the date(s) of separation, and the reasons for the separation. I quote directly from the statements made by each of the parents regarding the causes of the separation. Such quotations may occupy a page or two for each parent. I do *not* go into a detailed description of the various denials and counteraccusations. Rather, I make a simple statement like:

> Mr. MT states that the majority of the aforementioned allegations of his wife are false, with the exception of the drinking problem, which he readily admits to. However, he claims that even there she is exaggerating the extent of his alcohol consumption and the degree to which drinking interferes with his functioning.

It is particularly important to include here allegations that relate to child rearing. For example:

> Mrs. RT claims that one of the many reasons she asked for a separation was her husband's "incessant berating of the children." She claims that he would frequently call John "a stupid moron" or "the village idiot."

I then make a statement about whether or not the parents are divorced and make comments about remarriage(s). I include here pertinent information about stepparents (usually listed already in the aforementioned list of parties interviewed), "significant others" who may be involved in the conflict, children from other marriages who may be living in the home, grandparents who are involved with the children, and any other data important to the understanding of the custody dispute.

However, only skeletal material is provided here because the examiner is conducting a custody evaluation, not a full psychiatric evaluation. This section, then, provides the reader with a concise statement of the origins and the present status of the custody dispute.

For a sex-abuse evaluation I will trace the evolution of the sex-abuse accusation from the very first time the accuser came to believe the child was sexually abused until the present. This may involve a few pages, especially in complex cases where there has been a long history of repeated accusations with examinations by multiple evaluators.

The Heart of the Report

Here, the primary substantive data from which the conclusions have been derived are presented. Child-custody/visitation evaluations generally focus on each parent's assets and liabilities, especially as they relate to parenting capacity. I also include information derived from the interviews of each of the children as well as significant other parties significantly involved in the children's lives, e.g., stepparents, grandparents, and (when possible) the housekeeper. This data-collection process is described in detail in my book, *Family Evaluation in Mediation, Arbitration, and Litigation* (Gardner, 1989). When I conduct a sex-abuse evaluation, I use the protocols described in my book *Protocols for the Sex-Abuse Evaluation* (Gardner, 1995). It is beyond my purpose here to describe the specific details regarding the data-collection process in each of these types of evaluations. I will present, however, some advice and caveats that should prove useful for evaluators who are planning to testify.

Avoidance of Psychiatric and Psychological Jargon Throughout, the examiner should avoid, whenever possible, the use of psychological jargon. There are those who compensate for their feelings of professional inadequacy by using abstruse terminology. There is no concept in all of psychology and psychoanalysis that cannot be understood by the average child of twelve or thirteen. After all, we are only talking about human relations, not chemical and mathematical theories. Examiners who use an abundance of jargon compromise their credibility because the court may sense that they are trying to hide ig-norance with verbiage. In addition, they risk subjecting themselves to a common courtroom ploy. Specifically, the cross-examining lawyer may suddenly appear with a medical or psychiatric dictionary in hand. The attorney will ask the examiner (often in wise-guy fashion) to define a particular word that he (she) has used. No matter how experienced the evaluator may be regarding that particular word (possibly even more than the person who wrote the dictionary), it is not likely that the evaluator's definition will coincide with that in the dictionary. This is especially true in the fields of psychiatry and psychology, in which con-cepts are often vague and ill-defined. The layperson's inordinate respect for the written word is such that the dictionary's opinion may be taken over that of the expert's. Or the expert may not be familiar with some of the abstruse minutiae that the dictionary describes. It is rare that an evaluator will come out ahead in such a confrontation; therefore, one does best to avoid jargon. Again, we see here an example of how the court is used for the purpose of making an expert look foolish, rather than for its ostensible purpose of establishing what is best for the chil-dren and/or litigants.

Avoidance of Hyperbole   In the course of writing the report the examiner should avoid the use of hyperbole. Overstatement and "over-kill" generally weaken rather than strengthen a report. As a college freshman, I recall an English professor telling the class, "The adjective is the enemy of the noun." The statement has relevance to the final report. The more adjectives one uses to modify a noun, the weaker the statement becomes. Although readers of the report may not be con-sciously aware of this principle, they are likely to respond negatively to overkill. Lambuth (1923), one of Dartmouth's most revered English professors, often said: "If you're going to hit a nail, hit it on the head." There is great wisdom in this statement and it is useful for the examiner to remember it when writing a custody evaluation.

Anticipation of Refutation   It is a good idea to place in the final report defenses or arguments against anticipated refutations. It places on the record the reasonable refutation that the examiner may not be given the opportunity to provide on the witness stand. In essence, it punctures the balloon before the cross-examining attorney has a chance to blow it up. For example, a mother once complained that it was a sign of serious parental deficiency on her husband's part to have brought their 12- and 14-year-old boys to his attorney in order to make statements and sign affidavits criticizing her. She somewhat condescendingly stated that she would never do such a terrible thing to her children. Although I am in agreement that there are times when utilizing the children in such capacity can be psychologically detrimental to them, it is not always the case, especially for children in their teens. In this situation, the children were strongly desirous of living with their father because their mother entertained a parade of lovers in the home. Although she did not actually have sexual relations in front of the children, they were exposed to a series of men friends sleeping overnight with her. The mother, however, flatly denied having lovers in the home. The children were the only witnesses to these visitors, and the father needed their testimony to support his position. They welcomed the opportunity to provide testimony because of their strong desire to live with their father. In this case, I did not view the father's bringing the children to his attorney to be a sign of parental deficiency (as the mother would have wished me to believe). Rather, I viewed it as a manifestation of his affection for his children and his desire to do everything reasonable and possible to remove them from their mother, who, in my opinion, was clearly the less effective parent.

Accordingly, in this situation I quoted the mother's criticism of her husband and then stated my own opinion that in this case it was justifiable for the husband to have the boys interviewed by his attorney. I described them as relatively healthy and stable and quite capable of handling the situation in the lawyer's office. I stated that I did not consider the experience to have been psychologically traumatic to them. And I went further and stated that I considered it a psychologically salutary experience in that it provided them with a sense of power in a situation in which most children generally feel impotent. Not surprisingly, the mother's attorney did not ask me any questions about this alleged deficiency of the husband.

Use of Direct Observations and Quotations The strongest points in the final report are those based on the examiner's direct observations and direct quotations of the various parties involved. The same principles hold in the courtroom. And, when there have been third parties in the room who will confirm the examiner's observations, such statements become even more compelling. This is especially the case if the observation or statement provides strong support for the examiner's conclusions, conclusions that the party being quoted does not wish to support. An example of such a strong statement in a child-custody dispute might be:

> During my interview with Mrs. Esposito on July 12, 1993, she stated, "I never wanted to have children. I always found them a burden."

Another example:

> In the meeting of August 17, 1994, with regard to his involvement in the children's extracurricular activities, Mr. Thompson stated, "School plays are boring. When I do go, I generally fall asleep."

Another example:

> In my initial meeting with the parents on August 12, 1994, I asked them if they had any pictures of the children. Mrs. Esposito took out her wallet and proudly showed me a half-dozen pictures of the two children. In contrast, Mr. Esposito not only did not have any, but claimed that he never carried them. Furthermore, when his wife was proudly showing them to me, he sat impassively.

An example of this principle from the sex-abuse evaluation:

> At various times during my three interviews with Gloria, she rubbed her genitals with her hand. This was not an occasional or superficial phenomenon. Rather, she rubbed her vulva vigorously and was clearly gaining pleasure from the act. When I said to her that such things are usually done privately, and not in public, she responded, "My mommy used to rub me there and asked me to rub her there too. When I told her that I didn't like it, she told me that I'd get to like it, and I did."

Another example from a sex-abuse evaluation:

> He told me that if I didn't go down on him he'd beat the shit out of me.

This statement provided compelling proof that the child had been sexually abused. Obviously, it does not include what I refer to as the "borrowed scenario," fragments so often seen in the descriptions of children who are falsely accusing sex abuse.

The Use of Diagnostic Labels Psychiatrists, almost reflexively, feel the need to provide diagnostic labels in their evaluations. Such indiscriminate use of diagnostic labels can cause trouble in a child-custody evaluation and often in a sex-abuse evaluation. (In contrast, they may be extremely important in sanity and competency evaluations.) In the custody evaluation, the court is basically asking, "Who is the preferable parent?" It is not likely that a diagnostic label is going to add a significant amount of information here. Is the schizophrenic a better or worse parent than a psychopath? Is the hysteric a better or worse parent than an obsessive-compulsive? These are absurd questions. In addition to comparative diagnoses being of little value, they open the examiner to criticism. For example, the cross-examining attorney might ask the examiner to define the word *schizophrenia*. Following the presentation of the definition, the attorney may produce a standard psychiatric dictionary. The attorney may then ask the examiner if he (she) recognizes that particular glossary or dictionary as one of the authoritative texts in the field. The likelihood is that the examiner will say *yes*. The lawyer will then read the definition of schizophrenia provided by that volume. Even if the examiner were to be an internationally famous authority on the subject, and even though the definition in the dictionary might have been written by a librarian, the court is likely to view the written definition as having greater validity than the examiner's verbal one. (After all, everyone knows that things in print are more likely to be true than things that are said!) Accordingly, there is much to lose, and little if anything to gain, by using diagnostic labels.

Such displays in the courtroom make a mockery of psychiatry. I often say that "God forgot to read DSM-IV before putting human beings down on earth." Not even the most astute diagnosticians are likely to agree about which diagnostic label best fits a particular person. As a result, no matter what diagnosis the evaluator provides, an opposing attorney is likely to find another serious and competent examiner who will come up with an entirely different diagnosis. Predictably, the lawyers will spin off on this issue in that it provides an ostensibly important reason to lengthen the litigation down this diversionary track. Accordingly, providing diagnoses only opens up a can of worms in the courtroom and the examiner does well not to provide attorneys with this time-consuming and wasteful ploy in their adversarial games. Accordingly, I rarely provide a diagnosis in my report. If I am asked on the witness stand what a person's diagnosis is, I will refuse to answer the question and claim that it is not relevant to this evaluation. If given an opportunity to explain (sometimes I am and sometimes not), I will speak about how symptoms and a variety of other behavioral manifestations are the criteria on which I decide who is the preferable parent. I describe how diagnostic labels do not provide significant information in this regard and can be a waste of time and money to focus on in the courtroom. Accordingly, my refusal to provide a diagnosis is in the service of courtroom efficiency.

The examiner should describe those symptoms and behavioral patterns that interfere with parental capacity—regardless of the diagnostic disorder of which they may be a manifestation. For example, in one report I stated:

> A family interview was conducted with the Smith family on September 23, 1978. As the parents and the two girls entered the room, Jane (age 3) tripped on the threshold. She fell down and began to cry. She quickly got up, however, and ran to her father and put her head in his lap. As she sobbed he caressed her head and made reassuring comments such as "Don't worry baby, everything will be all right" and "Daddy will kiss it and make it all better." Following a few such kisses and caresses Jane stopped crying, but remained sitting next to her father while her head rested against his arm. While this was going on Mrs. Smith sat staring into space, seemingly oblivious to what was going on. This observation tends to confirm Mr. Smith's allegation that when he leaves his home in the morning, his wife is sitting in the living room watching television, and when he returns at the end of the day, she is still in the same position, with no evidence that the house has been taken care of or the children supervised to any significant degree.

As I am sure the reader appreciates, such descriptions have far more clout than the diagnostic term *schizophrenia*. It is very difficult, if not impossible, for a cross-examining attorney to use such a statement in the service of discrediting the examiner. This attorney will just have to let it rest as one of the strong arguments against his (her) client's position and hunt for other issues on which to focus.

Another example of the superiority of the substantive description over the diagnostic label:

> In each of my three individual interviews with Mrs. ST and in each of the two family interviews, she rambled, at times to the point of incoherence. In response to a question she would often start on the topic, but then quickly verbalize a series of loose associations that became increasingly unrelated to the issue under discussion. In every one of the individual interviews she asked me whether the conversation was being tape-recorded. Each time I informed her that I never tape-record without permission. Yet, she insisted that I place my tape recorder in front of her, without an inserted cassette, so that she could be reassured that I was not deceiving her. Even after I did this, she searched under the chairs and couch in order to reassure herself that I was still not taping the conversations with a hidden tape recorder. I consider her rambling to the point of incoherence to represent a grave problem in her communication with her husband and her children, and this was demonstrated many times over in the family interviews. Her suspiciousness is likely to engender in her children a similar attitude toward others, and this will interfere with their interpersonal relationships.

At no point did I refer to this woman as a paranoid schizophrenic, which she clearly was. To do so would have invited unnecessary and time-wasting questions in the courtroom.

Others have come forth with the same caveat. Saxe (1975), for example, warns against the use of diagnoses in custody proceedings and discusses how misleading they can be and how they may complicate rather than elucidate the issues under consideration. He points out how the use of such diagnoses as *schizophrenia* and *psychosis* may mislead a naive court into believing that these disorders are invariably associated with the inability to function as a parent. Bazelon (1974), a well-known judge, deplores the psychiatrist's penchant for diagnostic labeling and describes how it can narrow options for patients once they have been put into a particular niche by a diagnosis.

Even in sex-abuse evaluations one must be extremely cautious with regard to a formal diagnostic label taken from DSM-IV. There are situations, however, in which one might want to use very specific symptomatic terms such as *hysteria* (interestingly not to be found in DSM-IV) and *paranoia*. These are well-defined symptoms and less subject to reasonable argumentation. One can use these terms without applying a specific DSM-IV diagnostic category, because the person satisfies the criteria necessary for the application of this symptomatic label. (A diagnosis usually includes a specific cluster of symptoms.)

The use of diagnostic terms can extend, at times, to labels that may be generally viewed as signifying pathology. For example, one may even get in trouble using a term like *obsessive*. As is true for most disorders, there is a continuum between the normal and the pathological—and there is often no sharp cutoff point between the two. For example, most people at times become obsessed with or "hooked" on an idea. It is within the normal range of human behavior to become so preoccupied, on occasion, and to have difficulty "unhooking" oneself. It is very difficult to define the exact point where the normal proclivity for preoccupation ends and the pathological degree begins—the degree that would justifiably be called an obsessional disorder.

Using such terms as *alcoholism* may similarly cause the examiner difficulty in the courtroom. Alcoholism, too, lies on a continuum from low-frequency drinking, through medium-frequency drinking, to heavy drinking. The point where normal and occasional drinking ends and a frequency warranting the label of alcoholism begins is a very blurred one. Accordingly, if one refers to a parent as "an alcoholic," the opposing attorney may ask the examiner to define alcoholism, to state exactly how one diagnoses it, and to state specifically exactly how much alcohol one must consume in order to be so diagnosed. There are people who can consume huge amounts of alcohol and exhibit no interference in functioning, and there are others who, after very small amounts, become incapacitated. The alcohol ingestion becomes a "problem" when it interferes with functioning in significant areas of life, e.g., work, family relationships, and social relationships. Accordingly, one does well to describe the incapacitation that is caused by the alcohol and avoid terms such as alcoholism or alcohol abuse. This may appear to be a very fine distinction to the examiner, but it is the kind of thing that an attorney might want to seize upon in cross-examination. Accordingly, it is preferable to focus on the behavioral difficulties that result from alcohol ingestion. One may, however, quote the interviewees who used such terms. By doing so, one "plants seeds" and gets across the message to the court.

Seed Planting I have found the "seed planting" principle to be useful. Occasionally, the examiner will have very strong suspicions about an undesirable personality trait manifested by a party being evaluated, but will not have enough evidence to make a definitive statement regarding this trait. One way to get such strong suspicion "into the record" and, thereby, plant a seed in the judge's or jury member's mind is to quote a party who makes the particular criticism. For example, in one case a husband, who was suing for custody of the children, was in a far less stable financial situation than his wife. Under state equitable distribution laws, the assets of the marriage are to be divided equally between the partners, regardless of sex. Under these laws, a husband can conceivably receive alimony from his former wife and, if the children are living with him, support payments for them as well. Under such circumstances it is even possible for him to remain in the marital house, especially if it is in the children's best interests to remain there with the primary custodial parent (the usual case). The examiner might have the tendency to be biased against the husband in such circumstances because it is so untraditional an arrangement and can easily be viewed as exploitation on his part.

In this particular case, I was convinced that the husband was exploitive and that his desire for this arrangement was just one manifestation of this defect. However, I could not use his claims for custody and child support as confirmation because he was operating with the blessings of state law and could claim, through his attorney, bias on my part. What I did here was to quote a number of the wife's statements in which she accused her husband of being exploitative. These were statements made to me in his presence. In this way, I was able to introduce the notion without actually claiming that I was supportive of the wife's position. I do not use this principle for devious purposes. I do not, as many lawyers do, utilize the principle in order to misrepresent. Rather, I use it in order to emphasize a point for which I have full conviction, but for which I do not have enough "proof."

In Chapter Five I will discuss at length the yes/no question and the ways in which the person testifying can, on occasion, "bend the rules" and "slip in" extra information in spite of the constraints of that type of question. Sometimes one can "plant a seed" in the context of one's response here. For example, a cross-examining attorney, while pointing to a statement I made in one of my books or reports, may ask, "Is it not correct, doctor, that you have stated the following. . . ." The attorney will then read a statement of mine that is actually valid, but is basically misleading the court because it is an out-of-context quote. Often I will respond: "This is correct, as an out-of-context quote." Here, I am planting the seed in the judge's mind that the attorney has not provided the full quote and there is the strong implication that the court is being misled (which is usually the case under such circumstances). In Chapter Five I will provide other examples of seed planting, especially in the context of responses to yes/no questions.

When the Parties Disagree People involved in lawsuits generally disagree. This is not only seen in the individual interviews but in the joint interviews. My general procedure is to shelve points in which both parties are in diametric disagreement. I do not take the position, "If we have to stay here all night, I'm going to get to the bottom of this. I'm going to find out who's telling the truth and who's lying." This could indeed take all night and one still might not know who is telling the truth and who is lying. Accordingly, after two or three rounds (at most) I interrupt the parties and shelve the issue. Nor does it generally appear in my report. It is an error for the examiner to accept one party's rendition over the other; to do so may be a manifestation of bias. One should only list those deficiencies that are admitted to by the interviewee and/ or are directly observed by the examiner.

Examiners should base their strongest arguments on issues about which *both* parties agree. In such situations the nonsupported attorney will not be able to provide a meaningful refutation because his (her) own client has agreed that the deficit exists. For example, a father may complain that his wife stays up drinking all night and, when the children return from school the next day, she is still sleeping in bed 90 percent of the afternoons. The wife may deny the drinking but may agree that she is a "night person" and therefore needs much sleep during the day. She may claim that she is only asleep on 50 percent of the afternoons when the children arrive home. In such circumstances, the examiner should quote each parent's rendition and then might state:

> Even if Mrs. Jones's more conservative estimate is valid, it still represents a deficiency in maternal capacity in that she is not available for her children half of the days on their return home from school.

These deficiencies, on which both parents agree, are very powerful arguments and are extremely difficult, if not impossible, for an attorney to refute in cross-examination.

The Use of Psychological Tests Just as psychiatrists reflexively believe that it behooves them to go through the motions of getting a family history, doing a mental status, and then providing "the diagnosis," psychologists reflexively administer psychological tests. At this time the ones that are most in vogue are the *Minnesota Multiphasic Personality Inventory-2 (MMPI-2)* (Hathaway & McKinley, 1989), the *Millon Clinical Multiaxial Inventory-II (MCMI-II)* (Millon, 1987), the *Rorschach Test* (Rorschach, 1921), and the *Thematic Apperception Test (TAT)* (Murray, 1936). These tests were *not* designed to determine which of two parents would better serve as the primary custodial parent, and they certainly were not designed to find out whether a child was sexually abused or whether an alleged perpetrator did indeed abuse a child. One *really* has to squeeze the data hard in order to come out with anything that is of probative value in a court of law regarding these questions. Psychologists who use them often remind me of the old saying, "When the only tool you have is a hammer, everything looks like a nail." I have seen reports in child-custody and sex-abuse evaluations in which the complete report consists only of these instruments. Unfortunately, courts of law are very impressed with them and somehow believe that they get to the deeper recesses of the unconscious mind and provide special information that is not observable to the interviewer. I do not deny that these instruments do have some value in certain situations. The MMPI-2 and MCMI-II can provide *some* information about underlying psychodynamic processes and personality patterns that may be of use in therapy. But this does not mean that they will be of use in a court of law for the aforementioned purposes. The four instruments might prove useful in sanity cases, and IQ tests might prove useful in competence cases. It is all a question of using the proper diagnostic tool for the proper situation.

Hearsay   *Hearsay* refers to unverified information gained or acquired from another and not part of one's direct knowledge. Courts, with justification, are very cautious about the admissibility of hearsay testimony. However, mental health examinations often, by necessity, include hearsay data. Let us take the situation in which a wife claims that her husband has beaten her mercilessly on at least 15 occasions. He denies ever having beaten her, even once. Obviously, somebody is lying here. Let us take the example further and assume that their one child (age two) is too young to provide credible information regarding these alleged incidents. Obviously, it is an issue that is pertinent to a custody evaluation, but it is not one in which it is easy to come to a definite conclusion. To accept either party's rendition involves providing hearsay testimony.

There are men who beat their wives mercilessly and who deny, even in courts of law, that they ever engaged in such behavior. And there are women who will fabricate such allegations, recognizing that they can cause their husbands significant grief by claiming such abuse. To accept as valid the wife's statement that her husband beats her is basically providing hearsay testimony because the examiner himself (herself) has not had the opportunity to observe such events.

Under these circumstances I might state in my report:

> If the court substantiates Mrs. Smith's allegation that her husband has beaten her on at least 15 occasions, while in a state of inebriation, then I would consider it yet another reason to deprive him of primary custodial status.

The reader should note that I leave it to the court to make the final decision regarding whether the hearsay evidence here is admissible. No matter how credible the disputed allegation may appear to be, the examiner does well to avoid accepting it as absolute truth. Evaluators who do so may be subjecting themselves to justifiable criticism in court and may look foolish on cross-examination.

Little Bullets vs. Big Bombs In the course of the evaluation the examiner does well to avoid detailed inquiry into situations in which people are making mountains out of molehills. This is commonly done in the course of litigation, and the litigious process often encourages it. People get so carried away that every little bit of information is considered to be useful data. Every little pebble is considered ammunition. Differentiation is not made between the little bullets and the big bombs. Often lawyers do not make these distinctions either, so carried away are they by the litigious process. However, it behooves them not to make these distinctions, especially when the clients are very rich. Accordingly, in the course of the data-collection process examiners should interrupt the parties if they are arguing over minor points on issues that are not crucial to the evaluation. Often, I will preface such interruptions with comments such as: "Please do not interpret my interrupting you now as discourtesy. It's really designed to save time and money. I do not consider this an important issue, so let's go on." In some cases such interruptions may take place on numerous occasions throughout the course of a single session. Forensic evaluations are not for the passive types. The final report, as well, should not include frivolous and inconsequential material. Rather, it should include only the important issues, issues that are going to have formidable weight on either side of the scale.

The Importance of Balance Evaluators do well to provide a balanced report. To present one party as having assets only, and the other liabilities only, compromises the evaluation. It cannot but produce a certain amount of incredulity in the minds of the judge and/or jury members. Such one-sided reports are the hallmarks of bias. The most credible evaluators are those who are truly balanced and unbiased. In a custody/visitation dispute each parent is seen as having *both* assets and liabilities and the question is which parent has fewer liabilities and more assets. In a sex-abuse evaluation one wants to consider the dozens of differentiating criteria and assess whether each one warrants the conclusion that the sex abuse did occur or that the sex abuse did not occur.

Lawyers have sometimes been very unhappy with me for including criticisms of their clients in my report. They consider these criticisms to weaken the report and fear that they will provide handles for the opposing attorney to weaken it even further. They consider such criticisms to represent "holes in the dyke" that risk a crumbling of the whole wall. I believe that such attorneys are being short-sighted. I believe that describing such weaknesses on the part of the client whose position I am supporting enhances my credibility rather than lessens it. I generally try to impress upon such attorneys my belief that the small disadvantages associated with my describing deficits in clients are small compared to the disadvantage of my appearing biased or so deeply committed to the client's position that I am blinding myself to obvious deficiencies. I have *never* allowed a lawyer to talk me into removing descriptions of such weaknesses from my preliminary report. (I am referring here to situations in which all attempts at my serving as an impartial, or even as one side's expert with cooperation with the other side, have proven futile and I have decided to serve as the expert of the requesting party because, after interviewing the party, I have developed the conviction that my services are warranted.)

Comments on the Reports of Other Examiners

In many cases reports of other examiners are provided. The evaluator does well to read these carefully and to comment on them, with regard to both areas of agreement and areas of disagreement. As mentioned, the ideal way to comment on these reports is to review them together with the clients and give them the opportunity to comment on each point as it is read. This is far preferable to the usual procedure in which the examiner reads these documents alone and then presents the clients with the opportunity to comment on isolated quotations. Sometimes the examiner may miss important points in the course of such solitary review, points that are readily picked up by the clients.

In the course of such reviews, my sharpest criticism is often directed to those evaluators who make custody recommendations without evaluating *both* parents. Even sharper criticism has been directed against those who come to conclusions regarding sexual abuse and who do not attempt to interview the accuser, *and* the alleged perpetrator, *and* the alleged child victim. I have seen dozens of sex-abuse evaluations in which the accusing mother is seen briefly or not at all, the child is seen alone, and the father was never even invited to be interviewed. Yet, the conclusion is made that the father did indeed sexually abuse the child. Sometimes this conclusion is based on information collected during only a half-hour of interviewing (accusing mother and child combined). Furthermore, I am extremely critical of evaluators who do not conduct joint interviews—my richest source of information in custody and sex-abuse evaluations. On occasion, a previous examiner comes to a conclusion based on what I consider to be erroneous information. Review of that report gives me the opportunity to provide input about this error to the court.

Early in my work in custody evaluations I was somewhat hesitant to comment on the reports of previous examiners. I suspected that I might be criticized for having gone beyond the confines of what a report should include. However, there were really no precedents regarding what should be in reports, and in many ways the field is still open territory regarding how to conduct an evaluation and what to include in a report. There were a few cases in which it was clear to me that my comments would provide a definite service to the court because of what I considered to be egregious errors made by previous examiners. My report provided me with an excellent vehicle for bringing these to the attention of the judge. My experience has been that my earlier hesitations were not justified. I have not once had the experience in which an attorney criticized me on the stand for having commented on the reports of other examiners. Accordingly, I strongly recommend that evaluators devote a section of their report (preferably at the end) to a discussion of the findings of previous examiners. Again, it is important that examiners mention that their findings are based on their own evaluations and that the information derived from other reports was ancillary and served only as a point of departure for their own inquiries.

Probably one of the easiest ways to make a lifelong enemy is to come down heavily upon a colleague in one's report. It matters not whether this person is an acquaintance, or a friend, or someone who is living in another part of the country. To roundly criticize another professional in a legal report, a report that is entered into evidence in a court of law, a report that may be criticized from the witness stand, is bound to produce strong acrimonious feelings in the criticized person. Evaluators who are hesitant to provide such criticisms because they fear this animosity should not be involved in forensic evaluations. To hesitate to provide such criticisms because one fears that the professional relationship will be compromised is going to inevitably compromise the commitment that the evaluator has to the patient. This is a choice that every examiner must make. Lawyers often do this with impunity. In the courtroom they become the vicious antagonists of one another and yet will often still remain friends. Of course, there are some situations in which their being adversaries escalates to the point where they come to hate each other, but this usually only takes place when one has engaged in egregious behavior that goes beyond the expected degree of legalized and ethical psychopathy required for the practice of law. (I will elaborate on this statement in the final chapter of this book.)

Conclusions and Recommendations

I summarize my conclusions in a section entitled *Conclusions and Recommendations*. There I restate my final conclusions and outline some of the main arguments for them. I elaborate here on the *summary* of the conclusions and recommendations provided at the beginning of the report.

Consistent with my position not to provide diagnoses in my report, I may make a statement in this section about my failure to provide a diagnosis. I usually make a comment along these lines:

> I believe it would be injudicious on the court's part to devote itself to inquiries regarding the specific diagnosis of each of the parties. Most often such diagnoses do not shed light on the primary issues confronting the court. Furthermore, different examiners are likely to provide different diagnoses and even the most competent examiners may have differences of opinion—such is the nature of the art/science of psychology and psychiatry. Accordingly, I would consider it a waste of the court's time to provide diagnoses and have therefore omitted them from this report.

This statement protects me from the kind of cross-examination I might have been subjected to if I simply omitted diagnoses without providing an explanation. If such a statement is omitted, a cross-examining attorney might ask me (with intonations of utter incredulity), "Doctor, isn't it *unusual* (stated slowly and emphatically, preferably with eyebrows raised) not to have a diagnosis in a psychiatric report?"   We see here yet another example of using a report to protect oneself in advance from predictable criticism in a courtroom.

I will generally make a statement as well about my failure to give a name to the custody/visitation arrangement. I often made a comment along these lines:

> The court may note that I have not given any *name* to the custody/
> visitation arrangement recommended here. This was purposely done be-
> cause it is my belief that deliberations over the *name* of the arrangement are
> often wasteful of time and money. I believe I have answered the court's re-
> quest that I provide information about parenting capacity as well as who shall
> be designated the primary custodial parent and who shall have primary deci-
> sion-making powers in each of the important areas. Accordingly, I have
> provided what should best be referred to as a *parenting plan.*

This too protects me from an incredulous attorney asking me in the courtroom, "Isn't it *unusual*, Doctor, for an examiner not to give a name in a report to the custodial arrangement?" Again, my comment provides advance protection from what the attorney might have enjoyed exposing in court as a deficiency in me and my report.

In this section, as well, I comment upon the advisability of treatment. Courts almost routinely order treatment for one and all parties involved in child-custody and even sex-abuse lawsuits. Little thought is given to the person's motivation for therapy and insight into whether or not there are psychological problems—two provisos for meaningful therapy. Rather, there is a rubber-stamp, automatic recommendation that the various parties go into treatment, generally with separate therapists. Not only is it rare for everyone to follow through with this recommendation, but even if it were implemented, in most cases it is not likely to prove useful in that litigating parties have interpersonal problems that are not likely to be resolved by separate therapies. Courts generally have much more of a commitment to the efficacy of psychotherapy than I do. If a party exhibits absolutely no interest or motivation for therapy, I emphasize to the court the futility of ordering treatment for such a party. Generally, this statement is completely ignored by the judge.

Typically, a report ends with a statement along these lines:

> I hope the court finds this report useful. Enclosed please find a sum-
> mary of my curriculum vitae, which provides a statement of my qualifications
> for conducting this evaluation. A full CV is available on request.

The report concludes with a signature as well as a list of the persons to whom copies of the report are being sent. Most often these include the parents, the attorneys, and (when appointed) a guardian ad litem.

SOME IMPORTANT FINAL CAVEATS

As mentioned, it is important for evaluators to continually envision themselves on the witness stand when writing their final reports. Every sentence (and I literally mean that) may be used as a point of departure in cross-examination, the main purpose of which may be to embarrass and discredit the examiner. The issue of truth here is far less important than the issue of winning the conflict. The astute attorney will be ever looking for such "holes in the dike," and the examiner does well not to provide any (and I do mean *any*). The best way to avoid such a compromise in one's testimony is to be thinking of oneself being cross-examined as one writes and reviews the report.

There are examiners who destroy their primary clinical handwritten notes. In fact, I have come across clinics in which this is routinely done; in fact, it is the clinic's policy to do so. There are no *good* reasons for this practice, only *bad* reasons. Destroying notes communicates an extremely important message, namely, *cover-up*. No judge, no jury can possibly look favorably upon an examiner who engages in this practice. It indicates that the party who destroyed the notes has been doing something that he (she) is wary of exposing in a court of law. Such a practice *must* compromise the examiner's credibility and reputation as a responsible professional. I myself have never done this and cannot imagine myself ever doing so. However, there is nothing I ever write down in my notes that I am ashamed of and so have had nothing to hide. Unfortunately, I suspect that such practice is widespread, although one can never know the exact ubiquity of the practice.

FOUR
PREPARING FOR COURTROOM TESTIMONY

INTRODUCTION

Because there is usually a significant time gap between the completion of the evaluation and the time the examiner is asked to testify in court, some preparation is generally necessary. Obviously, examiners who merely ruffle through their notes while waiting to be called to the witness stand are not likely to provide as effective testimony as those who prepare properly for providing testimony. Evaluators have a strong moral obligation to dedicate themselves assiduously to this task; not to do so represents a compromise of one's ethical and professional responsibilities.

THE UPDATE CONFERENCE

In most forensic evaluations in which I have been involved, there has been a 6- to 18-month gap between the time I have submitted my final report and the time I have gone to court. Because this delay is psychologically detrimental to the involved parties, it generally entrenches the various kinds of psychopathology produced or intensified by involvement in litigation. Because of my appreciation that important things can happen during this hiatus, things that might be pertinent to my testimony, I include a proviso in my provisions document that stipulates an update meeting, prior to my court appearance. The stipulation states:

> 11) When there has been a significant passage of time between the submission of my report and the trial date, I will generally invite the primary participating parties for an interview update prior to my court appearance. This conference enables me to acquaint myself with developments that succeeded my report and ensures that my presentation in court will include the most recent information. All significant adult participants will be invited to this meeting and on occasion one or more of the children (especially teenagers). This conference will be held as long as at least one party wishes to attend.

This stipulation enables me to provide the most up-to-date and therefore meaningful presentation in court, one that takes into account factors that might not have been operative at the time of my evaluation. An extremely important fringe benefit of this meeting is that it places me in a stronger position in the courtroom than examiners who do not hold such a meeting. Often, some of these examiners' reports are one to two years old at the time of their testimony, and this places them at a serious disadvantage.

Generally, the nonpreferred parties are unreceptive to this update meeting and are often discouraged from attending by their attorneys. However, the provisions document makes it clear that even if only one party attends the meeting, it will still take place. Invariably the preferred party meets with me because of the appreciation that the updated information cannot but strengthen my testimony and put me at a significant advantage over adversarial examiners with out-of-date information. The attending parties also appreciate that the failure of the adversarial party to attend can be used to their advantage. They recognize that that party's absence prevents them from refuting whatever is told to me. Parties who do not attend, whether or not as the result of their attorneys' advice, are generally making a mistake. They deprive themselves of the opportunity for input into issues that are generally crucial to my decision. For example, they deprive themselves of the opportunity to comment on and even refute information provided by the parent who attends— information that might not be accurate. Furthermore, they deprive themselves of the chance to change my mind, a possibility that still exists—especially because changes in circumstances can bring about an alteration of my conclusions. I cannot emphasize strongly enough the importance of such meetings and consider them crucial to the thorough evaluation. Examiners who fail to conduct such meetings are voluntarily placing themselves at a disadvantage when they go to court and, with regard to the focus on this chapter, are depriving themselves of an important mechanism for assuaging fears they may have about courtroom testimony.

ASSUAGING FEARS OF PROVIDING COURT TESTIMONY

One of the reasons mental health professionals hesitate to involve themselves in custody litigation is the fear of a court appearance. The prospect of being cross-examined on the witness stand chills the blood of most mental health examiners. In fact, this is probably the most common reason why the vast majority of mental health professionals refuse to involve themselves in cases that may involve providing courtroom testimony. Such dread is not necessary. The more thorough the evaluation has been and the more familiar the examiner is with the family, the greater will be his (her) conviction for the recommendations made. And such conviction is the best allayer of these fears. Knowledge is a powerful weapon against fear. The more familiar we are with a situation, the more we know about it, the less likely we will fear it. Evaluators who dedicate themselves to the task of doing a thorough evaluation and who have a full grasp of their data arm themselves with the best defense against courtroom fears. To have "the facts at one's fingertips" is the most powerful antedote to such concerns. To know exactly where in one's files to look when one is asked a question is also a powerful assuager of these anticipatory fears. And to have full conviction for one's opinion, without significant lingering doubts about the validity and veracity of one's opinion, is also extremely useful for reducing courtroom anxiety. Knowing that there is absolutely nothing in one's notes or file that should cause embarrassment in the courtroom can also serve to protect oneself from such fears.

Evaluators have heard stories about attorneys trying to compromise the credibility of the testifying expert by such methods as trickery and hairsplitting. They have heard about attorneys becoming aggressive—to the point of being insulting and sarcastic. They know about lawyers who attempt to make them look like fools. They know about courtroom antics and histrionics. These are some of the reasons why examiners avoid getting involved in testifying if they possibly can. The evaluator may be honest, direct, and confident of having a valid position. He (she) may be trying to be of service to the family and may feel strongly that the testimony can be helpful. Yet the prospect of being involved in courtroom games whose main purpose is to degrade—professions of the "best interests of the child" notwithstanding—significantly discourages the involvement of many mental health professionals.

Although some witnesses are intimidated by a lawyer's pomposity and bombast, I generally welcome such displays. I come to the court after having conducted an extensive and time-consuming evaluation. I have gathered an enormous amount of information, am convinced of the validity of my conclusions, and am confident therefore when on the witness stand. I appreciate well that an attorney's histrionics and expressions of incredulity are maneuvers typical of lawyers whose positions are weak. Such displays are often provided for the benefit of clients and give the impression that the lawyers are working vigorously to earn their fees. One should take much more seriously attorneys who are well prepared and have logically and consistently thought out their arguments. They have a definite plan for their inquiry and the points logically follow one another. The people we should take most seriously in life are generally those who "speak softly and carry a big stick." But even here, if the examiner has done a solid evaluation, there is little to fear. He (she), too, should also "speak softly and carry a big stick."

The examiner's testimony, as well, will gain or lose credibility in accordance with the same principles. The more volatility, the more sermonizing, the more harangues and histrionics, the less credibility the evaluator will have. And if the examiner becomes hostile, it suggests that a "sore point" or "soft spot" has been touched upon by the cross-examining attorney. Such overreaction and defensiveness will give an astute attorney a good "handle" for an effective and possibly humiliating line of inquiry. The sensitive attorney recognizes that such emotional displays and defensiveness are compensations for basic deficiencies in the testifier's arguments and will exploit this knowledge to full advantage. At the point where the examiner has exhibited such defensiveness, the lawyer will recognize the "soft spot" and "hammer away" relentlessly. These attorneys may not know exactly what they are looking for, but they recognize that a detailed inquiry into all aspects of this particular area is likely to prove useful for their position.

Examiners may not only be fearful about what the cross-examining attorney may ask them, but even about what questions they may be asked in the course of direct examination, i.e., examination by the attorney whose position they are supporting. In situations in which one is serving as an impartial examiner, one cannot speak with that attorney privately to review the questions to be asked in court. One can, however, speak with both attorneys simultaneously, but this generally is not feasible. When I do serve as one side's expert (again, after having made every attempt to serve as an impartial), I am free to discuss with that party the basic plan of inquiry. In the course of such discussions, most attorneys invite my input with regard to the important points to be focused on in the course of the direct examination. However, my experience has been that most attorneys, even the most dedicated ones, do not cover all the points to the depth that I consider proper and warranted. Sometimes they get sidetracked by the objections and side issues that are so common in the courtroom. Sometimes they have to work under time pressures and cannot indulge themselves a full exploration of all the points that would be useful to present to the court.

One way of circumventing this problem is to ask the attorney if he (she) would be interested in your providing him with a specific list of questions to be asked in the course of direct testimony. My experience has been that the secure ones welcome this opportunity. The insecure ones may feel threatened that a nonattorney is providing them with a line of inquiry and will balk at the suggestion. I am not requesting that attorneys reflexively follow my recommended line of questioning; rather, I suggest that they give serious consideration to incorporating my questions into their own inquiry. If the attorney is comfortable accepting the examiner's suggested line of inquiry and specific questions and if he (she) can also incorporate them with conviction into his own line of inquiry, then the examiner's fears will be reduced.

I have found this practice of direct examination to be particularly useful in sex-abuse cases. At the time I write this (early 1995), I have been involved in such cases for over 12 years. Most of the attorneys cannot claim such a long "track record" in sex-abuse cases. In fact, the sex-abuse case that we are involved with together may have been the attorney's first or second. They have been brought in not so much for their expertise in the field of sex abuse but for their expertise in other legal areas that have led the client to believe that the attorney might be useful in this case as well. Secure attorneys have been quite receptive to my input into many of the details involving the direct examination.

In my early years, I too was fearful of providing testimony in court. As my competence increased and as I became ever more confident of the value of my evaluations, I became progressively less fearful. Furthermore, as I became familiar with ways of dealing with the aforementioned courtroom antics, I also found my fears reduced. In recent years, I have found that I actually enjoy going to court. I often compare providing courtroom testimony to a fencing match between the attorney and myself. However, it is not a fencing match between equals; rather, it is a fencing match between a party with a short sword and poor protection (the testifier on the witness stand) and a party with a long, sharp sword and superior protection (the cross-examining attorney). Because I enter the conflict at a disadvantage (or handicap) and because I am still required to play by rules in which I am viewed as an equal, the challenge becomes even greater and more enticing. Such an attitude, I believe, has also played a role in reducing my fears of providing testimony in court.

PREPARATION FOR THE COURT APPEARANCE

The Time Frame of the Testimony

Examiners should strongly request that their appearances be scheduled for a particular time on a particular day. Law courts are notorious for their lack of concern for witnesses' time and noncourt obligations. Witnesses can literally sit for days outside the courtroom waiting to be called. Whereas I recognize that one cannot know in advance how long a particular witness will be on the stand and that it is necessary to avoid a situation in which the court is available and there is no one standing by to be examined, the courts still show great insensitivity in this area. Although professional examiners are generally afforded a little more courtesy than parents and attorneys, they still do well to make every attempt to impress upon the lawyers their desire to appear at a particular time.

The Importance of Prepayment for Court Testimony

The issue of trying to delineate the time frame of one's testimony cannot be separated from the issue of payment for one's courtroom services. As the reader may recall, in my list of provisos for involving myself in custody litigation, I specify that I will be paid in advance for my time in court. There is no differentiation made between time on the witness stand and time waiting to testify. There are two reasons why my fee is higher for court appearances: (1) testifying is a more demanding experience than conducting an evaluation and (2) it "helps the client remember" that I am in court and increases motivation to get the attorney to put me on the stand as soon as possible. However, in spite of requests for such consideration, the examiner will often end up sitting in the courthouse for many hours, waiting to be called.

On the subject of being paid for my time in court, I also ask to be paid in advance. I generally submit a written estimate of the anticipated expenses and indicate, of course, that this is only an estimate and that after my appearance the fee will be adjusted accordingly, in either direction. I require all parties to pay me in advance for such services, and in many cases I ask that the payment be by certified or bank check. This is especially the case when I have reason to believe that the payer is less than enthusiastic about my testimony or when there is only a short time gap between the issuance of the check and my day of providing testimony. Examiners who believe that I am being extra cautious and even "paranoid" in this regard have never involved themselves in cases of this kind. Those who have, I am certain, have had their own bitter experiences and will, I am sure, fully support this precaution. In most cases, once the examiner has provided testimony, his (her) services are no longer needed, expenses are usually quite high, and money is likely to be prioritized to those upon whom the client is still most dependent. Enough said! I think I have made my point.

The Value of Charts

Charts, especially blown-up charts, can be particularly useful adjuncts to one's testimony. They provide a "visual aid" that might clarify one's testimony and often enhance its value. For example, I have recently found that blown-up charts of my *Sex-Abuse Time-Line Diagrams* (in Gardner, 1995) are particularly effective in association with my testimony in sex-abuse cases. Such testimony often involves my differentiating between a true and a false sex-abuse accusation. One of the ways of differentiating between these two types of allegation is to trace the evolution of the sex-abuse accusation from the very first time the accuser thought that the child was being sexually molested until the time of the evaluator's examination. One is particularly interested in those symptoms alleged to be the result of sex abuse that occurred during the time frame of the exposure to the alleged perpetrator and those symptoms that began after disclosure. Interestingly, these symptoms may be similar, especially in situations in which the child has been subjected to coercive interrogations (legal-process trauma) or indoctrinating therapy by overzealous mental health professionals (therapy trauma). Because in both cases the child has been subjected to a trauma, the symptoms may be the same or very similar. Only by delineating very specifically the time frames during which the symptoms manifested themselves can one know whether they are the result of bona fide sex abuse or legal-process/"therapy" trauma. The charts serve well to make these delineations to the court in a way far more compelling than mere verbal presentation.

Videotapes

Courts are becoming increasingly appreciative of the value of videotapes as an adjunct to testimony. Many courts routinely have video equipment readily available, to be brought in at a moment's notice. In fact, I would consider a court that does not have such equipment available to be compromising the value of the proceedings. In sex-abuse cases especially, I generally videotape because certain selected segments can provide compelling evidence in the course of testimony. Obviously, such demonstrations leave no question as to what was actually said or what transpired. Furthermore, videotaped segments of other examiners can also prove useful. This is especially the case when a child alleged to have been sexually abused has been interviewed by an overzealous examiner who uses anatomical dolls, leading questions, and other coercive techniques. The videotapes generally demonstrate these practices quite dramatically. And this can be especially useful in a court of law. Accordingly, if the examiner plans to use videotapes, then he (she) must arrange through the lawyers beforehand for the availability of such equipment.

Utilization of Depositions

As mentioned, the deposition, although a source of information for the cross-examining attorney, can also be a source of information for an examiner. It provides the evaluator with useful information regarding the lines of inquiry that the attorney is likely to follow in the course of testimony. The attorney conducting the deposition is likely to learn about the examiner's weak points. The examiner can also learn, at the same time, exactly what his (her) weak points are. Astute examiners, then, take pains to rectify these weaknesses between the time of the deposition and the time of courtroom testimony. In most cases in which I have been involved, the time gap between these two events is usually a month or two. Accordingly, the examiner generally has ample time to deal with the weaknesses that may have been disclosed in the course of the deposition.

For example, an attorney, during deposition, may ask the examiner exactly where in the various reports submitted a particular statement was made. The examiner may have a general belief that the statement was made, but does not recall exactly its source. Following the deposition the examiner does well to track down the exact source, because the attorney may repeat the question during the course of testimony.

Another example: Often I am asked for the scientific references for a particular statement I have made. This is a common maneuver utilized by cross-examining attorneys in an attempt to weaken the testimony of an examiner. The "scientific literature" in the mental health professions is such that one can find an article to support anyone's position, so weak is the alleged science on which most of our theories are based. Yet, the rules of the game are to provide such "scientific proof" of what one is saying. Sometimes I can come forth with a specific reference; on other occasions, I have admitted that I was unable to provide the specific reference(s) at the time. However, I have learned something from the attorney and, invariably, when I am asked the same question on the witness stand, I come forth with a few selected references. Although the articles do not generally provide "proof" of anything (as mentioned, our field is such that practically nothing has been "proven"), the response not only serves to frustrate him (her) but makes me look good in a courtroom. Whereas in the deposition he has "won a point," in the course of testimony, the more important "battle" (and I use the word without hesitation), I have won the point. Examiners involved in forensic psychiatry do well to have access to computer searches that will enable them to access articles relevant to their testimony.

Review and Preparation of Records

On the night prior to the court appearance, examiners should review all their material to the point where the major facts are easily recalled. If the examiner has prepared a comprehensive report (the far more preferable procedure), this will be the primary source of refreshing one's memory. If the report has been properly prepared, it will contain all the salient information, information that one is likely to make reference to in the course of one's testimony. If properly prepared, it will have selected the most compelling arguments in support of one's position. It is for this reason, as mentioned, that it is not uncommon for a report of mine to be 70 or 80 pages, or even longer. And this is especially the case in sex-abuse evaluations where I evaluate in depth the accuser, the accused, and the alleged child victim.

In addition, examiners should have their notes well organized so that they can quickly refer to particular points. Impartials compromise their credibility if they have trouble recalling important data or if they cannot readily refer to the material in their notes on a particular issue. An examiner hunting through disorganized notes does both the supported client and the court a disservice. Ideally, the examiner should be so familiar with the material that little direct reference to written notes is necessary. The most impressive testimony is that which is given verbally, freely and spontaneously, by one who "has the facts at his (her) fingertips." As mentioned, a thorough grasp of the material is one of the best ways to reduce fears related to court appearances. And having the full conviction that one's position is valid and that one has compelling support—with material that can be readily conveyed—is the most predictable way to reduce fears of a court appearance. However, one cannot be expected to be a walking encyclopedia, to have every single fact, no matter how minute, in one's memory. Accordingly, the examiner is generally allowed reasonable access to notes, especially for verbatim and/or extensive quotations. But one still must know where the material being referred to is to be found, and such material should be accessed *quickly*. In the service of this goal, I generally divide my files into the following categories:

> 1. Administrative File. Here I include the early correspondence related to my being brought into the case, my provisions document, subsequent correspondence with attorneys and other professionals, and any other information that is generally of an administrative nature. I

include here my own letters as well that are of an administrative nature.

2. Gardner Clinical Notes. I also include here my own clinical notes taken during interviews.

3. Gardner Clinical Report(s). Here I include not only my original report but update reports.

4. Reports of Other Examiners. In this file I not only include the reports of other examiners, but my commentaries, generally dictated at the time I review these reports.

5. Legal Documents. This may be a pile of anywhere from 1 to 12 inches (sometimes even more) of depositions, affidavits, certifications, motions, and even transcripts of former trial testimony. Also in this file I would include transcripts of videotaped interviews. Again, I attach my commentaries, often dictated at the time the document is reviewed. Also in this file I will include school reports, diaries, letters from the clients to other parties, doctors' reports, and police reports.

6. Additional Documents. I might include here detailed hospital charts, nurses' notes, complete doctors' files, and other material that I did not believe warranted a detailed review. Materials of this kind that *do* warrant detailed review are included in files #4 and #5. In a sense, this is a "dead file."

The commentaries on the materials to be found in files #4 and #5 are best conducted with the concerned parties. This is the most efficient way to assess these documents. My usual practice is to review the documents with the concerned parties and to dictate my comments in their presence. The comments also include specific page, paragraph, and line references. These are then attached to the document, and those that warrant direct inclusion in my final report are easily accessed. Accordingly, within the courtroom, I have an efficient method for pinpointing exactly where and when particular statements were made. The reference to the important items is to be found directly in my final report. If I recall a particular reference, but did not include it in my final report, the aforementioned file organization provides me with the best route of access to the particular point.

I recall well an experience I had while being cross-examined by the prosecutor, who was quite vigorous in her examination, even to the point of being arrogant and condescending. This was a very complex case in that there were over 20 accusing children in a nursery school situation, each of whose parents were claiming vociferously that their children had been subjected to the most vile abominations at the hands of the caretaker. At one point, in the course of my testimony, I stated that one of the mothers of an accusing child had made a particular statement. Immediately, with very cocky and incredulous overtones, she said to me, "Tell me, Doctor, exactly *where* and *when* did she say that?" It was quite clear that, when she asked this question, she was confident that she "had me by the balls," so sure was she that the statement had never been made. I knew that she had not recalled this particular statement made by the child's mother. I knew well that the mother had indeed made the statement in her deposition, and I knew also that I considered it important enough to make a notation of that statement in my commentary, which I knew was attached to the original document.

Accordingly, I immediately reached for the pile of depositions and pulled out the transcript of the mother's deposition (there was only one) and then stated, while looking at the face sheet of the deposition, "This was said by Mrs. X in her deposition dated August 12, 1989." I then scanned my three-page commentary, which listed all of the mother's important statements, to ascertain the exact page and line number where the statement could be found. It took me less than ten seconds to spot the quotation. I then stated, "This comment is to be found on page 23, lines four through eight." At that point, I read verbatim what the mother had said, and it provided compelling confirmation that my recollection was indeed accurate.

The prosecutor was temporarily dazed. She lost her composure and said something like, "How in the world did you ever remember that?" I said nothing and did not allow my "victory" to be compromised by any further statement. I just sat there and gloated, which psychologically rubbed salt in her wounds. There is another point here that is quite important. What the examiner says is often less important than the judge's and/or jury's respect for the expert. Lawyers know this well and will try to compromise the credibility of experts in any way they possibly can. One way of doing this is to catch them off guard or to try to impugn them not only in the voir dire but subsequently in the course of cross-examination. Here I was able to turn the tables and compromise the prosecutor. So I not only got across a crucial point but, more importantly, enhanced significantly my credibility to the jury.

Work Product

In some cases, especially those in which my attempts to serve as an impartial have not been successful and I am thereby serving as an adversarial expert, I will have notes in my files that are generally referred to as "work product." These are materials that are of interest and value in the collaborative work that the expert may have with the attorney, but that the attorney might not wish to have revealed to the adversary. They may involve, for example, suggestive lines of inquiry when cross-examining an opposing professional. I generally do not like to involve myself with work-product materials. In the days before word processors, the earlier versions of a report might be considered work product, especially if they contained material that the expert has decided is not to be included in one's final version. Sometimes, one was asked for these earlier versions. With the word processor, however, the earlier versions are often "evaporated" in the course of the computer updates, but the preliminary versions may still be on paper. In recent years, I have not been asked about these preliminary versions. There might be three or four such versions, and to save them is not practical. Furthermore, it is also extremely cumbersome to try to detect what are often minor differences between the various versions. I do not consider throwing out these earlier versions to represent the kind of cover-up already described when one discards or shreds primary clinical notes. Nothing is being hidden here. There is nothing in the discarded files that I am ashamed about. It is just not efficient to save them and spend time detecting the minor differences between the various versions.

As mentioned, work product is often the designation given to material that the attorney does not wish to reveal to the opposing side. My experience has been that such hesitation is most often not warranted. Attorneys have a way of reflexively not giving any information that is not necessary to provide. Obstructionism is the name of the game in legal proceedings. This is the opposite of the name of the "game" that I play. The name of my game is complete openness and honesty in the belief that this is the best way not only to learn the truth but to deal with courtroom testimony. I conduct my evaluations in such a way that there is nothing in my file that I have to be ashamed of.

In fact, some of the material in the so-called work product might often be of value to the attorney, but the reflexive desire to withhold all information may blind him (her) to this reality. For example, I might have a critique of an opposing examiner labeled as "work product," at the request of the attorney. This may include comments on weaknesses in his (her) curriculum vitae, questionable credentials, or "fluff" incorporated therein. Whereas the attorney might consider this the kind of information that he would not want disclosed, I personally welcome it. If the opposing attorney were to select this document from my file and ask me to address myself to what is contained therein, it might compromise the position of the attorney who is examining me because he has unwittingly given me the opportunity to say critical things about his adversarial expert. Accordingly, I usually keep work-product materials in my file. If the opposing attorney asks for them on the witness stand, I let the lawyers and the court decide as to whether or not they are to be disclosed. I therefore maintain my honesty and my dignity and protect myself from any embarrassment, defensiveness, or compromise in my composure that would be associated with trying to hide something that is in my chart or not talking about something that transpired.

The Rules of the Game

The courtroom has much in common with a spectator sport, especially when there are outside observers. Like all sports, it is important that one knows the rules of the game before one competes. These are sometimes referred to as courtroom procedures. One of the procedures relates to the practice that the attorney who is conducting the direct examination will provide the witness with great latitude and flexibility regarding the answering of questions. In contrast, the cross-examining attorney is going to generally restrict the examiner, often by confining him (her) to answering only yes/no questions. My experience has been that courts vary enormously with regard to this stringency of the cross-examination. In some jurisdictions (such as the Greater New York City area, where I live and practice), the courts tend to be somewhat stringent with regard to these questions, and cross-examining attorneys are likely to be quite hard-nosed with regard to imposing them upon a witness—especially a witness who may be providing very compelling testimony against their clients. In contrast, I have testified in jurisdictions where the courts allow an expert great flexibility with regard to answering questions, even under cross-examination. However, even in the same jurisdiction, judges themselves vary significantly with regard to such stringency, from the most relaxed to the most rigid. And lawyers, too, tend to vary in this regard.

Accordingly, it behooves examiners to find out exactly what the "rules of the game" are in the courtroom in which they will be testifying. Not to do so is to deprive oneself of an important bit of information relevant to one's testimony. As will be described in the next chapter, examiners do well to (1) formally subscribe to the rules and submit to the procedures and (2) at the same time, while submitting in accordance with dictum #1, get away with as much as they can. Accordingly, bending the rules as much as one can is also part of the game. However, one must know first what the rules are that one is trying to circumvent. The attorneys are the best source of information, and the examiner does well to make inquiries along these lines prior to the day of testimony. Specifically, one should ask about the particular court's pattern regarding the elaborations that are permissible in response to yes/no questions.

One could argue that I am suggesting deceit here or demonstrating lack of respect for courtroom procedures. I do not see this as deceit. I do have *some* lack of respect for *certain* courtroom procedures because they are not worthy of respect. Yes/no questions are a good example. Yes/no questions are *not* the best way to find out the truth in any matter, civil or criminal. Under the guise of being a method for finding out the truth, they are generally used to obfuscate and hide the truth. They are not used in direct examination, where the attempt is to elucidate. Rather, they are generally confined to cross-examination, where the goal is to obfuscate and suppress information. Accordingly, they inevitably lengthen the proceedings, make them much more complicated, and, not incidentally but predictably, earn more money for the lawyers. However, I must work within the system. There is no other choice if I am to be of help to the people who come to me. Accordingly, I work within the system but try to get away with as much as I can when on the witness stand. I will elaborate upon this in Chapter Five.

One should also inquire about the particular court's rule regarding witnesses speaking with attorneys in the course of breaks in one's testimony. My experience has been that most courts permit such communication, and it is common practice during the lunch break. However, there are certain jurisdictions in which one may not have any substantive discussions with anyone whatsoever during breaks in one's testimony. And this includes the lawyer whose position one may be supporting. When I am a court-appointed impartial examiner, this would include both lawyers. And when I am serving as an expert for one party, but still communicating with both lawyers, I still am not permitted to discuss substantive issues with them. Although we may go to lunch together, we are strictly required to conform to this rule. Examiners who break this rule will generally find themselves sorry when, after the break, they are asked by an opposing attorney if there were any conversations of a substantive nature during the course of the break. To deny such a discussion is basically perjury. To admit it is to compromise oneself significantly. There is nothing further I need to say on this point.

There are some jurisdictions, admittedly uncommon, in which an expert is allowed to sit in a courtroom and observe the testimony of clients and/or other experts. Although it is an uncommon practice, it is certainly done. Generally, it requires the permission of the judge as well as agreement by both attorneys, each allowing the other side's witnesses and/or experts to observe testimony. Obviously, if this were only allowed unilaterally, we would not be witnessing a "fair trial." On those occasions when I have been permitted to observe the testimony of others, lay persons or professionals, I have found the experience extremely valuable and cannot recall a time when I did not learn something very useful. Examiners should make inquiries, therefore, regarding the possibility of such observations and avail themselves of such opportunities whenever possible. Although this may entail extra expense to the client(s), my experience has been that it is generally money well spent.

"Meanwhile, Back at the Office"

One of the questions facing the examiner who is in full-time private practice is how many patients to cancel for a court appearance. One cannot know at the outset exactly how long he (she) will be required to remain in court. Generally, one can expect to stay longer than anticipated. The method I have found useful is to request that I be scheduled to appear as the first witness in the morning or the afternoon (for shorter testimony). In this way I lessen the likelihood that my appearance will be delayed by an unpredictably protracted testimony by someone appearing before me. Being the first person to testify makes it more likely that I will begin at an appointed time. I generally cancel all of my morning patients when my expected time in the courtroom is two to three hours. About a week before, I tell all my afternoon patients that I am not certain whether I will be back in the office because I have to appear in court in the morning. I explain to them that I cannot know beforehand exactly when I will be able to return to the office. I advise them to call my office about one hour prior to the session time in order to learn from my secretary whether I will be back. During breaks in testimony I call my office and apprise my secretary of developments and the likelihood of the time of my return. In this way I protect myself from the loss of income that would be entailed if I were to cancel the full day and then find myself required to appear only in the morning. Another solution to this problem is not to schedule any patients throughout the course of the day, testify in the morning, and devote one's afternoon to paper work, dictation of reports, and other professional matters that allow for flexible attention. Over the years, I have progressively shifted into the latter plan, but I recognize that this may not be financially desirable for many practitioners.

The Value of Selected Duplicate Documents

The evaluator does well to bring to the courtroom extra copies of the written report, curriculum vitae, and the provisions document (if used). Although the examiner may have already sent copies of these materials to the court, the attorneys, and the clients, these have a way of disappearing. My experience has been that this is especially the case with regard to the material sent to the court. In earlier years I thought this related to my failure to have placed the docket number on the first page of the report. My thoughts were that some clerk misfiled my report because of this oversight on my part. However, for many years I routinely (and even compulsively) placed the docket number on the first page of every report and every addendum. Even then my reports were often not on the judge's desk at the time of the trial. I suspect that the main problem was the judge's lack of interest in reading it and/or its being placed among thousands of pages of other documents pertinent to the case. I have been involved in cases in which clients and attorneys come to court with many suitcases filled with files, or boxes that are carried in on their shoulders or luggage trolleys—all carried in caravan-like fashion.

As a result, it is not uncommon for a judge to ask me if I have an extra copy of my CV or report. If the examiner has only one copy to give the judge, then that copy will not be available for the examiner to use when giving testimony. Usually my copy is highlighted and underlined and has marginal notes placed there the previous day, during the time of my court preparation. Obviously, I would not want to have that copy given to the judge, especially because it would compromise my testimony. Furthermore, once that copy is given to the judge, it is not likely that it will ever be seen again. It will be assigned an appropriate exhibit number and submitted as evidence. These documents have a way of disappearing into the bowels of the courthouse—never to be found again. And I have had similar experiences with copies of the provisions document. The easiest thing, then, is for evaluators to make copies of all documents that they believe might be requested by the judge during the course of the trial. Most often, these include the primary report, the provisions document, and the summary of my curriculum vitae. A fringe benefit of having these readily available is that the examiner can, with a simple flourish, quickly hand the copy over to the judge. This makes a good impression and saves the judge the discomfort or embarrassment of searching around for his (her) copy. I am not claiming that the evaluator rely upon these impressions as the primary way of convincing the court. I am only stating that one should not lose sight of their importance.

How to Dress

Experts do well to dress conservatively when providing testimony. This is the tradition in most courtrooms in which I have testified. Men, therefore, do well to wear ties. If, however, there is a courtroom situation in which the judge and the lawyers are "looser" in this regard, then the examiner can be free to do so as well. I am not claiming that one should be a rubber stamp of other people in one's dress. I am only claiming that one should not want to stand out as being atypical in a court of law. One can express one's individuality elsewhere, in situations where it may not be detrimental to a client or patient who is dependent on the examiner.

In the 1960s and 1970s, many therapists considered "hippie" costumes (I use the word without hesitation) to place them at the forefront of the latest thinking in the field of psychology and psychiatry. Beads, pendants, sandals, and the most bizarre clothing patterns were *de rigueur*. (Needless to say, I never wore such a uniform, nor did I believe that such a costume was particularly therapeutic.) There are still people today in the field who have some commitment to that fashion. They do their patients and clients a disservice in the vast majority of courts of law. Lawyers generally recognize this and so may weed out such "independent thinkers" before ever recommending them to a client.

FIVE
THE DAY(S) IN COURT

INTRODUCTION

Serving as an Impartial, Regardless of One's Formal Designation

I begin this chapter with an important caveat: Always make every reasonable attempt to serve as an impartial, even when recognized as an expert of one of the litigating parties. If one does not make reasonable attempts to serve as an impartial examiner (whether or not one is so designated by the court), one risks being considered a "hired gun." This epithet generally refers to people who will testify in support of those who pay them, regardless of personal conviction. To me, it is a form of professional prostitution. Of course, no mental health professional is going to claim to be a hired gun; rather, most profess that they are truly impartial. However, the true test of such impartiality is the individual who has literally written a report that supports the nonpaying party and is even willing to come to court to testify in support of that party's position. People with a "track record" of such "jumping ship" are those who can truly say that they are not hired guns.

A common situation in which mental health professionals serve as hired guns is one in which the evaluator in a child-custody dispute is at the outset willing to serve in support of one of the parties without making reasonable attempts either to serve as an impartial or, at least, to interview the opposing party. By playing into the hands of litigating attorneys, hired guns prolong the clients' grief and frustration. In order to help dissuade such individuals from appearing in this capacity and to contribute thereby to the general discouragement of this deplorable practice, I generally recommend that the attorney, whose position the testifying mental health professional is *not* supporting, conduct this type of cross-examination:

> *Attorney:* Would you not agree, Doctor, that it is somewhat simplistic to categorize people as being either "good" or "bad" and that a more realistic view of people is to consider them to be mixtures of both assets and liabilities?
>
> *Mental Health Professional (mhp):* Yes. (The mhp must say yes here. If he [she] does not, credibility is compromised because the statement is so patently true.)
>
> *Attorney:* Do you agree, then, Doctor, that parents are no exception to this principle and that they too are mixtures of both "good" and "bad" qualities regarding their parental capacity?
>
> *Mhp:* Yes. (Again, one has no choice but to answer yes.)
>
> *Attorney:* Would you not agree, Doctor, that in child-custody disputes, we are *not* trying to find out who is the "good" parent and who is the "bad" parent, but who is the *better* of the two parents?
>
> *Mhp:* Yes. (Again, the answer must be yes, even though he [she] can now sense what is to follow.)
>
> *Attorney:* Would you not agree also, Doctor, that in trying to determine who is the *better* of two parents, it is preferable to see *both* if one is to determine most judiciously who is the *better* parent?
>
> *Mhp:* Yes. (Obviously, if the mhp says no, he [she] looks foolish.)
>
> *Attorney:* Would you not go further and agree that an evaluation of parental preference is seriously compromised if both parents have not been seen?
>
> *Mhp:* Yes. (Here again, it would be very difficult for the mhp to avoid a yes answer, even though he [she] recognizes that such a response weakens significantly his [her] position.)
>
> *Attorney:* Doctor, have you conducted a psychiatric evaluation on Mrs. Jones?
>
> *Mhp:* Yes.

Attorney: How many times have you seen Mrs. Jones?

Mhp: (The mhp states the number of interviews conducted with Mrs. Jones.)

Attorney: Can you tell us the exact dates of each of your interviews with her and the duration of each interview?

Mhp: (Mhp presents the dates of the interviews and the duration of each.)

Attorney: What was the total number of hours of interviewing?

Mhp: (Mhp states the total number of hours of interviewing.)

Attorney: Have you ever conducted an evaluation of Mr. Jones with regard to his parental capacity?

Mhp: No.

Attorney: Have you ever asked Mrs. Jones to invite Mr. Jones to be evaluated by you?

Mhp: No.

Attorney: Have you ever written Mr. Jones a letter informing him that you are conducting an evaluation on his wife and children in the custody dispute and you are thereby inviting him to participate?

Mhp: No.

Attorney: Have you called Mr. Jones, informing him that you are conducting an evaluation?

Attorney: To the best of your knowledge, is Mr. Jones in this court-room today?

Mhp: Yes.

Attorney: Can you please point to the person whom you believe to be Mr. Jones.

Mhp: (Mhp points to the person believed to be Mr. Jones.)

Attorney: Is it possible that the individual at whom you are pointing is not Mr. Jones?

Mhp: Yes, it's possible.

Attorney: As I understand it, Doctor, you are here today to testify that Mrs. Jones is a better parent than Mr. Jones. Is that not correct, Doctor?

Mhp: Yes.

Attorney: And is it also not correct, Doctor, that you not only have never conducted an evaluation of Mr. Jones, but are not even certain whether he is actually the person you suspect him to be?

Mhp: Yes.

Attorney: In accordance with what you have said before about a custody evaluation being seriously compromised if both parties are not seen, would you not have to conclude that *your own* evaluation in this matter must be similarly suspect?

Mhp: (If the mhp answers no, testimony is compromised because of inconsistency and the attorney would do well to point this out. If the mhp hedges or responds that he [she] cannot answer yes or no, the testimony is similarly compromised and invites the attorney to point out the inconsistency. If the answer is yes [the more likely response], the attorney does well to respond as follows.)

Attorney (turning now to the judge): Your honor, because Dr. X has, by his (her) own admission, stated that his (her) testimony has been significantly compromised by his (her) failure to evaluate Mr. Jones, I do not think anything useful can be obtained by further inquiry. Accordingly, I believe it would be a waste of the court's time to proceed further and I therefore have no further questions.

The cross-examining attorney does well to stop here. The attorney's adversary will already have questioned the examiner during the course of the direct examination and is not likely to have any further questions on redirect examination, so limited has the cross-examination been. At this point the judge, of course, may ask further questions. However, the judge may feel compromised by such an inquiry because of the admission made by the evaluator that his (her) comments should not be taken seriously. If the cross-examining attorney wishes to proceed, however, in order to "rub salt into the evaluator's wounds," my recommendation is that he (she) focus on all hearsay statements made by Mrs. Jones about her husband. The attorney's main emphasis should be on the doctor's accepting as valid the criticisms of her husband made by Mrs. Jones. Even if the evaluator has not accepted as completely valid Mrs. Jones's allegations, the conclusions are likely to be based on the supposition that at least some of them are true (otherwise he [she] would not be providing testimony in support of her position). Stopping at the earlier point would represent more of a denigration of the so-called expert's testimony than proceeding with a detailed inquiry into the report's contents. I believe that if more mental health professionals were exposed to such cross-examination, fewer would be willing to serve as advocates, and this would be a service to all parties concerned—the courts, the legal profession, the mental health professions, and the families themselves.

There are mental health professionals who will conduct a sex-abuse evaluation in which a mother, for example, claims that her husband has sexually abused their daughter. The mother may have spent only a few minutes with the evaluator and the child less than an hour. On the basis of such limited inquiry, the evaluator has no problem writing a report in which she (he) concludes that the child was sexually abused and that the abuser was the father. In addition, it is common to recommend that steps be taken to obtain a restraining order, preventing the father from any contact with the child—pending a courtroom hearing. In some cases this involves the father's being removed from the home (if he is still living there). I have seen cases in which such a report has contributed to a father's being imprisoned. This practice is very common among individuals who unashamedly refer to themselves as "validators." This is the type of cross-examination I recommend for such individuals:

> *Attorney:* Have you ever interviewed Mrs. Jane Smith?
> *Mhp:* Yes.
> *Attorney:* How many times have you interviewed Mrs. Jane Smith?
> *Mhp:* Once.
> *Attorney:* And what was the date of that interview?
> *Mhp:* March 15, 1992.
> *Attorney:* How long did you spend with Mrs. Jane Smith?
> *Mhp:* Approximately 15 minutes.
> *Attorney:* Did you ever interview Mary Smith?
> *Mhp:* Yes.
> *Attorney:* How old is Mary Smith?
> *Mhp:* Three-and-a-half.
> *Attorney:* How many times have you interviewed Mary Smith?
> *Mhp:* Once.
> *Attorney:* What was the date of that interview?
> *Mhp:* March 15, 1992.
> *Attorney:* How long was that interview?
> *Mhp:* Forty-five minutes.

Attorney: Is it correct to say, then, that the total amount of time you spent with both Mrs. Smith and Mary Smith was one hour?

Mhp: Yes.

Attorney (while handing the mhp her report): Is this the report that you wrote concerning your evaluation of Mary Smith?

Mhp: Yes.

Attorney: Would you please read the date of that report?

Mhp: March 15, 1992.

Attorney: Is this statement on page 2 your final conclusions and recommendations?

Mhp: Yes.

Attorney: Would you please read this to the court?

Mhp (reading): "Child has been sexually abused by her father. Recommend that visitation be discontinued immediately. Contacted Sergeant Jim Jones at the 13th Precinct, telephone: 123-456-7890. Mother also advised to contact her attorney."

Attorney: Is it your conclusion, then, that Mary Smith was sexually abused?

Mhp: Yes.

Attorney: And it is your conclusion that she was sexually abused by her father, Mr. Roger Smith?

Mhp: Yes.

Attorney: Accordingly, you are telling us that you have written here that Mr. Roger Smith has sexually abused his child and yet you have never seen him and have never even seen fit to invite him to participate in your evaluation?

Mhp: Well, I . . . you see . . .

Attorney (interrupting): Please answer the question, yes or no?

Mhp: Well, you see . . .

Attorney (turning to the judge): Your Honor, I would appreciate your directing the witness to please answer the question "yes" or "no."

Judge (turning to the mhp): Please answer the question "yes" or "no."

Mhp (reluctantly): Yes.

Attorney: Have you ever interviewed Mr. Roger Smith?

Mhp: No.

Attorney: Did you ask Mrs. Jane Smith to invite Mr. Roger Smith in for an interview?

Mhp: No.

Attorney: Did you ever write a letter to Mr. Smith informing him of your evaluation and inviting him to participate?

Mhp: No.

Attorney: Your Honor, I believe that Ms. X has been professionally negligent in that she has written conclusions and recommendations about someone she has never even interviewed and never even tried to interview. I believe, therefore, that she has disqualified herself as a witness in this court of law and I recommend that she no longer be qualified to testify.

Membership in Rights Groups

Most of us have sympathies for certain rights groups. I do not deny the value of such groups, especially because they may contribute to social progress. However, mental health professionals should be *very* selective regarding participation in such groups, especially in those groups related to issues on which they may be asked to testify. Participation in groups related to areas in which the mental health professional may testify as an expert may seriously compromise the evaluator's credibility as an impartial expert. I would go further and say that such membership may haunt his (her) professional life, even after resignation.

For example, evaluators involved in custody and sex-abuse cases should not be members of men's or women's rights groups. Such membership will immediately compromise one's expertise on a witness stand, especially if the evaluator is going to support a father and is, at the same time, a member of a father's rights group. This may serve as a useful referral source, but it provides the mother's attorney with a very valuable and, I believe, justifiable route of attack on the witness stand. Unfortunately, I have come across many mental health professionals who are not only members of such groups but enjoy significant referrals from them. Such individuals are setting themselves up for formidable criticism on the witness stand by the opposing attorney. Because the criticism is justified, the evaluator's testimony is likely to be seriously compromised. Accordingly, such membership is a disservice to the clients, the courts, and the evaluators themselves—the benefits of such member-ship notwithstanding.

Where to Sit in the Courtroom

It is important for impartial evaluators to appreciate that, although they are viewed by the judge and attorneys as impartial, they must par-ticipate in the courtroom in accordance with fairly strict adversarial procedures. In fact, an observer who was not aware that the examiner was a court-appointed impartial might not be able to perceive this to be the case from merely observing the witness-stand examinations. The impartial examiner becomes viewed as the advocate of the side whose position is supported and as the adversary of the side whose position is not supported. And all the procedural rules involving the providing of testimony operate within this format.

Once in court the "friend of the court" may find fewer friends than anticipated. Certainly the parent who may lose the children be-cause of the examiner's report is likely to be bitter and filled with rage. And that parent's attorney, even if secretly agreeing with the examiner, will often appear hostile—that, after all, is what the attorney is being paid for. Even the parent whose position the examiner supports may be dissatisfied. This parent may believe that the evaluator has not mani-fested the appropriate degree of hatred for the spouse and has not been properly appreciative of the partner's most obvious alienating charac-teristics. In addition, this supported parent may believe that the evaluator has not gone far enough in the recommendations—and this parent's attorney will often reflect these views. Although up until this time the impartial may have done everything possible to remain neutral and above the adversarial proceedings, he (she) is now very much in the thick of the battle.

These constraints notwithstanding, I have introduced certain prac-tices that enabled me to maintain my individuality and make a statement that I do everything in my power to maintain my position as impartial examiner. Accordingly, when entering the courtroom, as the impartial examiner, I do not sit and converse with *either* party alone, whether it be attorney or client. There are some impartials who immediately join ranks with the supported party, sit next to that person during courtroom procedures, pass notes, whisper in the ear of the supported client and/or lawyer, and engage in all the little maneuvers of the adversarial examiner. In contrast, I sit in a neutral place and refused to speak to anyone, client or attorney, without the adversarial party being present. From my neutral position I may approach attorney A, tell him I would like to converse with both him and attorney B together (sometimes including also the guardian ad litem), and have a conference with both sides. Sometimes I will invite the parents to participate in this conference as well. Of course, if there is only limited time and there is a brief question, generally a discussion with both attorneys together will suffice. This practice, although unusual in the courtroom, should come as no surprise to the attorneys because it was already mentioned in my provisions document and, if there has been a joint meeting of attorneys and clients (the usual case), it has been implemented at that time as well.

In those situations in which my attempts to serve as an impartial have not been successful, but in which I have been designated as the expert of one side, there are three possibilities regarding where I sit in court. Each of these deserves special comment:

1. Although formally recognized by the court as the inviting party's expert, the opposing side has been ordered to cooperate in my evaluation. Often this involves a parallel expert who has been engaged by the other side and both parties have been ordered to cooperate with both evaluators. Under these circumstances, following the data-collection process, I will generally meet with both parents and their lawyers together to apprise them of my final recommendations. If, following this conference, the nonpreferred side (both client and lawyer) still maintains reasonably cordial and professional relationships with me, and permits me to continue operating in as impartial a manner as possible, my formal designation as expert for the opposing side notwithstanding, I will in the courtroom continue to invite the opposing attorney and client into conferences.

2. My attempts to serve as impartial have not proven fruitful, I have been recognized by the court as the expert of the inviting party, and the court has ordered the participation of both sides with a parallel evaluator representing the other side. Following the conference in which I present my findings and recommendations to clients and attorneys, the opposing side has discontinued all contact with me. Whether this has been the re-

sult of the client's or the attorney's decision is irrelevant. Under these circumstances, my attempts to invite them into subsequent conferences, especially an update conference prior to trial, have proven futile. Under these circumstances I have no problem communicating unilaterally with the supporting side both prior to and during the courtroom proceedings. Not to do so would deprive that side of input. That side should not be deprived of input from me because of the refusal of the other side to accept my invitation for involvement. Under such circumstances, I have no problem sitting together with the supporting party's attorney in the courtroom and conferring during breaks.

3. My attempts to serve as an impartial have proven futile and the court has refused to order the cooperation of the opposing side. Under these circumstances, I will interview the party who has elicited my services, with no promises beforehand that I will support his (her) position. If, after the interview, I decide that the party warrants my support, I proceed accordingly as that party's expert. Under these circumstances, I have no problem sitting at the table of the attorney whose position I have supported and conferring during breaks.

Some Important Pretestimony Questions

Whether one is conferring with attorneys from one or both sides, it is important for the examiner to learn about certain procedural rules regarding the conduct of the trial in the particular courtroom in which the examiner is testifying. In the last chapter I mentioned the importance of learning about the court's stringency regarding yes/no questions. If this question has not been asked previously, the examiner does well to learn the answer at this point. Obviously, once on the witness stand it is too late to ask the question. In addition, one should have asked previously about whether the examiner can observe the testimony of other witnesses, both lay and expert. Courts differ enormously with regard to this practice. In most courts of law it is strictly prohibited, but in others it is allowed. Sometimes this can be done with the mutual agreement of both attorneys. I myself have found the practice very valuable. I have no objection to other experts witnessing my testimony, even if it is done from a hostile vantage point. In every situation in which I have done this, I have learned something useful that has enhanced the value of my testimony. One can read the report of an adversarial expert and critique it to some degree. However, observing that person on the witness stand invariably will provide other information that could be useful. The report is a formal document, may have gone through several versions, and does not generally reveal deficits. On the witness stand the cross-examining attorney is likely to bring out weaknesses and deficits not only in the report but in the individual himself (herself) that go beyond the substantive material in the document. The main drawback to my observing others' testimony has been the added expense to the client for such observation on my part.

In one custody case I saw the father and the children, but the mother refused to cooperate in an evaluation and the court refused to order such cooperation. However, the court did permit me to observe the testimony of the children. These were children who were suffering with a moderate level of parental alienation (Gardner, 1992a) syndrome and who, I was convinced, were being programmed by their mother to be alienated against their father. On the witness stand, not only did the girls provide exaggerated and even preposterous complaints about their father, but frequently glanced at their mother for corroboration (even though on the witness stand). The younger child requested that her mother sit close to her, allegedly because she was so upset. The court allowed this and this child provided even more compelling examples of the process of maternal prompting. When I subsequently testified I focused significantly on the child's previous testimony. My presentation was far more compelling than that which I provided about what had gone on in my office. Not only was the mother present, but the court had been witness to the exact same events that I had observed.

One must also learn about the particular court's rules with regard to discussions with various parties during breaks. My experience has been that there is significant variation here. Most often I have been permitted to speak with clients and attorneys during breaks— either bilaterally or unilaterally as the case may warrant (see above). In some jurisdictions, however, there are strict prohibitions regarding such conferences. Specifically, once on the witness stand one is prohibited from speaking during breaks to any party involved in the proceedings, client or attorney, about any substantive issues. Examiners do well to find out what rule is in force in the particular courtroom, and the pretestimony discussions with the attorneys will enable one to gain this information.

I cannot advise examiners strongly enough to obey this rule, as absurd as it may be. I say this is *absurd* because it is yet another example of the constraints and restrictions of the courtroom that work against free flow of communication. It is from the free flow of communication that one is placed in the best position to learn what is going on in a given situation. Courtroom procedures work in just the opposite direction, their claims of finding out "the truth" notwithstanding. The primary drawback of engaging in such "illicit" discussions is that they may come to haunt the examiner subsequently while on the witness stand. The opposing attorney may very well ask the examiner if anything was said to the opposing clients or attorneys during the break. One is on the witness stand and one is under oath. One must answer honestly. I am not merely saying this from some commitment to some higher authority or higher sense of ethics. I am saying it for practical reasons as well. One may have said something to a client at that point and both agreed to "hush it up." However, on the witness stand the client might then quote the examiner as having said something specific during that time frame. Then all suffer. My memory is not good enough to remember well the differentiation between those things that I am free to repeat and those things I am supposed to cover up. I do not have a good enough memory to be a good liar, both for lies of omission and lies of commission. Perhaps there are some who can separate these things out very well and be reliable liars. Because I am not, it would be particularly dangerous for me to keep separate files and separate lists of things I should lie about and things about which I can tell the truth. I believe that most examiners are probably in my category. In short, this compromise of noncommunication is best tolerated because there is more to lose than to gain by breaking it.

If the examiner has not provided the supporting attorney with a list of suggested questions for presenting one's qualifications, these should be given at this point. Generally, I send these on during the week prior to my providing testimony (Addendum V). Below, in the section on the presentation of one's credentials, I will elaborate upon this document.

SWEARING IN (THE VOIR DIRE)

The Oath

The swearing in is usually referred to as the *voir dire*. The term is derived from Old French and means *true to say*. It refers to the oath in which one swears to tell the truth, not only with regard to one's qualifications to serve as an expert but also with regard to the questions that one will be asked in the course of the examination.

The voir dire generally begins with the examiner's being asked to raise his (her) right hand and swear to tell the truth. Sometimes I have been asked to place my left hand on a Bible and sometimes not. Sometimes the oath includes reference to God and sometimes not. Examiners do well to go through this ritual, regardless of their religious beliefs, commitments to the deity, and their opinions about the Bible. Or the examiner may object to this because it is a clear abrogation of the separation of church and state, emphasized so much by the founding fathers. In fact, requiring a person to swear on a Bible in a court of law is one of the best examples of how the allegedly revered separation of church and state is routinely ignored.

These considerations may be of great importance in other realms, but objections to this ritual in the courtroom at that point are a disservice to the client. At times, I personally have had some reservations about the ritual, not the basic principle of promising to tell the truth. However, expression of such disagreement has no place in the courtroom at that particular point. One does not wish to do anything to compromise one's testimony. The ritual represents the opinions of those people in that particular region and these must be respected by the examiner, regardless of his (her) site of origin and regardless of personal convictions in this realm. It is basically a matter of respecting the rituals of that particular area and it should not represent a significant compromise for the competent examiner. If it does, then the evaluator should not be involving himself (herself) in evaluations that involve courtroom testimony.

The Examiner's Credentials

In recent years I have found it useful to provide the examining attorney with a list of suggested questions. This practice evolved from the following considerations. As the years went on, my full curriculum vitae (which consists of background biographical material, publications, and presentations) became progressively longer, to the point where just the key items comprise about 85 pages (at this time). No one (I repeat no one) is going to pore through this volume. Accordingly, I have prepared an eight-page summary. However, even here, the attorneys generally did not select what I consider to be the important items. Accordingly, in recent years I have prepared a list of suggested questions. Usually, I ask the attorney if he would be interested in such a list. No one has yet turned me down. The problem with such a list is that one wants to have a proper balance between overkill and underkill. Examiners who have very few qualifications may try to include frivolous qualifications that may often be seen as "fluff." These might include such listings as a presentation to a local school PTA meeting, a letter to the editor, etc. These may do more harm than good. In contrast, examiners who have extensive experience run the risk of "overkill." The human brain can only tolerate so much data before it short-circuits. Under such circumstances information is not processed and the listener may fall asleep. I believe that the list I give the attorney provides a proper balance between overkill and underkill. Generally, it requires about 15 minutes of testimony. I refer the reader to Addendum V, which reproduces the list of questions I recommend to the attorneys. As can be seen, it covers educational background, teaching appointments, books, articles, professional lectures, and previous court testimony.

The whole purpose of this presentation is to ascertain whether the examiner is qualified to be considered an "expert" by the court. It is important for the evaluator to appreciate that there are generally no exact criteria for deciding what qualifications one needs to be an *expert*. For example, within the field of psychiatry, being board certified would certainly increase the likelihood that the individual will be viewed as an expert. However, the attorney might point out that the evaluator's boards are in psychiatry in general and not in the subspecialty of child psychiatry, a qualification that would obviously enhance expertise in child-custody litigation. But even if an evaluator has boards in child psychiatry, this does not necessarily mean that the individual would be viewed as an expert in a particular case because the focus is on a particular issue, e.g., custody litigation, sex abuse, competence, insanity.

I was once asked, in cross-examination during the voir dire, what my *training* was in doing custody evaluations. My response: "None!" I said this nonapologetically, but recognized that the judge was not too happy with my response. During a break I suggested that the attorney whose position I supported ask me to elaborate on that response. Accordingly, when back on the witness stand he asked me to elaborate on my statement that I had had no formal training in performing custody evaluations. My response was:

> During my residency training in the late 1950s custody/visitation litigation was extremely rare, to the point of being practically unknown. Accordingly, there was absolutely no reason to train anybody in this area. To criticize me in 1992 for not having had training in custody/litigation evaluations in 1957 is the same as criticizing in 1992 a physician who is giving testimony about AIDS for not having had training in the disorder during his residency in 1957 (when, obviously, the disease was unknown).

On another occasion a cross-examining attorney said to me: "And who, may I ask, designated you an 'expert'?" My response: "People like yourself have often used this term when making reference to me. I myself rarely use the term with regard to my qualifications." The important point here is that examiners do well to avoid referring to themselves as "experts." Rather, they should list their qualifications and experiences and let the attorneys and the court argue about whether their documentation warrants the label *expert*.

If the impartial examiner is extremely well qualified, then the attorney whose client this impartial is supporting will try to elicit the most detailed elaboration of this examiner's qualifications. The opposing lawyer may interrupt, even before the examiner has had a chance to begin, and say to the judge, "My client and I accept Dr. X's qualifications. Your honor, I suggest we proceed." At this point the well-qualified evaluator may not even have had the opportunity to tell the court that he successfully completed the first grade. Accordingly, the court will have been deprived of knowing the examiner's qualifications—information I believe the judge is not only entitled to have, but *should* have in order to weigh properly the testimony of conflicting experts. Following such an attempt to squelch the examiner's providing his (her) qualifications, the original lawyer (whose position the examiner is supporting) should say to the judge, "I believe, your Honor, that it would be helpful to the court if Dr. X *were* to present his qualifications, especially as they relate to the particular issues being addressed in this case."

While the judge and the two attorneys are trying to decide this question, the evaluator can do nothing but sit and hope that "justice will prevail" and that the court will allow the presentation of the examiner's credentials. All would agree that the court has every right to know the qualifications of those who conduct custody evaluations. However, as the reader can well appreciate, this consideration may take second place to an attorney's attempt to lessen an examiner's credibility in order to enhance a client's position. So from the beginning of the trial the interests of the children, the parties, and "justice" become less important than the interests of the client in winning the case. My experience has been that most often judges have not allowed an attorney to squelch the presentation of my qualifications. However, my guess would be that in 10 to 15 percent of cases the judge complied and instructed the attorneys to proceed. This in itself has given me advance information about the judge's receptivity to me. It tells me that, in this case, he is already unreceptive. And this may be more important than the substantive information that I have provided. As will be elaborated upon, the examiner does well to be sensitive to these important elements in courtroom procedures, elements that are not formally focused upon in the deliberations.

The reader should note that on the list of suggested questions to the attorney (Addendum V), there is no question: "What are the specific areas in which you consider yourself an expert?" The only question that actually mentions the word "expert" is the last one, "Has a court ever ruled that you are not qualified to provide expert testimony?" This omission was not a chance oversight. It is a deliberate omission. Listing the specific areas of expertise may serve to limit the examiner's testimony. In a typical custody/sex-abuse case, I might just say that I am an expert in child-custody disputes and child sexual abuse. I have written books and articles in both of these areas and have testified in these areas on many occasions. I also consider myself an expert in the field of child psychotherapeutic techniques and have written books and articles on this subject. In fact, it is the major area that I have been focusing on in my teaching at the Columbia Medical School for the last 35 years. Yet, if I did not designate it at the outset, I might not be able to testify in this realm if it were to come up in the course of the testimony, e.g., if I were to comment on the therapeutic techniques of some of the people who consider themselves to be doing "therapy" with allegedly sexually abused children. I have also written books on learning disabilities and have testified on that subject, especially in school cases. If I had not mentioned that during the voir dire, and the issue of learning disability came up, my failure to have mentioned this area of expertise at the outset might have prevented me from providing testimony in that realm. And this would be especially the case in a stringent courtroom situation.

I am quite knowledgeable on the subject of medical findings in sex-abuse cases. I have even written a chapter on this subject (Gardner, 1992b). Yet, I am not a pediatrician, especially one with expertise in genital examinations of children who have been alleged to have been sexually abused. The last time I conducted a physical examination on a child was in 1962. Obviously, I cannot formally designate myself an expert on physical findings of child sexual abuse. I have, however, been allowed by courts to provide testimony in this realm, especially in more flexible courtroom situations. To raise the question of whether I am an "expert" in this realm might prove to be to my disadvantage and deprive the court of information that could very well be useful.

Accordingly, the attorney conducting the direct examination does well *not* to pinpoint specific areas of expertise and hopefully have the examiner merely recognized generally as an "expert in child psychiatry." If the cross-examining attorney wishes to pinpoint the areas of expertise, the examiner should show no modesty and list every single area that he (she) possibly can and close with a comment along these lines: "These are the areas that come to mind at this point. It may be that there are other areas that I can consider myself qualified to testify on, and I would like to reserve the right to add to this list if such areas were to come up in the course of the trial." This request will certainly be backed up by the attorney whose position the evaluator is supporting, and the court in most cases will recognize this request.

Following the presentation of one's credentials, the opposing attorney has the opportunity to cross-examine the expert and try to convince the court that the individual is not qualified to be so designated, and even not qualified to testify. No matter how qualified the examiner may be, there will be attorneys who will try to discredit him (her). In fact, the stronger the qualifications, the greater may be the desire to embarrass and/or discredit the evaluator. Accordingly, evaluators do well to be aware that their curricula vitae may be subjected to detailed scrutinization, especially in lengthy trials and/or those that may come to public attention. It may come as no surprise to the reader that I myself have been subjected to some of the most vicious attempts to discredit me. Examiners do well to learn those areas that opposing attorneys are likely to focus on, areas that they consider weaknesses (whether justifiably or not). Then, the examiner should have available that information that will serve to counteract the attempts at discreditation.

A common maneuver is to try to present the examiner as a "hired gun." As stringent as the examiner may have been in trying to serve as an impartial (and I consider myself to be very much in that category), attorneys may try to convince the court that the examiner is a "hired gun." The best defense against this is to have spelled out at the beginning of one's report the steps that one took to serve in this capacity and to provide verification of these procedures. The court may not know of these steps. And so it is at that point that the lawyer may have the best chance to be successful with regard to this alleged criticism. In one case in which I was unsuccessful in serving as an impartial, primarily because the opposing lawyer fought vigorously such appointment, the following interchange took place at this point in my voir dire:

    Attorney: Doctor (said in a very condescending way), are you familiar with the term *hired gun?*
    Gardner: Yes.

Attorney: Will you please define the term *hired gun*? (Obviously, his intent here was that I would provide a definition that would apply to myself.)

Gardner: A hired gun is a professional who is willing to testify in support of any party who pays his fee, regardless of his or her own convictions. Most attorneys fit this definition perfectly!

At that point he dropped the inquiry and, I suspect, was sorry he brought it up. He did, however, provide the opposing attorney with the opportunity for me to describe at that point in the voir dire the steps I had taken to serve as an impartial examiner. In the course of that description I was able to make specific reference to the letter that the opposing attorney had written in which he refused to join in with the inviting party to have me so designated.

After the completion of the presentation of credentials and the examiner's being recognized as an expert by the court, the examiner does well to have a copy of his (her) curriculum vitae available for submission to the court. It is important to have this on hand in order to be given immediately to the attorney, who will mark it appropriately and submit it to the court. As mentioned, I generally use an eight-page summary rather than my full curriculum vitae.

THE DIRECT EXAMINATION

Introduction

The direct examination refers to that part of the testimony in which the examining attorney is the one whose position is being supported by the evaluator. He is "the friend," in contrast to the cross-examining attorney, who can reasonably be referred to as "the enemy." As mentioned, prior to trial I generally ask the supported attorney if he (she) would like a list of questions to serve as guidelines for direct examination of me. This is separate from the standard list of questions recommended for the voir dire. These questions are specific for the particular case. Secure attorneys are likely to be receptive to this invitation; those who are insecure will consider the examiner to be usurping their role. I generally take the position that in a battle (which is what court-room litigation is), one should not turn away help from any reliable source.

Generally, I have my comprehensive report in front of me when I testify. As mentioned, this report generally includes the most important data that I wish to impart to the court. However, the examiner does well to use the material contained therein as a point of departure for his (her) testimony. First, it is not likely that the court will allow the examiner to read directly from this report and, even if such "testimony" were allowed, it would be injudicious of the examiner to do so. A person who speaks directly and spontaneously is much more persuasive than someone who has his (her) nose in notes that are being read. On the night before trial, I may underline or highlight key words that I may have the opportunity to glance at in the course of my testimony. Courts will generally permit occasional glancing at notes but usually frown upon reading long extracts.

Background of My Involvement

I generally ask the attorney to give me the opportunity to spell out the provisions of my involvement in the case, especially when I have not been successful in serving as an impartial. In this way, I let the court know what my position is regarding serving as an advocate. This is even more the case when I have been designated by the course as the expert of the attorney who is directly examining me. The court may have forgotten the initial overtures to have me brought in as an impartial, and this part of the testimony helps refresh the judge's memory. It also has the fringe benefit of protecting me from questions during cross-examination, the purpose of which is to get the court to view me as a hired-gun expert, in the hope that the court will have forgotten my earlier attempts to avoid serving in this capacity. These steps, of course, have already been spelled out on the first page of my report, but the report generally has not yet been submitted into evidence. (Usually this is not submitted until after I have completed my testimony, or at least my direct testimony.)

Persons Evaluated

Next, I generally state the names of the parties interviewed, the number of times each party was seen, and the time frame of the evaluation. When this is lengthy it is generally not necessary to pinpoint every single appointment. Rather, one just wants to give the court some general idea about the intensity of the evaluation. Because I generally conduct in-depth evaluations over many weeks—and sometimes months—imparting this information puts me in a more credible position than an opposing expert who may have conducted a far more limited examination.

Documents Reviewed

Next, I usually list the documents I reviewed in the course of my evaluation. It is important at this point for the examiner to emphasize that data was collected from these documents but that the examiner's conclusions and recommendations were based on his (her) own evaluation. I cannot emphasize this point strongly enough. Ideally, the examiner reviews this material carefully, gives serious consideration to the data provided therein, but bases his (her) findings and recommendations on the basis of his (her) own observations. If one has relied significantly on other people's opinions, one compromises oneself as a bona fide expert.

Presentation of One's Findings

Next, the evaluator is given the opportunity to present in depth his (her) findings. This is the heart of the evaluator's testimony. Here one does well, when possible, to look at the judge in an attempt to establish some kind of a relationship with him (her). Of course, if the judge is sitting to the side and often behind the witness stand, such attempts at contact may not be possible. In jury trials it is best to talk to the jury directly and frequently make eye contact with various members of the jury. I cannot emphasize too strongly that the relationship the examiner establishes with the judge (jury) is a far more important determinant of their reactions and receptivity than the actual content of what is said in the course of one's testimony.

The Importance of "Balance" Evaluators do well not to provide a testimony that is too one-sided. One does not want to praise only the party whose position is being supported and just criticize roundly the party whose position is not being supported. Most situations are not that clear-cut, and in most cases each party has both strengths and weaknesses, both assets and liabilities, that should be addressed. Examiners who believe that the best kind of testimony is one in which the supported client is provided with praises only and the nonsupported with criticisms only is likely to compromise his (her) credibility and be viewed as biased (which is probably really the case). Competent experts are truly balanced and call the shots as they see them. Quite frequently, when discussing an issue, I will present it in balanced form and then come up with a conclusion on that point. In the service of that goal I might say something along these lines: "On the one hand, A, B, and C factors argue for this conclusion. On the other hand, D, E, and F factors argue for this conclusion. All things considered, I believe that the arguments supporting the latter conclusion outweigh the arguments supporting the former." One's recognition of the complexity of the situation will generally be appreciated by the judge (jury), even though most people prefer simple answers.

I am not recommending anything deceitful here, especially with regard to a conscious and deliberate inclusion of some defect that does not exist. The more common practice is for examiners to consciously and deliberately omit defects they observe under the misguided belief that such omissions strengthen their reports and testimony. In actuality, just the opposite takes place in that the judge (jury) is likely to be suspicious of an examiner who sees absolutely no defects in the client being supported.

On occasion, in situations in which I am serving as one party's expert, an attorney will ask me to omit the critical comments about the client under the misguided belief that their presence compromises the client's position. The concern is that the opposing attorney will use these defects as "handles" for cross-examination and thereby compromise his (her) position. Generally, I try to impress on these attorneys that there is compelling evidence to support their client's position and that rather than weakening my arguments, the inclusion of a few deficiencies actually strengthens them. Usually the attorney is dubious, but I do not let this dubiety result in my omitting the client's deficiency(ies).

The Opposing Lawyer's Objections It is in this phase of the direct examination that one can expect the most objections by the opposing lawyer. Lawyers vary from those who hardly ever object to those who compulsively do so and will take every opportunity to squelch the examiner's testimony. The more compelling the examiner's testimony, the greater the likelihood the opposing attorney will try to squash it. It is in this phase that the examiner will be in a position to gain some objective information about possible judicial bias. A judge who is biased in favor of the opposing attorney will support (sustain) a very high percentage of that attorney's objections, even the most frivolous ones. A judge who is receptive to (or even biased for) the examiner will reject (overrule) a high percentage of the opposing attorney's objections. In the latter case, the judge genuinely wants to hear what the examiner has to say, is receptive to learning from him (her), and will view all these objections as irritating intrusions and distractions and as interfering with the search for the "truth."

Videotapes It is in this phase of the direct testimony that the examiner may wish to demonstrate selected segments from videotaped examinations, both his (her) own as well as segments of evaluations by other examiners. Here, one does well to select *short segments* that provide the most compelling evidence for one's position. As mentioned, the human brain has limited capacity for sustaining attention, and putting the judge (jury) to sleep certainly does not help one's testimony. It is here also that blown-up charts might also prove useful. These visual aids add clout to one's testimony and often provide information in a format not possible with direct verbal testimony.

Generally, this segment of my testimony takes about two to four hours, depending upon the number of interruptions by the opposing attorney. Even then, I have often not had the opportunity to put in all the data contained in my report, thus the importance of a comprehensive report.

"Scientific Evidence"

A favorite maneuver of the cross-examining attorney is to ask the expert for "scientific evidence." There is a generally held assumption that scientific evidence is more likely to be valid than evidence that is not scientific. Although the concept of scientific proof may be of importance in such fields as chemistry, physics, and biology, the concept is not as applicable in the field of psychology—especially with regard to issues being dealt with in such areas as child-custody disputes and sex-abuse accusations. I am not referring here, of course, to such situations as when the DNA found in the sperm sample of the child's vagina matches the DNA found in the sperm sample of the accused. This, obviously, is scientific proof. (Of course, even here there are those who claim that DNA testing has a long way to go before being truly worthy of being considered scientific.) For every article in the psychological literature that provides scientific proof for a particular point, there is another article that provides scientific proof for its opposite. Accordingly, it is not a prejudice to refer to psychology as a "soft science" in comparison to mathematics, physics, and chemistry, which are often referred to as "hard sciences."

Unfortunately, courts of law and juries are very much beholden to so-called scientific proof, feel more secure when they believe that they have it, and selectively ignore information that sheds discredit on this common myth. Accordingly, lawyers may ask the examiner whose position they are supporting for scientific proof, and the cross-examining attorney is likely to try to discredit the examiner by trying to demonstrate that his (her) position is not supported by scientific proof. Unfortunately, I have never had a good opportunity to lecture the court on the weakness of so-called scientific proof, especially when it comes to psychology and psychiatry. Rather, I have had to go along with the "game," provide alleged scientific proof, and refute the so-called scientific proof of adversarial mental health professionals.

I am not claiming that all the scientific articles I have ever brought forth have been of no value in supporting my position. I am only claiming that I recognize their weaknesses and do not have as much faith in them as do many judges and juries. My bottom-line recommendation to testifying experts is to get their "scientific proof," recognize its weaknesses, and know that in a court of law the cross-examining attorney is going to question the validity and reliability of whatever proof one has. The best response is to quote the most compelling segments from the best articles one has. Usually this suffices. My experience has been that courts of law do not go into detail on the relative merits of the various articles that are presented as scientific proof. They know, however, that the opposing side is going to be coming in with its pile of references, providing scientific proof for its position.

Up until recently, the Frye test was the criterion by which courts presumably determined whether or not scientific evidence was admissible. This principle, formulated in 1923 by the Court of Appeals for the District of Columbia, was formulated in Frye v. United States. The case involved the admissibility of a systolic blood pressure deception test, a precursor of the polygraph. The court declared:

> Just when a scientific principle or discovery crosses the line between the experimental and demonstrable stages is difficult to define. Somewhere in this twilight zone the evidential force of the principle must be recognized, and while the courts will go a long way in admitting expert testimony deduced from a well-recognized scientific principle or discovery, the thing from which the deduction is made must be sufficiently established to have gained general acceptance in the particular field in which it belongs.

One of the problems with the implementation of the Frye test is the question of exactly who in the scientific community is to be designated as the deciding authorities of what is to be generally acceptable. In any scientific community there are factions, and each side may consider itself to hold the "generally acceptable" viewpoint and may claim that the opposing views are the ones that are not acceptable. Nowhere is this more apparent than in the fields of psychiatry and psychology. There are dozens of fields of therapy, each of which claims that its approach is the valid one and the others are not. Each brings forth what it considers to be "scientific proof" of its therapeutic approach. Obviously, some have to be right and some have to be wrong; in fact, more of them are wrong than right. What usually happens is that the judge and/or the jury makes the decision as to whether or not the testimony is admissible. Obviously, this cannot be made on the basis of knowledgeable assessment of the various theories, but on criteria having absolutely nothing to do with this, such as whether they like or dislike the person who is testifying or whether they want to find the defendant guilty or not guilty.

In 1993 the Supreme Court of the United States in Daubert v. Merrell Dow Pharmaceuticals replaced the Frye test with more specific criteria to serve as guidelines for the admissibility of scientific evidence. The Daubert ruling is more restrictive than the Frye test. The plaintiff stated that the Bendectin she took as an antinauseant during her pregnancy caused congenital anomalies in the fetus. The defendant, Merrell Dow Pharmaceuticals, claimed that Bendectin does not have this particular side effect. Both sides brought in scientists to provide supporting evidence. Daubert does include the Frye provision that the theory or technique be generally accepted by the appropriate scientific community. However, Daubert, as was true of Frye, does not specify how one determines which school of thought is "generally acceptable" or which peer-review publications are required, and this of course is a significant weakness in its utilization. It also advises the trier of fact to consider whether the theory or technique has been subjected to peer review. Again, the question arises as to which peers and publications.

A central element in the Daubert decision is that the trial judge should consider whether "the theory or technique has been or can be tested." And this, of course, is central to a scientific principle. Basically, this consideration relates to the potential of the theory or technique to be falsified, i.e., to be disproven. This is sometimes referred to as "falsifiability." In order to allow for falsification, the technique must provide well-defined procedures that other examiners can follow in order to test the theory or procedure to determine if it is valid. Strong theories and procedures will survive this testing mechanism and be confirmed over and over again as other examiners, using the same testing methods, are able to confirm the validity and reliability of the theory or technique. However, if the theory or technique is not valid, then the method for demonstrating its falsification will have been precisely outlined. A theory or technique that does not provide guidelines for its own falsification cannot properly be considered scientific.

Underwager and Wakefield (1993) have provided an excellent description of the value of the falsification criterion in sex-abuse cases. Using first an example from the purely medical model they describe bloodletting, a practice that was in vogue in Western medicine for over 200 years. The theory was that bloodletting was curative. If, after the procedure, the patient recovered, then the bloodletting theory was considered proven. If, however, after bloodletting, the patient died, the assumption was made that the patient would have died anyway. Obviously, this is not the kind of theory that can be disproven because all outcomes are considered to be verification. Not surprisingly, this theory went out of vogue when more predictably successful methods of treatment were utilized. Under the falsification criterion, bloodletting would not be admissible in a court of law.

Next, they describe common practices in the "diagnosis" of child sex abuse. If the child admits abuse, then the abuse has been substantiated. If the child denies abuse, then the abuse has still been substantiated because the child is considered to be in "the phase of denial." If the child admits abuse and then recants, the recantation is not considered valid because the child is presumed to have retracted under pressure from the perpetrator. If the child does not recant, then the abuse is confirmed. If the pediatric examination finds general trauma, then the abuse is considered confirmed. If the examination is normal, then the examination is considered "consistent" with sex abuse or "abuse by history." Again, these common ways of dealing with the problem allow for no method of proving the conclusion false.

Underwager and Wakefield (1993) also describe similar phenomena for the accused. If he admits the abuse, he is guilty. If he denies the abuse, he is considered to be in the "phase of denial." If he fails the polygraph, he is guilty. If he passes the polygraph, then he is considered to be a psychopath or in a phase of "formidable denial," so much so that he can even fool the lie detector. If he shows no emotion, he is considered a psychopath or master manipulator. If he shows emotion, he is considered to be overwhelmed with guilt and disgust over his behavior. These no-win situations for the accused again are derivatives of the inability of one to falsify the system.

Underwager and Wakefield (1993) then describe how the application of the falsification principle makes Summit's child sexual abuse accommodation syndrome (CSAAS) inadmissible. It is not diagnostic of child sex abuse because the same symptoms can be seen in nonabused children. Similarly, those who claim repressed memory of childhood sexual abuse could not hope to admit this theory in a court of law because there is no way of falsifying the theory. If the adult woman remembers abuse, then the abuse has presumably been confirmed. If she forgets the abuse, then she has merely "repressed the memory of it," and the abuse is again confirmed. When both verification and lack of verification prove verification, there can be no scientific validation or falsification.

Daubert also recommends that the promulgator of a theory or procedure make known the potential rate of error. In sex-abuse cases this would relate to the rate of false positives. This provision, if strictly enforced, will produce significant difficulty for evaluators—from the most sober and conservative to the most zealous and incompetent. To genuinely assess the error rate of such procedures, one must have some kind of an external, final, and valid proof against which to measure the particular assessment instrument. This is sometimes referred to as *external validity*. Because pedophilia is a criminal act, the vast majority of child abusers will not admit that they have perpetrated the crime. Furthermore, there are rare individuals who may "confess" to such a crime when they never perpetrated it. Accordingly, statements by the perpetrator cannot be a reasonable source of external validity. Nor can statements by the child, especially younger children, because of children's gullibility, suggestibility, and manipulatibility. The rulings from a court of law cannot be a source of external validity because bona fide perpetrators may be found not guilty because of lack of evidence and those innocent of this crime have sometimes been found guilty of having perpetrated it, especially in recent years under the influence of hysteria that we have been witnessing (Gardner, 1991c). Last, there are certainly borderline situations in which the determination as to whether abuse has taken place is subjectively determined by the alleged victim, as well as by others who make the decision as to whether the particular act warrants the label *sexual abuse.*

Although the Daubert decision may be viewed as an advance in that it requires scientists to provide more stringent evidence for their theories and techniques, if strictly enforced by the courts, it is likely to result in the inadmissibility of evidence provided by the vast majority of mental health professionals. Most of the procedures that we use to assess for child sex abuse will not stand up to such rigorous requirements as "falsifiability" and error rate. The main reason for this is that we cannot compare our diagnostic techniques with any known standard or proof. There is no external validity by which one can compare an evaluative technique. No matter what the protocol one uses for assessing for child sexual abuse, there is nothing to compare it with that is "the standard of proof." There are many bona fide cases for which our assessment techniques cannot provide enough evidence to "prove" the abuse in a court of law, even by the more lenient preponderance-of-evidence principle. Even the most sober and conservative evaluators cannot claim a high degree of validity to their protocols, especially in borderline situations.

In short, even though Daubert may prove beneficial in excluding repressed-memory therapy and the child sexual abuse accommodation syndrome from the courtrooms, if applied stringently it can have the effect of excluding the testimony of just about every mental health professional. What is likely to happen, then, is that the courts will do the same thing they did with the Frye test. If the judge wants to admit the testimony, Daubert will be ignored; if the judge wants to exclude the testimony, he (she) will have many opportunities to do so because Daubert provides a much longer list than Frye to justify such exclusion. To the degree that judges utilize it will courts deprive themselves of testimony from mental health professionals.

Conclusions, Recommendations, and Degrees of Medical Certainty

After the basic body of my testimony has been presented I am generally asked to summarize my conclusions and recommendations. Often attorneys ask me if each of these conclusions is based on a "reasonable degree of medical certainty." The attorney is making reference here to a hierarchy of certainty required in legal proceedings. This hierarchy, from the least exacting to the most stringent, is:

1. Probable cause. This is the least exacting level of certainty. It often involves just a suspicion and is not generally enough to bring about a definitive conclusion in a court of law.

2. Preponderance of the evidence. This can be quantitatively expressed as 51 percent certain. In civil cases, this is enough for a court to come to a conclusion.

3. Clear and convincing proof. This is stronger than preponderance of the evidence. Although clear and convincing proof may bring about a decision in a civil case, it is not enough to bring about conviction in a criminal case.

4. Beyond a reasonable doubt. This is the requirement in criminal cases in which there needs to be an extremely high degree of certainty for conviction.

The reasonable-degree-of-medical-certainty criterion generally applies in civil cases, at levels 2 and 3. It must be applied at level 4 in criminal cases. Usually, I am only asked if I can express my conclusions with a reasonable degree of medical certainty, but occasionally I am asked to be more specific with regard to the legal degree of certainty as described above. Examiners do well to appreciate these levels. There are examiners who will say that they are "100 percent certain" that their findings are valid. This is very risky, especially in fields like social work, psychology, and psychiatry. Even statements like "99 percent" may be risky and even "turnoffs" for some judges and juries. It is safer, even in civil cases, to use such terms as "beyond a reasonable doubt."

Submission of the Report Into Evidence

Before leaving the witness stand the examining attorney will offer to submit the evaluator's complete report into evidence. Most often there is no problem with such submission. On occasion, the opposing attorney will object and then the judge will listen to the arguments on both sides. It would indeed be unfortunate if a long and detailed report was not admitted into evidence. I am sorry to say, however, that there have been occasions in which my report has not been accepted. I do not believe that on any of these occasions the reason had anything to do with any real deficiency in my report. Usually this occurred in situations in which the judge was obviously biased against the side that I was supporting and allowed the opposing attorney to use some kind of legal maneuver to justify the report's not being admitted. This is just one example of my repeated observation that the adversary system has less to do with the administration of justice and more to do with other factors, like allowing attorneys to prove themselves in battles of wits at their clients' expense.

THE CROSS-EXAMINATION

"Speak Softly and Carry a Big Stick"

This principle, popularized by Theodore Roosevelt, is a very important one, not only in life, but in a court of law. People who speak with high emotion, especially those who rant and rave, are generally far less credible than those who speak calmly and deliberately. The former are generally trying to compensate for weaknesses in their position, whether or not they realize it. The latter are much more likely to be speaking from a solid foundation. I am not suggesting that the impartial evaluator artificially "play it cool." Such advice implies that there may be strong underlying feelings that the evaluator does well to hide. Ideally, examiners should have such a full command of the material and such conviction for their position that they will be genuinely secure when testifying in court. Under such circumstances, they will have few feelings to hide and will not have to create any false impressions of calmness. Nor am I suggesting that the evaluator ideally be free from tension. A cross-examination is an extremely difficult experience and one must be alert and "on top of it" at all times. Mental health professionals, especially, are in strange territory in the courtroom. They may be dealing with attorneys with years of experience in cross-examination who may be quite clever in utilizing maneuvers that attempt to make examiners look foolish, change their testimony frequently, get upset, or exhibit other qualities that will compromise credibility. The evaluator's best defense against such formidable adversaries is to have a firm and full grasp of his (her) position, to be clear on the issues, and to be able to state them as calmly and concisely as possible. Furthermore, examiners who have had the opportunity to interview the primary parties from both sides of the conflict do well to appreciate that they are likely to be more knowledgeable about the case than anyone else in the courtroom because only the impartial has had the opportunity to conduct the most extensive evaluation of all parties concerned.

Who to Look at in the Courtroom

In civil trials it is the judge who obviously has the most power and who is the person the examiner is most interested in impressing. Ideally, this would be done in a face-to-face discussion, where there is opportunity for the maximum amount of eye contact. Courtroom situations, however, generally preclude such an opportunity. Usually, the witness stand is to either side of, and often in front of, the judge's bench. Witnesses, therefore, must turn sideways, and even look a little behind themselves if they are to have any direct, face-to-face confrontations with the judge. This constraint should not, however, result in the examiner's losing sight of this important principle. On many occasions, following the completion of the interrogations by the attorneys, the judge will conduct his (her) own inquiry. Each time, it behooves the examiner to shift around and speak with the judge directly. To continue facing into the courtroom at that point is injudicious. The examiner should appreciate that the judge is not required to conduct such an inquiry; in fact, judges cannot do so frequently or at length lest they risk being criticized. The judge is supposed to be the referee, the trier of fact, not an interrogating lawyer. Although the judge is often referred to as the "finder of facts," it is the lawyers who are supposed to elicit and extract factual information from the witnesses.

Throughout most of the testimony the witness will be facing the interrogating attorneys. In jury trials, the jury is generally off to the side, but usually very much within the visual range of witnesses. Under such circumstances the witness has a choice between looking at the interrogating attorneys or looking at the jury. Examiners who choose to look at the attorneys are generally making an error. As mentioned throughout this book, more important than the content of what one says is the relationship one has with the people who are going to decide the fate of the clients. Examiners on witness stands should do everything possible to establish a relationship with a jury. I generally do this by talking directly to the various jury members, often with direct eye contact. One does not want to single out any particular person but roam from person to person, somewhat randomly.

During cross-examination there may be situations in which one might want to have direct eye contact, rather than just general, face-to-face confrontation, with an opposing attorney. This is in accordance with the principle of "staring him (her) down" and letting an opposing attorney know that you are not being intimidated by the interrogation. Sometimes, such face-to-face interrogation is especially useful when one has "won a point."

At times, there may be a strong temptation to look at the clients, especially for the purposes of getting some kind of nonverbal communication. For example, in cross-examination a yes/no question may be asked to which the examiner does not know the answer. A subtle hand gesture or facial expression might immediately communicate to the examiner what the correct answer is. It is generally an error to involve oneself in such communications. These will be picked up by an opposing attorney and, if he (she) is doing his (her) job, will bring this to the attention of the court who, invariably, will criticize the examiner and the client. Often, the required information can be obtained during the breaks. The gains of such communications from the witness stand are often far less than the losses.

Last, there are examiners who stare into space during the course of their testimonies. They are like robots. This is an error. People who do this are depriving themselves of the opportunity of forming relationships with the various important figures of the courtroom and are compromising their testimony. In addition, it just does not look good, and appearances play a role in one's credibility.

There are some examiners whose noses are ever in their notes. This too is a serious mistake. Not only does it "look bad," but it implies that the examiner is insecure and/or unsure of the facts (which is probably the case on both points). This, too, cannot but compromise credibility.

The Yes/No Question

The Three Possible Responses to the Yes/No Question Most of the questions posed by the attorney whose position the examiner supports will be open-ended and will thereby provide the evaluator with the opportunity to elaborate on the findings and justify the conclusions and recommendations. For example, in the course of the direct examination the lawyer may say, "Please state to the court your reasons for recommending that Mrs. Green be designated the primary custodial parent" or "Can you tell us why Mr. Cohen should not be designated the primary custodial parent?" The opposing lawyer, however, during the course of cross-examination will generally pose most questions in such form that the expert witness will have little opportunity to elaborate on the answers. They are so structured as to warrant, and even require, answers that are simple, short, and often yes or no. The questions are often so worded that evaluators may be required to provide responses that do not reflect their true intent or position. Evaluators do well to avoid such distortion of their position by not falling into the trap of answering yes or no when the issue is too complex to warrant such a response. The examiner, in such cases, should not hesitate to respond with "I cannot answer yes or no." Generally when one answers, "I cannot answer yes or no," the cross-examining attorney is not likely to ask, "Why, Doctor, can't you answer yes or no?" To do so would give the expert an opportunity to elaborate in a way that might compromise the cross-examining attorney's position. Generally, he (she) will not "open that door" under cross-examination. Usually, he (she) will move on to another question or try to pose the question in a different way.

I cannot emphasize strongly enough the importance of evaluators not answering yes or no unless they are 100 percent certain about the answer. If only 99 percent certain they should answer, "I cannot answer yes or no." Answering yes when only 99 percent certain is likely to compromise the evaluator when the one percent possibility becomes a reality. The lawyer who asks this question may be very well aware of that one-percent situation and is therefore setting a trap. The procedural rules in courts of law allow three possible answers to the yes/no question: "Yes," "No," and "I cannot answer yes or no." One should be comfortable with answering "I cannot answer yes or no" as many times as the lawyer poses questions that warrant such a response. On occasion, I have done this up to a dozen times and then the lawyer knew "I meant business" and was not going to fall into any of his (her) traps. To do otherwise may result in the court's coming to oversimplified and even erroneous conclusions. In spite of these precautions, questions will often be so worded and selective that the evaluator's true intent may be distorted or misrepresented. It is here that one sees most clearly the hypocrisy in the attorney's claim to be "only interested in what is best for the child."

The examiner may feel quite frustrated on the stand when prohibited from elaborating on responses and clarifying the kinds of misleading conclusions that are often conveyed by the simple yes/no response. An evaluator who tries to elaborate will be interrupted by both the questioning attorney and the judge and instructed to strictly confine answers to the questions posed. With such questioning the attorney hopes to get the evaluator to selectively present and reveal items and material that will support his (her) client's position and withhold from the court that which will weaken the client's cause. Examiners do well to appreciate that most judges are well aware of such antics and are not so easily taken in by the cross-examining attorney's maneuvers.

For example, I once served as an impartial examiner in a case in which I recommended that the mother have primary custody. One of my main reasons for coming to this conclusion was that the father was far more committed to his work than to his children. His wife and children viewed him as a "workaholic"—which he was. In the cross-examination the attorney asked: "To the best of your knowledge, Doctor, is Mr. X an alcoholic?" I answered no. He then repeated the same question with regard to drug addiction, wife beating, gambling, and philandering. Again, I had to answer no, that he was none of these things. He then continued and asked me questions about whether Mr. X had ever been in jail, been committed to a mental institution, received electroshock therapy, or had attempted to kill himself. Again, I continually answered no to all of these questions. The attorney, of course, refrained from asking about any of the deficiencies that the client did have— deficiencies that contributed to my recommending custody to his wife. I suspected that the judge was not taken in by all of this game playing and that the inquiries were conducted for the sake of the client, who the attorney hoped would be impressed by the "brilliance" of this cross-examination. The judge's decision in favor of the mother supported my belief that he had not been taken in by the attorney's antics.

Most often, however, such a line of inquiry would not be permitted. Courtroom procedures do not allow an attorney to bring in information that is patently false, data for which there is absolutely no foundation. If an attorney tries to bring in such material, the opposing attorney generally objects and the objection is usually sustained by the judge. On occasion the judge himself (herself) will interrupt the inquiry and ask if there is any justification for such questions. Unfortunately, my experience has been that attorneys all too frequently get away with this kind of introduction of false and misleading information. My experience has also been that such depravity (and I do not hesitate to use this description) is much more commonly seen in civil trials than criminal trials, which are usually far more stringent.

Another example of how the cross-examining attorney uses the yes/no answer to mislead the court is demonstrated by the case of Mr. Y, a philanthropist, who was quite neglectful of his children. This was an important factor in my decision to recommend that his wife be given custody. The lawyer was able to elicit a long stream of yes answers from me regarding the various charities to which Mr. Y had made generous contributions. He then asked, "You will agree that Mr. Y is a very generous and giving person?" The lawyer here was obviously trying to get the court to generalize from Mr. Y's social benevolence and conclude that he was equally benevolent to his children. Without hesitation I simply answered no—because the statement was not basically true. I could have answered, "I cannot answer yes or no." The attorney did not ask me to give the reasons *why* I answered no, because he suspected that I would use the why question as an opportunity to make a comment along these lines: "In the area of public contributions, Mr. Y is, without doubt, a generous man; however, when it comes to the care of his children, I do not consider him generous because. . . ." It is rare for an attorney to ask evaluators to elaborate on *why* they answered no or could not answer yes or no. To do so might open the floodgates and invite a barrage of responses that might compromise the client's position. At best, the attorney might try to rework the question in order to elicit a response that is more to his (her) liking. My general advice to examiners is that they provide as many "cannot answer yes or no" responses as they feel warranted, even if they provide 15, 20, or 30 in a row. Such perseverance gets across the message to the cross-examining attorney that the examiner is not going to be tricked or bludgeoned into providing an oversimplified answer—an answer that will distort his (her) position.

"Bending the Rules" I have provided testimony in courts in various parts of the United States and Canada and have found there to be significant variation with regard to how stringent courts are with regard to confining the examiner to yes/no questions. And even in the same jurisdiction there may be significant variation, depending upon the judge and the attorneys conducting the trial. As mentioned, my primary problem with these questions is that they are designed to bring about a distortion, oversimplification, or compromise of the evaluator's position. Attorneys justify them under the procedural rules of the adversary system. They recognize that their purpose is to obfuscate and distort, but they justify the procedure as serving the higher goal of providing the judge and jury with each side's best position. They believe that this is the best way to learn "the truth." As mentioned in various places in this book, I do not agree with this, but I am not going to change the system at the point when I am testifying on the witness stand on behalf of a client. Accordingly, evaluators who go into the courtroom must play by the rules of the lawyers' games. But like most rules, there is a certain amount of flexibility, and the rules can be "bent" at times.

Bending rules around the yes/no questions presents the examiner with a conflict. If one subscribes strictly to the yes/no constraints and responds accordingly in automaton-like fashion, one may create a good impression by virtue of this strict compliance with courtroom procedures. But such submission may allow for the perpetuation of misrepresentations and distortions that the cross-examining lawyer is trying to promulgate by the use of such questions. Furthermore, such strict submission to yes/no questions may deprive the evaluator of the opportunity to "slip in" extra messages, while still working within the confines of the system. Accordingly, the client whose position is being supported is thereby best served by such "bending of the rules."

There are a variety of subtle ways of adding additional communications to the yes/no response. For example, one can say the word yes in such a way that it implies, "Why that's obvious! How can you be so stupid as to ask such a foolish question?" Sometimes that message can be communicated by the examiner's looking incredulously at the attorney and saying, "Of course!" Sometimes additional messages can be communicated by substituting "Yep!" and "Correct!" These responses are provided in a very clipped way to imply: "I have absolutely no problem at all agreeing with you on that point." The implication is that the examiner has absolutely no embarrassment or hesitation agreeing and therefore his (her) position is not in any way being weakened by the yes response. This type of retort is especially useful when the attorney believes that the evaluator is unsure or hesitant to provide a strongly affirmative response. Sometimes the examiner may be able to stretch the yes answer further with such responses as "You're 100 percent correct" or "Absolutely true!" This can have the effect of taking the wind out of the sails of the cross-examiner, yet still be in basic compliance with the courtroom procedure. I never had the experience of an attorney asking the judge to instruct me to change the intonation of my yes/no answers or to order me not to use the aforementioned kinds of substitute responses.

Similarly, one can often get across additional messages with "no" answers. For example, one can say no in such a firm way that one is transmitting the additional message: "There is absolutely no way in the world I could possibly consider an alternative response." This might be communicated by saying, "Absolutely not!" Such minor alterations to the basic yes/no responses are generally allowed in the courtroom, even under the most stringent circumstances.

However, there are times when I have found that I can "get away with more" and quickly insert a few extra words in order to protect myself from the inevitable distortions of my position that the cross-examining attorney is trying to bring about with yes/no questions. For example, during one trial an attorney asked me a question about the mother that was clearly designed to give the impression that she was, at the time of the trial, a woman subject to frequent outbursts of hysterical rage. In actuality, that description was applicable at the time of my evaluation. However, by the time of the trial, one year later (a not uncommon hiatus), she was remarried, had quieted down, and that description was no longer applicable. I knew this from my direct observations of her during my update meeting one week before the trial. In the courtroom the attorney, while holding my report in hand, said, "Have you not stated that Mrs. X is a 'woman subject to frequent outbursts of hysterical rage'?" Instead of merely saying yes, the answer he expected, I, in a matter-of-fact way, responded, "Yes, at *that* point." The word *that* was emphasized strongly. I was attempting to get across the message that the statement was valid at that point *in the past* but was no longer valid *now*. Immediately, the judge interrupted me and asked me why I had said, "At that point." Had he read my original report and the recent update, he would not have asked that question. He would have known from my update report that she no longer exhibited this symptom. I knew, from my earlier experiences on that day, that the judge had not read my reports (the usual case) and so I quickly added "at that point" in my response in the hope (which was realized) that it would provide me with an entrée to present the clarifying and more reliable data.

Often, the cross-examining attorneys will quote passages from some of my books that they believe will cause me embarrassment or are designed to mislead the court. One way in which they do this is to select a passage out of context. Had the whole passage been read, an entirely different message would be sent to the court. Typically, the attorney will first present me with the book from which he (she) is quoting and get me to agree that that is indeed my book, and then the title will be read into the record. Then he (she) will ask me, "Have you not written here, Doctor, on page xyz, the following. . . ." Sometimes they will read the passage. Sometimes they will ask me to read it myself. In either case, if I believe that the quotation is out of context and that if the whole statement were read, an entirely different message would be sent to the court, I will respond, "Yes, as an out-of-context quote!" Most often, I am allowed to get away with this expansion and sometimes the judge will ask that the whole passage be read. Under more stringent conditions I might say, "Yes, that is exactly what is *written* there." I might say this with a very affirmative tone with emphasis on the word *written*. Or I might say the same thing in singsong fashion. In either case I am trying to get across the message that there is much more going on here than just what is written. I might get across the message by saying, "Yes, you have read that correctly" or preferably, "Correct as read!" It is extremely important that the examiner be certain that the lawyer is reading precisely what has been written. My experience has been that many lawyers will drop a crucial word or two or insert some words of their own and try to fool the court into believing that they are reading exactly what the examiner has written. Prosecutors especially are prone to do this. Accordingly, the safest thing for examiners to do is to either read the specific passage themselves or to insist upon reading along with the attorney.

My general way of dealing with the dilemma regarding strictly adhering to yes/no questions (and thereby looking professional and complying with courtroom procedures) and trying to "bend the rules" (and thereby risking one's professional status, but serving the client) is to carefully and gingerly test the waters regarding how much I can "get away with." All this is part of the fine art of the fencing match of cross-examination. In short, I try to get away with as much as I can without going so far that I compromise my credibility or status as a competent witness. The more I "get away with," the more satisfied I am that I am providing the court with more accurate data.

"I Have No Recollection" Although the three responses, "yes," "no," and "I cannot answer yes or no," are generally considered the only acceptable responses, on occasion there are other responses that are acceptable under the rules. One such response is "I have no recollection." This is a far safer answer than a flat no and should sometimes be used. It is especially useful when one is suspicious that a no answer might get the examiner into trouble. This is particularly the case if the testimony is being provided after a significant time gap between the evaluation and the time of trial. Of course, the examiner should review meticulously one's report and other pertinent documents. However, no one's memory is perfect and so the "I have no recollection" response is occasionally justified. However, a series of such responses will seriously compromise the examiner's credibility in the courtroom. Obviously, the superiority of this response over the flat no is that if the attorney does come up with data that would embarrass the examiner in light of the no answer, he (she) is covered with the "no recollection" response. I am *not* suggesting that one use this response to lie (which is commonly done), that is, when the admission of a yes response might seriously compromise the examiner's and possibly the supported client's position. I am only suggesting this response when one genuinely does not have a recollection and one basically feels that the answer is no but one suspects that there is the small possibility that a yes answer might be appropriate. Other ways of saying the same thing while still providing a generally acceptable response are: "That would not be consistent with my usual policy" and "I am *very* dubious."

The Multiple-Question Ploy The examiner should also be aware of the simultaneous presentation of multiple questions presented as a single question for which a yes or no answer is requested. The lawyer here may be trying to sneak in a question that, if asked alone, would receive a different answer. The lawyer may have a question he knows the therapist will answer negatively. By mixing it in with a collection of questions he (she) knows the evaluator will answer positively, the lawyer hopes to get a yes answer for that particular question as well. If the examiner detects even one misstatement in a barrage of accurate facts, he (she) does well to answer no or state that he (she) cannot answer yes or no. Again the lawyer will usually not ask *why* the examiner has responded in this manner, because the attorney suspects that the examiner will use such an open question as an opportunity to focus on the single misleading statement hidden in the series of accurate ones. Sometimes, under such circumstances, I will respond crisply, "Multiple question!" or "Multiple question. Please break it down." Invariably, the judge will support the request and the lawyer will submit and break down the question into its components. I have never encountered a judge who directed me to submit to the request that I answer a multiple question. Furthermore, the examiner "wins a point" here by pointing out the lawyer's poor cross-examining technique. The reader will also note the manner in which I point out this deficiency. I am not humbly saying, "Excuse me sir (ma'am), it would be most helpful to me if you would be good enough to break that question down into its component parts so that I will be in a better position to answer it." Rather, I quickly "shove my fist down his (her) throat" decisively, and crisply state, "Multiple question!"

Words to Avoid

Most junior-high-school English teachers know that there are certain words an instructor does well to avoid using in a classroom situation. A few of these are *mastication* (chewing), *formication* (an hallucination that insects are crawling under the skin), and *frigate* (a kind of boat). To use such words in the average junior-high-school classroom is to invite pandemonium. Similarly, there are certain words that the evaluator does well to strictly avoid using in the courtroom. Two examples are the words *always* and *never*. All of us do well to avoid the utilization of these words, but such words are especially risky in the courtroom because of the likelihood that there will be exceptions. And a cross-examining attorney will attempt to get the examiner to agree that there *are* indeed exceptions, thereby compromising him (her). Accordingly, examiners do well *never* to use the word *never* and *always* to avoid using the word *always*.

Another word that the examiner should studiously avoid is *speculate*. Although there is a significant amount of speculation in every evaluator's report or testimony, the speculations should not be labeled as such. Lawyers love to jump on anyone who is foolish enough to use that word. They like to profess that court decisions are made on the basis of "hard facts" and "evidence." They like to believe that there is absolutely no place at all in the courtroom, or even in the legal process, for *speculations*. The reality is that most of the examiner's conclusions and recommendations are justifiably considered speculations. They involve extrapolations from present data to future events. They involve the hope that the conclusions derived from the present experiences will subsequently apply. However, one is not likely to have an opportunity to

THE DAY(S) IN COURT 153

elaborate on this point in the courtroom. Even if the supporting attorney gives the examiner the opportunity to state what I have just stated regarding speculation, the evaluator's credibility will be compromised. The judge, and even the supporting attorney, has been deeply imbued with the idea that examiners who speculate in the courtroom are seriously compromised in their ability to provide meaningful testimony. Accordingly, if the reader wants everyone to jump down his (her) throat, just say, "I would speculate that . . ." or "It is my speculation. . . ."

In certain jurisdictions, using the word *credible* may get the expert into deep trouble, especially in criminal trials. In such jurisdictions, there is a strict principle that only the trier of fact can assess credibility of a witness, and not an expert. (I am *not* referring here to the credibility of the expert witness per se but to the credibility of the parties the expert has evaluated.) And this is especially applicable to child witnesses who allege that they have been sexually abused. In such jurisdictions, it is not the expert's role to assess the alleged victim's credibility; it is up to the jury or the judge. Accordingly, if the expert says that the child's sex-abuse scenario is not credible, that testimony may become disallowed. An overzealous cross-examiner and/or prosecutor may try to get much mileage out of that statement and aggressively claim that the expert is trying to take over the role that should properly belong to the jury or judge. Such an attorney will try to portray the expert as someone who is grandiose and overstepping his (her) proper boundaries.

At every point, all the people who are interrogating witnesses—judge, jury, police, detectives, lawyers, and mental health professionals—are assessing credibility. All, consciously or unconsciously, wittingly or unwittingly, are continually concerned with whether the information being provided by the interviewee is valid, and that consideration cannot be separated from the credibility of the person who is making the statement. One cannot divorce a statement from the party who is making it.

However, courts often operate for years in accordance with such myths, and the evaluator is not going to alter this view or change the "official" rules. Accordingly, in such jurisdictions, it is judicious for the evaluator to strictly avoid using the word *credibility*. However, one should still present the data that demonstrate the interviewee's lack of credibility. In this way, the incredibility of the statement is communicated to the court without the risk of the testimony being disallowed because of its label. For example, rather than testifying that a child's sex-abuse allegation is incredible, one can say, for example, "The child, age four, stated that when her teacher tried to put his penis in her vagina—on the lawn in front of the school as they were going to the bus—she pulled a tree out of the ground and threw it at him. The teacher then started to cry and ran away." All one need do is present this preposterous statement and it speaks for itself as patently incredible. Fortunately, in most jurisdictions in which I have testified, the principle that the expert not assess credibility does not operate. However, examiners need to know of its existence and do well to make inquiries of the attorneys prior to testimony in order to avoid this complication to one's testimony on the witness stand.

The Open File

Generally, during the first session of an evaluation in which I am seeing parties from both sides, I inform them that my files are completely open and that, at any point, both parties may have access to them. I advise each party to give copies of all submitted documents to the other side in the service of this goal. When anyone asks to review copies of my written notes, I will, with a flourish, invite the party to look at them. Photocopies are readily provided (at the going rate for photocopying). And, if one wants to pay for the time and effort of my transcribing my written notes into readable English, such a service is readily provided. At no point do I hesitate or obstruct. There is absolutely nothing in my notes that is a secret, nothing that I could consider worthy of withholding. However, my experience has been that those who have demanded typewritten transcripts of my written notes often have a harassment motive operative in the request. At the same time that the requester is informed that I will comply with the request, I inform him (her) that I charge my usual hourly fees for such services, the same fees that I ask for preparation of written reports, and, as is my policy, I ask for payment in advance. I then provide the party with the anticipated cost of such transcription. It is a rare person who then comes forth with the significant amount of money necessary to pay for this tedious and generally unnecessary service.

The same flourish should also be used when responding to a cross-examining lawyer's request to peruse material from the evaluator's files. The chart material should be so well organized that a particular document can quickly be found. More important than the good impression that this makes is the examiner's state of total relaxation when providing it. One of the worst things an examiner can do is to be hesitant or defensive about providing certain material to a cross-examining attorney. Under these circumstances, all the red bulbs in the attorney's head are likely to flash simultaneously and all the antennae that stick out of his (her) head are likely to start buzzing.

An attorney who senses that the examiner is tense about revealing a certain document is likely to focus on the acquisition of such, ask questions about why it is not available, and, when it is received, review it in great detail, hoping to find some issue with which to embarrass or compromise the examiner. The best attitude the examiner can have is this: "Here's my chart in front of you. It's available to you in its entirety. Throughout the course of my evaluation, any and all documents contained in my file were available for scrutiny by the clients. In fact, my instructions have been that they make copies for each other of all documents submitted to me. There is absolutely nothing in this chart that I fear you will see." If the examiner communicates this attitude, the attorney is not likely to ask to look at any document at all! The rug is pulled out from under him (her), and searches of this kind are thereby discouraged from the outset. The response quickly pulls the wind out of his (her) sails. However, I am not suggesting that the examiner create a false impression here and hide tension regarding revelation of the material. Rather, the evaluation should be so conducted that the examiner has full confidence that nothing compromising is contained in the file.

"Is It Possible, Doctor, That . . ."

This is a common question used by cross-examining attorneys. Its purpose is to get the examiner to admit to something absurd and even stupid. Because anything is possible, a yes answer is the only one that the examiner can reasonably give. One cannot answer no to the question, no matter how infinitesimally small the possibility, no matter how high the unlikelihood. For example, an attorney might say, "Is it possible, Doctor, that Mrs. X's belief that she was repeatedly raped by space aliens is indeed a fact and is not part of a paranoid delusional system?" One must answer yes even though there is absolutely no evidence that space aliens have visited people on Earth, either for the purpose of fornicating with Earthlings or for any other reason. An attorney might ask, "Is it possible, Doctor, that Mr. Y's belief that in a past life he was an Egyptian king is true and that this is not part of a delusional system?" Again, one must answer yes to this question. A more common question: "Is it possible, Doctor, that you are wrong and that Mr. X did indeed sexually abuse his child?" Again, one must answer yes, even though there is absolutely no evidence that the abuse occurred and even though the examiner is convinced that the accusation is a conscious and deliberate fabrication on the part of the client's former wife.

My usual response to the "Is-it-possible" question is: "I'm going to save the court reporter a lot of time and trouble." I then look toward the court reporter and say to him (her): "Every time he (she) (pointing now to the cross-examining attorney) asks me a question beginning with 'is it possible,' just put down yes." I have never yet been interrupted before the completion of this response. Nor has an attorney yet asked of the judge, "Please direct Dr. Gardner to simply answer yes or no." My response makes a mockery of the question and generally puts an end to it, although some lawyers are so compelled to use it that they will ask it a few more times before they get my message that this is the response I am going to give repeatedly.

On occasion, I will answer the "Is-it-possible" question this way: "Of course, *it's possible!*" My response is made with the intonation of incredulity, especially by emphasizing the words *it's possible*. Usually, while saying this, I will simultaneously raise my eyebrows, open my eyes wide, stretch out my arms, sink my head between my humped-up shoulders, and raise my hands up in the air. (It's easier to do this if you're Italian or Jewish!) I do all this while looking the attorney straight in the eyes. All this communicates the message, "You must be some kind of an idiot if you can possibly believe such a stupid thing." Another way of accomplishing the same thing is to provide the same response in singsong fashion: "Yes, it's possible." The word *possible* here starts loudly and ends softly. The implication here is that a person must be very stupid to believe such a thing.

Sometimes, I can get away with the answer: "Of course, anything is possible. The question here is not what is *possible* but what is *probable.*" In most courts of law, that's about as far as I can go. However, if the "waters have been tested" and I see that there is greater flexibility with regard to the yes/no restrictions, I will add, "In this case, it is so extremely improbable that for all practical purposes the possibility does not exist." An alternative of the "Is-it-possible" question is the "Could-it-be" question. The latter is basically another way of saying the former, and so I deal with it in exactly the same ways as described for the "Is-it-possible" question.

"If You Were to Learn, Doctor . . ."

On occasion an attorney will attempt to cause expert witnesses to lose their composure—and thereby compromise their credibility—by asking questions that suggest extremely abnormal behavior manifested by the client, behavior not appreciated by the evaluator in the course of the examination. For example, under cross-examination I have been asked, "If you learned that Mr. X had a series of homosexual lovers during the course of his marriage, would that have changed your opinion?" "If you found out that Mrs. X had been hospitalized in a mental hospital prior to her marriage, would this have changed your opinion?" "If you learned that Mr. X would undress his 5-year-old daughter and ask her to dance naked in front of male friends, would this have affected your opinion?" These allegations are gross exaggerations and distortions of what had really gone on or were invented by the attorney and had absolutely no basis in reality. They were designed to get me flustered and seduce me into thinking that I had missed some extremely important points. The attorney here was trying to compromise me with such questions, and the examiner should be aware that this is occasionally done in the courtroom. Under these circumstances I generally try to bend the rules a bit in my response in order to get across my parallel communications. Accordingly, I respond, "Yes, you're absolutely right! If I did *indeed* learn that Mr. X *actually* asked his daughter to dance naked in front of a group of his male friends, I would *certainly* have reconsidered my conclusion!" The response is said in such a way that I communicate the message: "If indeed I have been so misled and if indeed he would engage in such a preposterous activity, I would have reconsidered my position. However, the absurdity of the allegation is so formidable that I am incredulous that such an activity ever took place." Usually, the opposing attorney will interrupt and object to the question as having no foundation. Sometimes the judge will do the interrupting or sustain the opposing attorney's objection. Attorneys cannot frivolously bring in such hypothetical questions unless there is some nidus of truth or unless there has been some previous testimony supporting the allegation. However, I have been in courtrooms in which such preliminary material was not presented and the attorneys were allowed to get away with this kind of horseplay.

"Did You Not Write, Doctor, That . . ."

As most readers appreciate, this is not my first book on the subject of forensic psychiatry. On the one hand, I am flattered that attorneys have often taken the trouble to read at least some of my previous publications. When cross-examining attorneys do this, they are generally sifting through my publications in order to find something that can compromise me on the witness stand. A common maneuver is to present me with one of my books, ask me to state its name, and then ask me whether I am the author of that book. That done, the attorney flips to a particular page and will either read a segment directly or have me read it. Most often (if not always), the selected statement is quoted out of context and thereby misrepresents my position. Attorneys do not ask me to quote material that they believe will support the other side's position. Rather, they are trying to make some point about me as a person or make some point that will support their position. Following the submission of that segment into the record (either by the cross-examining attorney or me), the attorney will ask, "Did you not write that, Doctor?" Obviously, I did write it and the attorney believes that my saying yes will somehow compromise me and support his (her) point. If I recognize that the out-of-context quotation totally misrepresents me, I will generally not simply say yes and let him "get away with it." Sometimes I will say, "Yes, you have read accurately what it says right there." My intonation implies that there is more on that subject that is not being read, but I have satisfied the structure of the yes/no answer. While saying this I *very quickly* touch the page with the tip of my index finger. This gesture gets across the message that only a very small fragment of the material has been quoted. Again, we see a little "bending of the rules" here. A common answer that I provide is, "Correct, as an out-of-context statement." If I have more flexibility I might add: "You have conveniently omitted the previous sentences, which put into proper context the meaning of that statement." Sometimes the judge will allow me to provide the elaboration that then rectifies the misrepresentation. Sometimes I will say, "I am in *full* agreement that it says exactly what you have read." While saying this, I will generally point to the book, possibly moving my finger back and forth. I try to get across the message that there is much more to the story than what is contained in that fragment.

On occasion, attorneys have presented me with critical reviews of some of my publications. As every author knows well, one cannot expect uniformly positive responses to one's work. Cross-examining attorneys relish the opportunity to bring these criticisms to the attention of the court in the hope of compromising the examiner's credibility. When confronted with such material, the examiner does well to request that the exact source of the material be placed on the record. My experience has been that the most distorted misrepresentations of my work have been found in newspapers, magazine articles, and nonprofessional publications—often written by people who have some axe to grind or some special agenda. I might also ask for the name and qualifications of the writer. Generally, the court will support such requests, and it behooves the supporting attorney to point out to the court that the document is less than reliable. When the criticism appears in a more reliable publication, one still can take opportunities to bend the rules and slip in a few extra words like, "Yes, that was indeed written by Dr. X, who is well known for his work in *academic sociology*." The implication here is that he has never seen a patient and that this is his view from an ivory tower. Or, I might say, "Yes, that was indeed said in *that* particular review." The implication here is that there are other reviews that have different, more positive things to say. As is true of all criticisms of the witness perpetrated in the context of yes/no questions, it behooves the attorney whose position is being supported to give the examiner the opportunity to correct during redirect examination distortions that may have been promulgated by yes/no questions. Accordingly, if the examiner has not had the opportunity to provide the rest of the quote in the context of cross-examination, it should be provided in the process of the redirect.

"With All Due Respect, Doctor . . ."

It is not uncommon for cross-examining attorneys to preface their comments or questions with: "With all due respect, Doctor. . . ." When an attorney prefaces a question with "With all due respect," it generally means that there is *no* respect at that point. The cross-examining attorney may have been questioning the examiner for many hours and, throughout the course of the interrogation, not once use this preface. Then suddenly the attorney prefaces a statement with this introduction. At that moment the word *respect* is being used in the service of reaction formation. The attorney—at that point—has absolutely no respect at all for the evaluator's opinion and is now moving in to try to humiliate, expose deficits of, or otherwise compromise the evaluator. The same introductory words are often used when addressing the judge under similar circumstances. At that point, the attorney's level of frustration may be formidable, his boiling rage enormous, and his hatred for the judge at its peak. Yet, even though his respect at that point has reached its nadir, he will begin his comments with, "With all due respect, Your Honor. . . ."

I have found it amazing that most attorneys do not appreciate this mechanism. In fact, I had two experiences in which attorneys actually said to me, after I explained to them what I considered to be going on, that such thoughts of denigration were "the last thing in the world" in their minds. My attempt to impress upon them that "the last thing in the world" is often "the first thing in the world" proved futile. Also, although the all-due-respect introductory phrase generally includes the word "Doctor," the way the lawyer says "Doctor" conveys even less of a feeling of admiration for the evaluator. One should generally not make any comments to the cross-examining attorney about one's thoughts regarding his (her) use of the term; rather, the examiner should appreciate that at that point one may have "gotten to him (her)" and caused frustration. Or, one should recognize that it might be used as the "buttering up" phase prior to coming in for "the kill."

"Fishing Trips"

At times a lawyer may bombard the examiner with a barrage of questions that appear to be irrelevant or only peripherally relevant to the issues at hand. In my experience, one of two things is going on in such a situation. The first, and less likely, is that the lawyer really has an important point to make that the evaluator does not understand. Ultimately, the attorney may reveal the track down which the questions are leading. The more likely alternative, in my experience, is that the attorney has no ultimate point in mind, is not really laying a foundation, and is flooding the therapist with questions in the hope that some response might provide a useful issue to pursue. Such attorneys are being paid for their services, and it behooves them to get up there in the courtroom and perform for their clients. If they cannot provide *quality* services, then they believe they should at least provide *quantity* services.

One would hope that the judge or the opposing lawyer would interrupt early such time-wasting and often pointless inquiries. Unfortunately, my experience has been that they may take considerable time before doing this. Courts traditionally allow wide latitude regarding the length and depth of cross-examination. The nonsupported party is thereby given the greatest opportunity to strengthen his (her) position. In such cross-examination (which can last hours and even days), the examiner should appreciate that the judge is generally not naive and will not be impressed by the lawyer's antics, misleading questions, attempts to deceive the court, etc. At times I have seen judges interrupt the attorney who is going on such a fishing trip with such comments as, "Mr. X, where are you going with all of this?" At this point the attorney might respond, "Your Honor, I'm laying a foundation." My experience has been that people who go on "fishing trips," like all fishermen, sometimes come home without any "fish." My experience also has been that more competent attorneys do not go on fishing trips and they recognize that this compromises them in the courtroom.

Presenting Projective Tests on the Witness Stand

Use of projective tests is "risky business" on the witness stand. There is probably no other place where evaluators are so vulnerable as they are in their interpretation of projective material. Our field has not reached the point where there is unanimity regarding the interpretation of any ink blot, figure drawing, self-created picture, dream, or fantasy. There are a wide variety of opinions regarding the meaning of such material, and the less familiar the examiner is with the patient, the more likely his (her) opinion will diverge from that of another professional. Accordingly, no matter what interpretation the evaluator provides, the attorney is likely to be able to present an alternative that is equally credible to the court—which may be naive with regard to such matters.

There are judges who routinely order psychological tests on parties embroiled in child-custody and sex-abuse litigation and use the findings from projective tests as crucial determinants of their decisions. This is a grave mistake. Projective fantasies have much in common with dreams, although there are certainly some differences. It is very difficult, if not impossible, to differentiate the dreams of the normal person from those of the psychotic. Dreams may tell much about psychodynamics, but they tell very little about diagnostic status and even depth of pathology. In fact dreams, by the very nature of the logical (or, more correctly, illogical) processes they utilize, *are psychotic*. Even the most highly maternal parent will have death wishes, on occasion, toward the children, and these may be symbolically represented in projected fantasies.

Projective instruments were designed to provide information about underlying psychodynamics; they were not designed to be of particular value in child-custody and sex-abuse evaluations. One really has to "squeeze the data" in order to extract from these instruments information of probative value in a court of law in which a custody dispute or a sex-abuse accusation is being litigated. It is therefore naive and injudicious on the part of courts to utilize such material in these deliberations, and it is a disservice to the courts for evaluators to provide it. There are judges, however, who recognize the weakness of these instruments and are very dubious about their value in the courtroom. This is especially the case when they experience parades of mental health professionals coming to the courtroom and providing diametrically opposed opinions regarding the meaning of the same data.

Many years ago there was an article in *The New York Times Magazine* in which the author presented Rorschach Test responses to a series of internationally famous experts on Rorschach interpretation. These experts claimed they could make accurate statements about the personalities of the respondents without clinical data or other identifying information. Accordingly, the author presented to the experts Rorschach protocols of unidentifiable famous individuals and invited the experts to make guesses regarding who these people might be. The purpose of the article was to point out how far afield many of these *mavens* were. In fact, one was so far off that he begged the author not to reveal his name. I do not recall exactly the nature of his bizarre conclusion, but it was as if he had taken the protocol of Adolph Hitler and decided that the person was Mother Teresa. The author, out of pity for the "expert," complied with the request. Had I been the author, I would not have done so. People who involve themselves in such a project should have the balls to allow their names to be revealed, whether or not the guesses are good ones. I often regretted that I never saved that article. I would have quoted it directly in publications. Unfortunately, *The New York Times* was unable to track down the original, so long ago had it appeared. (I believe it was in the mid-1970s.) I mention the article here because it is an excellent demonstration of the weakness of conclusions derived from projective tests, even conclusions made by world-famous "experts."

The way in which the utilization of projective material can compromise an examiner's position in court is well demonstrated by the following vignette: A six-year-old boy, in the course of the custody evaluation, is given a piece of drawing paper and crayons. He is invited to draw anything he wants and then to tell a story about what he has drawn. This is standard procedure in child diagnosis and treatment and I routinely do this myself. The child draws a house and then draws a man in the middle of the house. The man is drawn in black crayon and as the boy fills in the human outline (again with black), there is a vigorous and intense quality to his work. He then takes a red crayon and says, "The whole house is burning down and so is the man." Again, there is a frenetic quality to his work as he covers the whole drawing with red lines. He then says, "The whole house is burned down. Everything is ashes. Even the man is ashes." The child is then asked how the house caught on fire. The reply is, "The boy's friend, who lives next door, burned it down. He was angry at the man who lived in the house. He didn't like him because he was mean."

Most examiners would agree that the drawing and its associated story reveal that the child is extremely angry at his father. Depicting his father as completely black, and drawing him frenetically, suggest that the child views his father as a fearsome and ominous figure, as anxiety-provoking and dangerous. Most would agree, as well, that the friend next door is merely a convenient device, an alter ego, for assuaging guilt over the boy's hostility. It is not *he* who kills his father, but his friend (his alter ego) next door. The boy's hostility toward his father is vented through a drawing in which he totally destroys the father by burning him to death.

Now let us imagine the situation in which the evaluator has included the above material in the report and considers the child's massive hostility toward his father as one argument (among many) for recommending that the mother be given custody of the child. The husband's attorney, during cross-examination, could ask the examiner to show the court the picture and explain its supposed meaning. Following this presentation, the attorney could ask the following questions, to which only yes/no answers could be required:

> *Attorney:* Is it possible, Doctor, that this child watched television before drawing this picture, either on the same day or one or two days previously?
> *Examiner:* Yes.

The examiner has no choice but to answer yes. A no response essentially says that there is absolutely *no* possibility that this child watched television over a three-day period. Even if there is no television set in the home, there would still be the possibility that he watched in another child's home. The attorney then continues.

> *Attorney:* Is it possible, Doctor, that the child observed a program in which a building burned?
> *Examiner:* Yes.

Again, the examiner has little choice but to answer yes, because to say that there was *no* such possibility is absurd. This is especially the case because most news programs routinely describe the major fires of the day. The attorney then proceeds.

> *Attorney:* Is it possible, Doctor, that such a program depicted people being injured and even killed in such a fire?
> *Examiner:* Yes.

Once again, the examiner has to answer yes to preserve credibility.

> *Attorney:* Is it possible, Doctor, that the picture that you've just shown us was suggested by his watching such a television program, a program in which a fire was described, a program in which people were burned to death in the fire?
> *Examiner:* Yes.

If the examiner tries to follow the one-word response with an explanation, the attorney will likely interrupt and instruct the testifier to confine responses to yes or no. This is likely to frustrate the examiner because of the deep-seated conviction that such environmental suggestions play a small role, at best, in producing such pictures and fantasies. The examiner firmly believes that it is the internal pressure of psychodynamically meaningful material, rather than external suggestive stimuli, that play the most important role in creating such fantasies in the child. But a skilled lawyer will not permit the testifier to provide this explanation. Even if the examiner were permitted to give explanations (and sometimes the judge might ask for them), the attorney could still extract a statement that such an explanation is "theory" and not "fact." And the attorney could then proceed with further inquiry designed to weaken the explanation:

> *Attorney:* Is it possible, Doctor, that your explanation is incorrect?
> *Examiner:* Yes.

If the examiner claims that there is absolutely *no* possibility that the explanation is incorrect, the examiner compromises credibility. So, once again, the examiner has no choice but to answer in the affirmative. The testifier has no choice but to agree that the explanation may be incorrect and there may be no opportunity at that point to elaborate and to explain that the possibility of being incorrect is extremely low, that well-established psychological principles would highly support such an explanation, and so on.

An astute attorney (especially one who consulted a knowledgeable and experienced psychologist or psychiatrist) might proceed as follows:

> *Attorney:* In the course of your practice, Doctor, have you ever treated children who have been exposed to psychological traumas such as divorce, accidents, injuries, hospitalizations, and death of a parent?

To this question, the examiner has almost no choice but to say yes. To a negative response, the attorney might justifiably ask about how long the "expert" has been in practice and what kinds of patients have been seen. Assuming then that the answer will be yes, the attorney could then continue:

> *Attorney:* Is it not true that children who are exposed to such traumas deal with them via reiteration because such reiteration contributes to the desensitization process? In other words, each time the child thinks about the trauma, talks about it, and emotes to it, the youngster experiences some relief from the psychological pain associated with the trauma?

Again, the examiner has no choice but to say yes. To answer in the negative would compromise significantly the examiner's credibility and degree of competence because the statement is a well-known principle in child therapy. Assuming, therefore, that the answer is again affirmative, the attorney might continue:

> *Attorney:* Isn't it possible, then, that this child was upset by watching a television program in which people were killed in a fire, and he attempted to deal with his untoward psychological reactions by a desensitization process?

Again, it behooves the examiner to say yes or else risk a loss of credibility. The attorney then continues:

> *Attorney:* Isn't it true, Doctor, that children commonly use their self-created drawings and associated stories as a vehicle for such desensitization?

Again, the examiner almost has no choice but to answer in the affirmative for the same reason. The attorney then continues:

> *Attorney:* Isn't it possible, Doctor, that this child's picture, then, was the result of an attempt to desensitize himself to his strong emotional reactions evoked by watching this scary program?

It is likely again that the examiner will have to say yes. The attorney may then continue:

> *Attorney:* Accordingly, Doctor, by your own admission you have agreed that an alternative explanation is perfectly credible and fits in with well-known psychological principles.

Again, the examiner has almost no choice but to agree with the attorney that there is a credible alternative to the examiner's explanation—an alternative that has nothing to do with parental capacity.

The lawyer whose position the examiner is supporting may provide an opportunity for a presentation of the rationale for the explanation. But it is important for the evaluator to appreciate that the judge may be extremely unsophisticated when it comes to understanding such psychological processes. And the cross-examining attorney may fully convince such a judge that the expert's interpretations are totally speculative creations not worthy of consideration.

All evaluators who use self-created drawings and associated stories have had the experience that parents will state that the examiner's explanations are not valid and that the story comes from a recent television program or experience. In earlier years I tended to go along with the traditional explanation that such parents were trying to deny a painful reality and that the child's selection of a particular television program or experience was of little importance. More important was the child's selection of that material because it lent itself well to utilization and incorporation in the child's psychological processes. In more recent years I have come to agree more with the parents than with those who taught me the aforementioned explanation. I have found that the vast majority of children (especially younger ones) often "lift" allegedly self-created stories from public media and personal experiences. Of course, I do obtain idiosyncratic material, but the contamination with external stimuli is often formidable. Accordingly, in recent years, in association with the diagnostic/therapeutic process, I often invite parents' input regarding the child's self-created stories elicited when administering the Draw-a-Person Test, Draw-a-Family Test, and many freely drawn pictures around which children spin fantasies. Such experiences have added strong support to the aforementioned warning against the use of these pictures and stories in the courtroom.

It would be an error for the reader to conclude that I consider such self-created stories to be of *no* value whatsoever. This would be a *reductio ad absurdum* of my statement. In the *therapeutic* situation, when one has an opportunity for ongoing elicitation of stories and close work with parents, then one is more likely to be able to differentiate stories that have been externally contaminated from those that are truly idiosyncratic. The former are of limited psychotherapeutic value; the latter serve well in the course of the therapeutic process (Gardner, 1992c).

There are judges who will frequently, if not routinely, order psychological tests on both parents and/or children. As mentioned, this is a manifestation of the judge's naïveté. It reflects the court's view (promulgated by mental health professionals) that these tests are "objective" and that they provide information that is much more accurate than "mere" clinical observations. The judge here has probably been duped into the belief that there is something more objective and scientific about an instrument such as the *Rorschach Test* (Rorschach, 1921) or the *Thematic Apperception Test* (TAT) (Murray, 1936) than the clinical interview. Such a request is probably also related to the judge's belief that these tests are more efficient and can get to the "roots" of personality problems more efficaciously than clinical interviews. There is no question that psychological tests can often provide much extra information in an expeditious way. But it is very unlikely that they are of greater value than clinical interviews in custody and sex-abuse evaluations. The tests were not designed for these purposes, and one really has to *squeeze* out the data to get information that is useful for such legal evaluations. They are, however, more valuable in sanity and competence cases, areas for which they have been found applicable. Accordingly, examiners who cooperate in such cases by complying with court dictates are doing their patients and the court a disservice. Unfortunately, such utilization of these tests is widespread and contributes, thereby, to each party's bringing in a parade of professionals to provide different explanations for the same projective data.

In spite of my strong criticism of the use of projective materials in custody and sex-abuse evaluations, I do not refrain entirely from their use in the courtroom. There are a few projective techniques that I do utilize, but I am careful to do so only as a vehicle for obtaining more objective and "hard" data. In short, I utilize instruments that allow themselves to be *points of departure* for the obtaining of overt statements that can be more useful in a custody or sex-abuse evaluation. For example, in my protocol for the sex-abuse evaluation of the child (Gardner, 1995) I do use the freely drawn picture, the Draw-a-Person Test, and the Draw-a-Family Test. However, I do not make speculations regarding the meaning of the drawings per se or the derivative stories. Rather, I merely confine myself to the question of whether the picture and/or story specifically and explicitly relate to sexual abuse. Speculations regarding the symbolic meaning of any of these items do not warrant the conclusion that the sex abuse occurred.

"Wisecracks" from the Witness Stand

There are times when the examiner will have a strong impulse to respond with a joke or wisecrack. This is especially true when one is being cross-examined by the more flamboyant type of attorney. Although the retort may be unusually clever and certain to make everyone in the courtroom laugh, the examiner does well to resist the impulse. The attorney is sure to ask the judge, in a very sanctimonious manner, to direct the examiner to observe courtroom decorum and to respect the dignity of the legal process. The judge will invariably honor this request, and the examiner's position will be compromised—the cleverness of the joke notwithstanding. For example, on many occasions I am asked by a cross-examining attorney: "Are you being paid for your testimony, Dr. Gardner?" The implication of the question, of course, is that I am a "hired gun," even though I was brought in by both sides as an impartial. I have no choice but to answer yes (except, of course, in situations in which I am pro bono). My impulse has been to say, "Aren't you?" or

"Are you doing this for nothing?" I have squelched my impulse (even though one wisecrack usually deserves another) because the lawyer would have predictably used it as an excuse to request of the judge that he quickly hit me over the head with his gavel (figuratively, of course) and require me to confine myself to simply answering the questions. I would not give him this opportunity to compromise me with the judge.

I recall one case in which the cross-examining attorney was a man who combined two deficits, each of which is bad enough alone, but when they coexist in the same person at the same time, they can have a devastating impact on all those around them. These qualities are *ignorance* and *arrogance*. The cross-examining attorney was basically a stupid man who did not recognize how ignorant he was of basic legal principles and he thereby compromised significantly the position of his client, a man involved in a child-custody dispute. Under cross-examination he said to me: "As I understand it, Doctor, what you are saying is that Mrs. Jones began this lawsuit because . . ." He then provided point by point my major arguments, one after the other, emphasizing the most compelling reasons that I had for my position. It took him about five minutes to ask this "question." Even before he finished I had the strong impulse to say:

> I want to thank you on behalf of Mrs. Jones and her attorney for having articulated in such a compelling manner her basic position. I think that they themselves could not have presented it in as convincing a manner. You have summarized their position eloquently, and we are all grateful to you for this.

I suspected that I could have gotten away with this "compliment" in the courtroom because the judge herself was irritated by this attorney. However, I squelched the impulse and merely answered, "Yes, that is my understanding of her position, and I agree with every point you have delineated."

Breaks in the Testimony

Inevitably, there are breaks in the testimony. As mentioned, in some jurisdictions an expert is not permitted to talk with clients or attorneys during breaks in the course of testimony. In most jurisdictions, however, I have been permitted to do so. In earlier years I suffered significant frustration during court breaks when I could not communicate with the attorney whose position I supported. As an impartial examiner, I suffered all the disadvantages of being an advocate and had none of the advantages. In more recent years I removed myself from such an impotent position. As mentioned, I circumvented this problem by making myself available to *both* attorneys, not only following the submission of my report, but right up through the trial—especially during the breaks in the course of the litigation. However, I strictly adhere to the position that I will not speak with one attorney without the other being invited to hear and contribute. This gives me the freedom to recommend lines of inquiry to either attorney. Of course, the attorney whose position I am supporting is generally quite receptive to my suggestions. As might be expected, the other attorney is generally interested in what I have to say but not too happy that I am providing ammunition to the other side. This invitation is rarely declined. My status as impartial examiner is thereby preserved, and my moral obligation to do what is in the best interests of the children is thereby gratified.

In the course of such discussion I am particularly interested in giving the supported attorney questions or suggestions to pose to me during the redirect examination in order to correct distortions and misrepresentations that came to the court as a result of the constraints of cross-examination. In that conversation I might also ask him to ask certain questions that have been brought to mind as a result of my cross-examination. Generally, these involve small points that may have passed me by, points that have been brought up in cross-examination. Sometimes I will request information related to misperceptions and distortions that the cross-examining attorney has tried to perpetrate upon the court. The presence of the client (or both clients if the invitation has been accepted) is useful here because his (her) (their) presence can be useful in providing input on many of these points. This procedure lessens the temptation to involve myself in the previously described nonverbal communication between a client and myself in the course of my providing testimony.

The above procedure is the one I utilize when I am formally designated by the court as an independent examiner. When this attempt has not been successful, I am usually recognized as the expert of one party, but the opposing party has been ordered to cooperate in my evaluation. Although recognized as the inviting party's expert, I conduct the evaluation, as much as possible, as if I were indeed the court-appointed independent examiner. This procedure is followed when I present my findings and recommendations to both attorneys and clients and give both sides the opportunity for input into my final report.

Once in the courtroom, there are two possible positions I then take. If the opposing side has been reasonably receptive and cooperative and has not then brought in "hired guns" to "shoot me down," I will meet with both attorneys during courtroom breaks. If, following the submission of my report, the opposing side has been obstructive and/or antagonistic, and/or has subsequently brought in the services of a hired-gun mental health professional, then I believe it would be a disservice to the party whose position I am supporting to meet with both attorneys during the course of the trial. The other side is sitting with the newly engaged hired gun, passing notes, and whispering to one another. Under such circumstances it would be a disservice to the client to continue to fully cooperate with the other side. It would be the equivalent of voluntarily, unilaterally, and unnecessarily providing ammunition to the other side. Under those circumstances, I will meet alone with the attorney whose position I support. I can do this without any problem because I have always been recognized by the court as the expert of the party.

There are situations in which I have seen fit to support the position of the party who initially refused to have me recognized as the impartial examiner but cooperated only in compliance with the court order. Although recognized as the expert of the inviting party, I concluded that the initially unreceptive party warranted my support. Accordingly, from the point of view of the inviting party I have "jumped ship." From my point of view, I have not been "a traitor" in that all were apprised at the outset that I would be conducting the evaluation, as much as possible, as if I were the court's independent examiner. Most of these cases have not gone to court, so weakened has the inviting party been made by my decision. In those cases in which I did indeed go to court, I have testified on behalf of the initially reluctant party, much to the frustration of the party who originally invited me. During court breaks I generally speak with both sides together under these circumstances.

Refusal to Answer a Question

There are certain situations in which the examiner should consider refusing to answer a question. One relates to questions involving previous cases that might involve divulgence of confidential material. The evaluator must appreciate that in many cases the court proceedings are public record and answering a question about a particular person (not involved in the proceedings) may represent a disclosure of confidential material. Under such circumstances the evaluator should openly state reluctance to answer the question because it would involve divulgence of privileged information. Usually, there is some discussion at that point as to whether the evaluator should be required to respond. Sometimes the court decides not to insist that the question be answered, and the inquiry proceeds. Or the court may decide that the question is permissible, and the examiner is ordered to answer it. Under such circumstances, the evaluator is usually protected from complaints of divulgence and disclosure. Sometimes, if the issue is unclear, I will turn directly to the judge and state, "Your Honor, I would appreciate your ordering me directly to answer that question, a question that involves divulging confidential material about clients in another case." My experience has been that judges most often provide the order. Examiners do well to protect themselves by obtaining that court order. They should appreciate that they are dealing with litigious people, one and even both of whom are probably going to be very angry at him (her) for not providing full support or enough support. And previous clients are likely to still harbor ongoing hostilities from their own cases. Inappropriate disclosure of privileged information provides such angry people with an excuse to complain to ethics committees and even to file malpractice suits.

Questions regarding one's fees in the particular case in which one is testifying are routine and they must be answered. In fact, the examiner does well to bring along photocopies of one's financial records, which all concerned parties are entitled to have. However, as a spin-off from this I have been asked questions about my own personal finances, especially my income from my practice, from involvement in legal cases, book royalties, etc. Although my feelings about such questions are "It's none of your business," I have unfortunately not been successful in my attempts to preserve my privacy. Often, my reluctance has not even been supported by the attorney whose position I am supporting and/or the judge, and so I have had to reluctantly answer such questions. I do believe that they are basically irrelevant to the case, but I would be in contempt of court if I refused to answer them. I suspect that the main reason for the failure of my attempts to withhold this information relates to curiosity on the part of both attorneys and the judge. Often, in response to a question about my income from various sources, I have turned to the judge and said, "Your Honor, I consider that question irrelevant and will only answer if ordered to do so by the court." Unfortunately, most often the court has ordered me to answer the question.

On occasion, I have had the following fantasy with regard to my answering this question: "Your Honor, I can see how questions about the fees I am charging these clients are completely relevant to this case and I have answered them without hesitation. However, I fail to see how questions about my personal income have any relevance to this case and I refuse to answer them. If the court deems me to be in contempt of court, then I see myself as having no other choice than to engage the services of an attorney to represent me on this point." I have never said this and cannot see myself doing so; however, I believe that if I were to go to that extreme, I would probably win the point.

There are questions, however, about the evaluator's personal life that may be relevant to the court. For example, when testifying in a child-custody dispute, it is reasonable for a cross-examining attorney to ask whether the evaluator himself (herself) has ever personally been involved in a child-custody dispute. If the answer is affirmative, then further questions about the details and outcome are relevant to ask. Examiners who have been deeply involved in such disputes, especially prolonged ones, and still have residual reactions are likely to be compromised when conducting a child-custody evaluation. And the party whose position has not been supported is justified in making inquiries along these lines. In fact, I would go further and state that attorneys do well to check out this point *before* recommending their clients for child-custody evaluations. Similarly, a person who has been sexually abused in childhood may be seriously compromised when conducting a sex-abuse evaluation. Accordingly, questions about whether the examiner himself (herself) has been sexually abused in childhood are relevant when the evaluator is testifying in a case involving child sexual-abuse accusations. As mentioned elsewhere (Gardner, 1991c), there are women who were sexually abused in childhood who have not worked through their residual reactions. One of the pathological derivatives of their experiences is to become overzealous in the diagnosis of sex abuse (seeing it when it does not exist) and overpunitive with regard to what should be done with sex-abuse perpetrators (whether or not they are actually guilty of abuse). Again, attorneys involved in enlisting the services of examiners should screen such people before commiting themselves to them.

I recall once testifying in association with my request that a child, alleged to have been sexually abused, should receive an examination by a pediatrician specializing in the realm of physical examinations of children alleging sexual abuse. The father was insistent upon such an examination and the mother resisted it strongly. Accordingly, in the course of my evaluation, I was asked to testify regarding my reasons for recommending this examination. In the course of my testimony the mother's attorney asked me to describe specifically the possible positions the child would be asked to assume during the course of that examination. I believe that I provided a fairly good description of what could be expected. The attorney then asked me to get off the witness stand, lie down on the floor, and demonstrate these various positions directly. I refused and asked the attorney whether she would be making the same request of the female pediatrician we were considering inviting in to conduct the examination. Amazingly, she said that she would ask of her the same thing. Accordingly, I turned to the judge and again stated that I refused on the basis that I considered this demeaning. The judge agreed and did not direct me to comply with this absurd request. Had he done so, I would have refused and told him: "Your Honor, I refuse to comply with your directive. I would consider compliance with this request demeaning, and I see myself as having no alternative but to engage the services of an attorney." Although one is certainly in a weak position under cross-examination, examiners should not let themselves be pushed around and be required to submit to unreasonable and even irrational demands.

THE REDIRECT AND RECROSS EXAMINATIONS

It is during the redirect examination that the supported attorney is in a position to question the examiner about points raised during cross-examination, points that warrant clarification and elaboration. This is the time when the distortions created by cross-examination are supposed to be rectified. In my 35 years of experience on the witness stand, I have not once (I repeat not once) been in a situation in which the supported attorney then covered all the material I considered warranted during the redirect examination. And this represents one of the serious flaws of the adversary system. The assumption is made that this will be done and that ultimately *all* the pertinent information will be brought to the attention of the court. I have never seen this happen. Even when I have given the lawyer written lists of topics to be covered during redirect, all the points have not been brought up. Part of this relates to a system that allows for frequent objections, which may or may not be sustained by the court. Part of this problem relates to the fact that what I consider important may not be considered important by the attorney. I am not claiming infallibility here. But I do believe that I know more about the psychiatric aspects of the case than the attorney and that the legal considerations often becloud the psychiatric ones. This problem is further compounded by the fact that often under direct examination the attorney does not ask me all the questions I believe are warranted, even when given a list. This is one of the reasons why my reports are so comprehensive. They get on record all the material I consider warranted, because I do not trust that all this information will be brought before the court in either the direct or redirect examinations.

I have often thought that it would be a good idea to jot down some notes during the cross-examination, notes that would serve as points of departure for questions under redirect. I would give specific attention to points brought up by the cross-examining attorney that are worthy of rectification and explanation. However, when on the witness stand, one cannot take notes. I have never done this, but

I suspect strongly that if I were to do so somebody, somehow, would object. However, considering the high pressure of the situation and considering the fact that my mind must be fully attentive to the cross-examination questions, jotting down such notes (even if allowed by the court) would be a distraction from the issues at hand.

Another compromise relates to the fact that the attorney cannot, during redirect, bring up issues that were not brought up during cross-examination. The purpose here is to put a limit on the amount of material in the deliberations. The theory is that otherwise they might go on forever. I appreciate the value of this constraint but, in many cases, it deprives the court of important information. It is based on the assumption that the attorney conducting the direct examination is infallible and never forgets or omits any important issue. In most other situations in life one does not have to "live with" such omissions. Afterthoughts may be brought forth, especially regarding issues that are highly significant to the topic at hand. Courtrooms generally do not permit this. My experience has been that sometimes an attorney might be allowed to bring forth questions during the redirect inquiry that were not originally covered during the time of the direct examination. Most often, however, the opposing attorney will object to the belated introduction of material not previously covered, and the objection is usually sustained by the court.

The recross examination is even more limited than the cross-examination in that the recrossing attorney must confine himself (herself) to issues covered during the redirect examination. Theoretically, there can be further rounds of redirect and recross, but in practice there are generally no more than a few rounds of each. My experience has been that after two rounds of redirect and recross examination my testimony ends and I am invited to step down from the witness stand. In these subsequent rounds I have rarely had the opportunity to give input to the attorney(s) because there has usually been no break between these relatively short elements in the examination. This too represents a constraint, because on occasion there has been information that I would have liked to have brought before the court via a suggested question to the attorney who is conducting the redirect examinations. We see here yet another weakness of the adversary system as a method of finding out "the truth."

PROSECUTORS

First, I wish to emphasize that the comments I make here about prosecutors are derived almost exclusively from my experiences in sex-abuse
cases. It may be that this group is not representative of prosecutors as a
whole, and that prosecutors in other realms do not conduct themselves
in the ways described here. It may also be that there are prosecutors
who work within the sex-abuse realm who do not exhibit the qualities
that I have encountered. Whatever the prevalence of those who do not
fit the description of the prosecutors I present here, there is no question
that there are enough who fit this profile to warrant my comments.

My experience has been that prosecutors represent a special category of cross-examining attorneys, especially with regard to the
viciousness with which they involve themselves in cases. Attorneys involved in child-custody disputes are generally not very much in the public
eye, with the exception of high-profile cases involving celebrities. Even
when there is a sex-abuse accusation involved in a civil-court custody
dispute, it is not likely that the case is going to attract significant public
attention, especially in recent years, when such accusations are so widespread. Prosecutors, in contrast, are typically involved in criminal cases
that are more likely to be brought to public attention. Furthermore,
their professional advancement is very much dependent on their track
record with regard to the percentage of cases they win and those they
lose. Accordingly, their commitment to the case becomes more formidable, and therefore there is the likelihood of even more erosion of values
than in other lawyers.

Prosecutors, like other professionals, exhibit a wide range of skill,
from the highest to the lowest. I focus here on those whom I have encountered in sex-abuse cases. I recognize fully that there certainly are
prosecutors who are not in the category described here, but there are
enough in this reprehensible category to warrant my comments. Examiners who testify in court should know something about the background
of the people who examine them, especially when their background is
likely to result in more vicious cross-examination in which conscious
and deliberate deceit is "the name of the game"—protestations of professional honesty notwithstanding. As the reader will come to see, my

"bending the rules" is BB ammunition compared to the war weapons that these people bring into the courtroom.

Notoriety

When a prosecutor concludes that no sex abuse has taken place, he (she) will enjoy little public attention. After all, there is nothing to talk about when the conclusion is that there is "no evidence." In contrast, if the prosecutor finds that there is "suggestive evidence" (no matter how remote and preposterous), then there is "much work to be done." The uncovering process (often with justification referred to as a "witch hunt") demands significant attention as interested parties (and they are everywhere) eagerly await the outcome of the investigation. All the details need be divulged if one is to have "a good case." Every remnant of sexual behavior must be "dug up." Young prosecutors, with no particular standing in the community, have an opportunity here to "make a name" for themselves. Other forms of investigation attract little attention in the public media or, at most, may receive occasional attention in the back pages of the newspaper (with the exception of murder cases, especially "juicy" ones). Sex-abuse cases in nursery schools and day-care centers attract widespread media attention. And, especially in smaller communities, people who were previously unknown may suddenly make headlines in association with a sex-abuse accusation against them. What a wonderful opportunity for a young prosecutor "on the way up." It is an opportunity for overnight fame. Typically, these prosecutors work closely with the accusers, and it behooves them to intensify sex-abuse hysteria in order to ensure their continually being in the public eye. The prosecutor becomes viewed as the hero who is protecting innocent children from perverts—certainly a noble calling.

In some cases, the prosecutor may have established a reputation as being in the Casey-always-gets-his-man category. Once Casey concludes that the alleged perpetrator is guilty, he never lets go. He will carry it up to the Supreme Court if necessary. Nobody escapes Casey once he is convinced that the crime has been committed (and Casey is easily convinced). He would like to maintain his "perfect record" in order to ensure his reputation as "one of the best, if not *the* best." And the accusers feel grateful that they have been lucky enough to have an individual of Casey's reputation on the case. Casey gets his fame, promotion, and higher salary; the accused goes to jail. Casey deserves everything he got for his efforts; the perverted perpetrator deserves what he got for his perversity.

The Prosecutor as "Civil Servant"

A prosecutor is basically a civil servant. It is a salaried position with the usual increments. In the crowded field of law today, the "best and the brightest" generally take jobs with prestigious law firms (sometimes after a year or two of "internship" with judges in high-level positions). Idealistic ones will often gravitate (usually for only a few years) to legal aid and other low-paying positions, through which they can gratify their humanitarian inclinations. Civil service jobs are generally not those sought after by the superior students. Rather, they are more likely to be taken by those who have been less successful academically. This intellectual impairment is an asset when one is working as a prosecutor in sex-abuse cases. It enables one to believe some of the preposterous things that they are told by hysterical accusers and the "validators" and thereby enables them to stay in the system and enjoy the benefits to be derived from such involvement. Other prosecutors, of course, are not justifiably placed in this category. They may be quite intelligent, but gravitate toward the work for other reasons—such as the potential for notoriety and the opportunity to gratify (in a socially approved way) sadistic urges via the deep involvement with criminal elements that the work entails.

Although some prosecutors I have encountered do appear to be ethical individuals who will not prosecute a suspect when the evidence is strong that the person is innocent, there are others who will do so vigorously, even fanatically. Some in the latter category, I suspect, know that the defendant is innocent, but they are so desirous of demonstrating their prowess in imprisoning people that they totally ignore ethical and moral considerations. Such individuals view defendants as objects to be locked up in prison, not as human beings. They blind themselves to the fact that the defendants are people who suffer enormous frustration over being accused of a crime that was never committed and who face the prospect of long imprisonment. By ignoring these obvious feelings of the accused party, these prosecutors can justify their relentless pursuit of "justice."

The major rationalization that prosecutors use is that they are "serving the people." Every one of their cases begins with "The people of the State of X vs. John Doe." Theirs, they would like to claim, is a noble calling in that they are protecting people from criminals who prey upon an innocent public. There is no question that we need individuals to protect us from those who perpetrate crimes upon us. But there is a better way of doing this. One does not have to engage psychopaths (see below) to utilize the adversary system, but this is exactly what we are doing.

Prosecutors as Psychopaths

Many of the prosecutors I have encountered are, I am convinced, psychopaths. They were probably prepsychopathic when they entered the field, and their involvement over the years has intensified their pathology to the point where I have no hesitation using this label. Such individuals use the law to legalize their psychopathic lifestyle, but they are psychopaths nevertheless. They satisfy the central elements for psychopathy, namely, lack of the ability to put themselves in the place of their victims and absolutely no guilt over the cruelties they perpetrate upon them. Their one main goal is professional advancement and, in the service of this goal, they care not how many innocent people they put in jail and/or how many lives and reputations they destroy. To them, defendants are like pieces on a chessboard to be knocked off and put in a box. And, when there is the possibility of achieving some public notoriety (often the case in sex-abuse lawsuits), they become even more ruthless.

I present some examples. In one case in which I was involved, the prosecutors decided, mainly on the basis of rumor and an anonymous tip, that a young woman in her twenties was sexually abusing pubertal boys in her housing complex. Each of her alleged victims denied vehemently that such was the case. Some of these boys were then taken to the police station, literally put in jail cells, and told that they would not be freed until they helped the prosecutors put this young woman in jail.

When the parents came to the jail house, they were told that their children would only be released *after* they had disclosed their sexual abuses by this woman. The boys again insisted upon their innocence of such acts. The boys and their parents all actually believed that the prosecutors could keep them in jail indefinitely unless and until they "confessed." Accordingly, they consciously and deliberately told the prosecutors what they wanted to hear, namely, that they had involved themselves in a wide variety of bizarre sexual activities with this woman. At the time of this writing, nine years later, she is still in jail. Some of the boys, now young adults, are recanting and describing what happened to them. I have carefully reviewed this case and am convinced that this woman's version of the story is valid, as is that of the recanting boys.

In another case in which I was involved, a four-year-old girl in "treatment" for sex abuse that never occurred spun out ever more elaborate and bizarre fantasies about the various people with whom she had been sexually involved. After a year of such "treatment" she "disclosed" a sex orgy in which were present her uncle, grandfather, grandmother, and two cousins ages six and eight. The prosecutor descended upon the uncle and his children and, when the children denied any such involvement, they were taken out of the home in order to be "protected" from a sexually abusing father. The children repeatedly refused to admit to any such encounters. Coercive interviews were utilized, both directly and via the use of anatomical dolls and leading questions. Still, the children adamantly refused to "disclose" that they had been abused, either by the father or the grandfather. Finally, after almost three months, they were told that they would be allowed to go home if they would "disclose" abuse of either the father or the grandfather. Accordingly, the older child "disclosed" that her grandfather had sexually abused her. The two children were then allowed to return home. Once home, the child soon "recanted" the allegation against her grandfather and stated quite clearly that the only reason she accused him was to return home.

Typically, prosecutors and their investigators have a deep commitment to the value of anatomical dolls. I am convinced that many of them know quite well that these dolls, when used along with coercion, suggestion, and leading questions, will result in "disclosures" from the vast majority of children who are subjected to them. One has to be very simpleminded not to recognize this, although there are certainly many simpleminded people who believe that the dolls actually assist in such evaluations. Many of the psychopathic-type prosecutors I am focusing on here recognize, I believe, exactly what they are doing and are happy to use this "scientific" instrument in the service of furthering their careers, their salary increments, and their notoriety. I believe that they recognize well the simplemindedness and naïveté of the social workers, psychologists, psychiatrists, and other "validators" who actually believe that these dolls can be useful and do not in any way facilitate the elicitation of false sex-abuse accusations. Psychopathic prosecutors are attracted to the adversary system like iron to a magnet. It is extremely well structured to enable them to perpetrate their psychopathic abominations under the guise of "serving the people" and "justice."

Examiners who involve themselves in forensic work, especially criminal trials, must be well aware that a certain percentage (I cannot tell how high it is) of prosecutors they will encounter are in this category. I do not know the percentage, but I firmly believe that if one administered psychological tests that identify psychopathy—especially the MMPI-II, the MCMI-2, and the Rorschach—to a group of prosecutors and administered the same tests to a control group of individuals who were not prosecutors, there would be more psychopaths among the prosecutors than in the randomly selected control group. Furthermore, I suspect that many of the prosecutors who were found to be psychopathic on these tests would be amazed to learn that they suffer with this disorder. They do not appreciate how they have been corrupted by the system to which they have dedicated themselves. But the need to blind themselves to their psychopathic behavior has been so great that they have been operating under the delusion that they have really been performing a public service. Others would probably provide a wide variety of rationalizations to justify the responses that resulted in the diagnosis of psychopathy.

Other Psychodynamic Factors
Operative in Prosecutors

I consider it worth repeating that I do not consider *all* prosecutors psychopaths; rather, I consider the field to draw psychopaths because it can provide them with social approbation and even notoriety for their psychopathy. There are other kinds of individuals who may gravitate toward the profession, again because it provides them with a socially acceptable expression of pathological needs. Angry individuals are likely to gravitate toward the field. Serving as a prosecutor can enable a very angry individual to express hostility and, at the same time, earn a living at it. The more crime one sees, the more defendants one sees to be guilty, the greater the likelihood one will have the opportunity to "punish" these defendants. If one were to recognize that *some* of those accused of sex abuse are indeed innocent, then one is deprived of the opportunity to vent such rage. Of course, just about all prosecutors are going to state publicly that there are indeed some innocent people who are being victimized by a false sex-abuse accusation. There are some prosecutors who genuinely believe this and will find "no evidence" for prosecution in many of the cases that come their way. There are others, however, and these are the ones I am focusing on here, who are likely to blind themselves to obvious manifestations of a false accusation, so great is their rage and their need to vent it on defendants. What they intellectually profess and what they actually do are two entirely different things.

Examples are readily available if one examines people who are career soldiers. From 1960 to 1962, while serving as a psychiatrist in the United States Army, I had the opportunity to meet many such individuals. As the reader may recall, the United States was not involved in any major war during this time frame. The Korean War was over and the Vietnam War had not yet begun. Very few people were drafted. Accordingly, those who chose to be in the military service were mainly volunteers, some of whom had remained in the service after World War II and the Korean War. It was during this period that I saw professionally many men who were clearly extremely hostile individuals who had gravitated to military service because it had provided them with an opportunity for a socially acceptable expression of their rage. Infantry training, especially, provided such an outlet. One is continually learning how to more efficiently and effectively kill people with weapons ranging from pistols to hydrogen bombs. The people who do this best are given medals and may often be referred to as "heroes." It is easy to see how such enraged individuals might gravitate toward the military service and even do well there. There are some, I was convinced, who were basically in the category of the criminally insane, so obsessed were they with killing the enemy; if they were discharged from the service, they might either decompensate or murder civilians. Some, after discharge, would gravitate toward police work, somewhat less prestigious, but still a social institution that allows for the release of murderous rage in a socially acceptable fashion.

Another psychodynamic factor operative in some prosecutors is the need for power. Being a prosecutor places one in a very powerful position. Indeed, one holds the fate of many individuals in one's hands. Many prosecutors are ruthless in their quest for power; defendants, in many cases, merely serve as pawns in this pursuit. One can decide which cases have enough evidence for prosecution and which cases do not. This places defendants at their mercy and cannot but enhance the feelings of power these individuals crave. As Lord Acton so wisely said, "Power corrupts, and absolute power corrupts absolutely." Many of the prosecutors in this category can justifiably be referred to as "little Hitlers."

The media knows well the attractive power of sex. Prosecutors are not immune to this phenomenon. For many, prurient interests are clearly operative in their obsession with sexual cases. These sexual gratifications fuel their commitment to the case and provide them with morbid forms of vicarious sexual satisfaction. And, when the violence element is operative, as in the case with rape, another morbid element is added to their commitment to the case. In some prosecutors, I am certain these elements are conscious; in others, these elements are at various levels of unconsciousness and subconsciousness.

Dealing with the Cross-Examining Prosecutor

Evaluators who are going into court to testify and who find themselves being cross-examined by prosecutors do well to appreciate that they may very well encounter the types of individual I have just described. What can a mental health professional do in such a situation? After recognizing that this is the type of individual with whom one might be confronted, one should operate under the principle: "Trust absolutely nothing this person may say." Recognize that within every statement there may be a hidden deceit. Duplicity is the name of the game for this type of individual. There is no trick, no matter how low or illegal, that he (she) may not stoop to in order to achieve the desired goal. Such individuals consciously and deliberately lie in the hope that they will get away with it. Slander, perjury, and libel mean nothing to them. They know well that in a court of law they enjoy absolute immunity and that there is no way that one can take legal action against them for anything they may say in the context of that setting. Accordingly, the name of their game is to fool the judge and jury into believing things that they know are not true. Lies of omission are standard in all courtrooms; in fact, such deceit is one of the provisos of the adversary system. Each side is instructed to withhold that information that may weaken its position and this in itself fosters lies of omission. Whereas it is considered unethical for attorneys to utilize lies of commission, i.e., conscious and deliberate deceits, they certainly do so. And it is far more likely that prosecutors will do so, especially the psychopathic types.

I present here some of the techniques prosecutors are likely to utilize. One common maneuver is to take a statement that the examiner has made and, when repeating it, insert one or two additional words that entirely corrupt the meaning. One way of doing this is to insert such words as *all*, *always*, and *never*. Another way of doing this is, while standing at a distance, to open up one of the examiner's own publications and have the examiner verify that it is indeed his (hers). Then the prosecutor might ask, "Is it not a fact, Doctor, that in this very book of yours you have said . . . ?" The prosecutor makes a statement, allegedly from the book, but does not read it verbatim. Obviously, the "selection" is designed to embarrass the expert witness because it implies that that the statement is just the opposite of what the witness is testifying to, or will in some other way support the prosecutor's position, or make the expert look foolish. Before answering that question, the examiner should insist upon the prosecutor's indicating the exact quote, page and line. Furthermore, it would be an error for the examiner to allow the prosecutor to read the passage because of the aforementioned maneuver of adding or deleting words. Rather, the examiner should insist upon being allowed to read the passage himself (herself). At that point the prosecutor may drop the whole issue immediately. He (she) recognizes that the publication does not provide any verification whatsoever for what was claimed.

Or the prosecutor may bring the book over and request that the examiner read verbatim the highlighted segment. While doing this the examiner may recognize that this is an out-of-context quote, the purpose of which is to misrepresent. Usually, I sense this immediately upon presentation of the book, where I see that only an isolated segment of the paragraph is highlighted. Before reading it I will say, "This is an out-of-context quote." It is best to "squeeze this in" *before* reading the passage rather than afterward. After one has read the passage, it may be much more difficult to make that statement. My experience has been that in civil cases the judge may very well require that the total statement be read. Unfortunately, my experience in criminal cases has been that the prosecutor may be successful in distorting the examiner's intent by confining him (her) to the out-of-context quote. Even then, however, the statement squeezed in by the examiner before reading the passage—that this is an out-of-context quote—has planted a seed in the mind of the judge and/or jury.

In one case in which I was involved, the prosecutor withheld all information from the defense lawyer, and it took a court order to get him to turn over the materials he had been legally required to transmit many months previously. He did this with impunity because he knew full well that there would be no consequences for his recalcitrance. Furthermore, he knew that the less time the defense attorney had to review this material, the weaker his position would be on the day of trial, which was impending. It also gave the defense experts (one of whom was me) less time to review the materials. In the batch were approximately 12 session reports of a child in "treatment" for having allegedly been sexually abused by one of her relatives.

At the time of trial the prosecutor asked me how many therapeutic reports I had on that particular child. I answered, "Somewhere between 10 and 15." He then said to me, "Wouldn't it surprise you, Doctor, to learn that there were many more such reports; in fact, I have a pile of them here." He showed me a pile that was quite thick and clearly contained many more than 12 or 15 reports. However, he held them upside down, at about five to six feet distance from me, and was presenting the batch to the court with the implication that *all* of those reports were indeed on that particular child. He did not give me the opportunity to say anything other than to agree with him that the number of reports in his hand was indeed more than 12. He then had me verify, as I watched him count them out, that there were a total of 40 reports. Nor was I able to say anything about the fact that they were *upside down*, and, as far as I could tell, some of them might have even been blank sheets of paper or reports of other patients. He led the court to believe that the defense attorney had selected from 40 reports approximately 12 that were given to me.

While I was on the witness stand (before the break), I did not really know what was going on. I believed that the defense attorney was sending me everything that he had, but it was certainly possible that he had not. The prosecutor was successful in getting me to doubt the honesty of the defense attorney and believe that he might possibly have sent me only selected reports. This has certainly happened to me in the past. While he was counting each item in the pile, I also made the assumption that all the papers in that pile were indeed reports on that child only. However, the thought did cross my mind that perhaps not all of these documents were reports on this specific child. I knew that there must be some reason for his having turned them upside down. Had I to do this all over again, I would have slipped in additional comments to my yes/no answers with such responses as, "Yes, *you* have said that all of those reports are of that child," or "Yes, it *may be* that all those reports are on that child, but the papers are upside down, so all I am counting are blank papers," and "I have absolutely no knowledge of what is in that pile; I will only agree with you that you have counted out 40 documents."

Fortunately, in the break I learned from the defense attorney that he had sent to me *all* of the reports that the prosecutor had given to him, and it was the prosecutor who had withheld the additional ones. Furthermore, he told me that the batch of materials the prosecutor was counting included reports of *other* children, not simply those of the child in question. Accordingly, when I returned to the witness stand, in the course of redirect examination, I was able to advise the court that the defense attorney had given me all that he had received from the prosecutor and that it was highly likely that the pile contained many reports other than those of the child in question.

One of the best things an expert can accomplish when subjected to such a psychopath is to try to reveal his duplicity to the court. If one accomplishes this goal, then the legal dictum, "Falsus in uno, falsus in omnibus" (Latin: False in one [area], false in [all]), although usually applied to a witness, can now be applied to the prosecutor. His (her) reputation, then, as a dishonorable person will have been established to the court. The prosecutor will thereby have weakened his (her) case.

When sitting on the witness stand, while being cross-examined by psychopathic types (not uncommon in the law), a segment of Rudyard Kipling's poem "If" sometimes comes to mind:

> If you can bear to hear the truth you've spoken,
> Twisted by knaves to make a trap for fools . . .

This is only one of a whole series of the poem's provisos to be satisfied if one is to truly consider oneself a Man (in the Victorian, if not the modern, sense of the word). It takes a certain amount of ego strength to expose oneself to such corrupt individuals. Any ego debasement one may feel over being subjected to such psychopathic types can be somewhat compensated for by the knowledge that one is being honest in helping a defendant who has been the victim of such an individual. In those cases in which the sex-abuse accusation is false, it is not the children who have been the victims, but the defendants.

I wish to emphasize again that my description of prosecutors is derived almost exclusively from the experiences I have had in sex-abuse litigation. As mentioned, it may be that prosecutors working in other areas do not function in this way and it may even be the case that there are prosecutors working in sex-abuse cases who do not justify the formidable criticisms I describe here. However, whatever the prevalence of prosecutors who do not fit my description, there is no question that there are many who do. Accordingly, mental health professionals who testify in court must be aware of this group, regardless of their prevalence, if they are to handle themselves effectively in criminal sex-abuse cases.

AND NOW, THE PAYMENT
FOR MY TESTIFYING!

Women's liberation and gender egalitarianism notwithstanding, men still have much more money than women. I am not claiming that this is justifiable, but it is the reality. Accordingly, in the vast majority of custody and sex-abuse cases in which I have been involved, the fathers have either paid the total amount or the major portion of my fees. Although legislative statutes in recent years have generally required courts to be "sex blind" in custody determinations, the realities are that mothers, much more frequently than fathers, will win a custody case. This does not relate simply to "old-fashioned" judges who subscribe to the traditional view that mothers are intrinsically the superior parent. Even the more egalitarian justices will often rule that the children would be better off remaining with the mother, after using such criteria as relative strength of bonding, availability, and the children's preferences.

In short, the father is usually the one who pays the money, and the mother is usually the one who is granted custody. Before this final decision is made, the father is likely to have to pay for a report that does not support his position and even pay a mental health professional to testify against him in court. Obviously, an examiner who believes that a father will fulfill financial obligations under these circumstances is naive. It is downright simpleminded to entertain such expectations. Anyone who is masochistic enough to enter the field and "trust" a person to pay for services involving testifying against him (her) in court will predictably gain gratification of these masochistic tendencies.

Because I am not a masochist (although it may be that I am one, after all, when one considers the fact that I have voluntarily involved myself in litigation), I have required an advance security deposit before agreeing to become involved in lawsuits. Over the years this deposit has risen from $1,000 to $3,500, depending on the type of lawsuit. This relates not only to inflation but also to progressively increasing reluctance by payers to fulfill their obligations to me. But this deposit is not the only mechanism I utilize for security. My provisions document (Appendix II) requires the payer(s) to pay at the time services are rendered. Frequently I have had to "remind" people that they are on the verge of defaulting, and sometimes such reminders involve the threat that I will remove myself from the case and report my reasons for withdrawal to the presiding judge (with copies of my letter to the attorneys and clients).

My policy of insisting on an up-front security deposit is especially reassuring to the party not paying for the evaluation. Usually this is the mother, and her fears that I might be biased against her—because her husband is paying my bills—are often relieved by this provision. But this security deposit is not only for the mother; it is for me as well. The likelihood that one (and even both) of the parents will end up being extremely angry at me is quite high. After all, their most cherished possessions, the children, are at stake. In the most common situation, the father is the one paying the bills and the mother is the one whom I am more likely to recommend as the primary custodial parent. This was in line with my belief that custody should be awarded to that parent (regardless of sex) with whom the child has established the stronger, healthier psychological bond. And that parent (regardless of sex) who was the primary caretaker during the earliest years of the child's life is more likely to be the one with whom the child has developed the stronger, healthier psychological bond (Gardner, 1989, 1992a).

In our society—women's expanded involvement in the workplace notwithstanding—mothers, much more often than fathers, have assumed the primary care of their children during the formative years. The application of this important principle often tips the balance in the mothers' favor, although certainly many other factors are operative—especially when there is a long gap between the infancy period and the time of the custody dispute. Even in child-custody cases in which there was a false sex-abuse accusation, I generally still recommend the mother as the primary custodial parent, with the understanding that she give up the campaign to prove that the father is a child molester. If she will not, or cannot, then I recommend transfer of custody. Again, all these considerations are in no way affected by financial considerations because of the security deposit. I do not care how noble, how pure, and how free from influence the examiner considers himself (herself) to be: recognizing that if one supports party A money will be forthcoming, and if one supports party B money is not likely to be forthcoming, is going to compromise the honesty of the vast majority of, if not all, evaluators.

Throughout the data-collection process I studiously avoid giving either party any information regarding "which way the wind is blowing." This is extremely important, especially if the wind shifts, as it often does in many evaluations. It is generally not until the conference with clients and attorneys described in Chapter Four that the clients find out what my findings are. The rage engendered by my decision sometimes results in sudden professions of inability and/or refusal to pay my bills. Up to that point most parents somehow find the money to pay punctually. If it is the nonsupported party who is being asked to pay for my report, that individual can be "reminded" that the provisions document allows me to hold up submission of my report to the court and attorneys pending payment. This "reminder" is usually enough to ensure such payment, because the payer does not want to be viewed as obstructionistic by the judge.

The provisions document also indicates that I will ask for payment in advance of courtroom testimony. Generally, about three weeks before testifying I submit an estimated bill, which includes travel time, any travel expenses, and my fee for court services. The provisions document allows me to ask that this payment be in the form of a bank or certified check. Sometimes, when the testimony is going to be in favor of the nonpayer, the payer has to be reminded of the final paragraph of my provisions document, which states clearly that the payer recognizes that he (she) may be asked to pay for testimony not supporting his (her) position. This requirement is a direct outgrowth of the predictable experience that *most people will resist strongly the demand that they pay money to someone who is going to court to testify against them.* The examiner who does not appreciate this phenomenon should not be involved in conducting custody evaluations.

I recognize that mine is a very "hardnosed" approach. Insisting on advance payment engenders hostility and criticisms of being distrustful and even "paranoid about money." The alternative is to trust people in a situation in which there is a high risk of defaults. Running after the clients to obtain money is ego debasing. Whether one wants to view it as threatening or begging for money (or any combination of the two), the experience cannot but lower the examiner's feelings of self-worth. Not asking for the money leads to exploitation, which in itself lowers self-worth. The choice then is between which path to lowered self-worth the examiner wishes to follow. Both involve a compromise in one's dignity. If I have to lower my self-esteem, I prefer to earn money while being humiliated rather than lose money while being humiliated.

SIX
THE JUDGE AND THE JURY

JUDGES

WHO ARE JUDGES AND HOW
DID THEY GET ON THE BENCH?

There was a time when many people became judges because it was viewed by the legal profession as a "high calling." The scholarly types gravitated toward the field, especially those who had a high sense of ethics and values and were willing to suffer financial privation in the service of performing this important work. There were others, however, for whom less noble reasons were operative. Many were attracted to the enormous power that judges wield. For many this could serve as excellent compensation for feelings of inadequacy. The whole courtroom performance provides such gratifications. The judge, in robes, enters the courtroom and everyone stands silently, presumably in deference. From the bench everyone in the courtroom "snaps to"; anyone who dares to openly defy the judge may be dragged off by the bailiff and even put in jail. But these two extremes do not exist in isolation and for many judges there is probably a combination of both factors operative in their choice of profession.

Of course, there are other factors operative (as is true of any kind of work). The judge enjoys formidable esteem outside the courtroom. Although people are not required to "kowtow," they often do so even though the judge has no jurisdiction over anyone outside the courtroom. A judgeship can be a political plum provided for service to the party. If elected, it can be a statement about the judge's popularity with members of the community. And, at the highest levels, it can be a source of enormous prestige. It can also be a civil service job for people who could not be successful in the private practice of law, a judgeship providing a secure niche, predictable salary increments, and ultimately a pension.

Over the course of the 35 years that I have been involved in providing testimony, I believe I have witnessed a shift toward more opportunists and incompetents entering the field, and fewer idealists. I suspect that, at this point, there are still many idealists, especially at the highest levels, but I am convinced that the opportunists, incompetents, and those with less lofty motives are very much on the scene. It would be an error for the reader to conclude that I view judges to be a lower breed than people in other disciplines and professions. Every field has its range from the most dedicated and skilled to the most incompetent and ignorant.

There is nothing in the U.S. Constitution that requires a judge to be a lawyer. Although most do have legal training, it is not a requirement of the office. Obviously, most would consider it desirable that the person at least be a lawyer. Judges are either elected or appointed. Those who are elected must ever concern themselves with their reputations, or else they might not be reelected. And those who are appointed must consider those who have appointed them. The appointments are often made along the lines of political parties, and often influential individuals in the party play an important role in a judge's appointment. And political parties are also very much concerned with their reputations. Accordingly, judges are very much in the public eye and recognize that unfavorable press may jeopardize their positions, whether it be for re-election or reappointment.

With regard to the burgeoning caseload of sex-abuse accusations, a judge who has a reputation for protecting us from perverts, who puts them behind bars if there is even the slightest suspicion that they have sexually abused our children, will generally be viewed with approval and gratitude. In contrast, the one who has allowed even one "pervert" to roam the streets may find himself (herself) unemployed. In our atmosphere of sex-abuse hysteria (Gardner, 1991c), most judges will take no chances. I have encountered judges who have openly made statements along these lines: "If there is one scintilla of evidence, no matter how remote, that this person sexually abused a child, I will do everything in my power to remove him (her) from society." In the service of this goal, constitutional protections of due process are ignored. The principle of our founding fathers that a man is innocent until proven guilty is basically shelved. In these cases, a man is guilty until proven innocent. The principle that it is preferable that a hundred guilty men be set free than one innocent man be incarcerated is reversed in these cases. The principle that *is* utilized is that it is preferable that a hundred innocent men be found guilty than one guilty person be allowed to go free. Such judges get positive feedback from hysterical parents and thereby enhance the likelihood of reappointment. There are judges, however, who are not taken in by hysterical parents, coercive "validators," opportunistic prosecutors, and others who parade before them in these cases. (Such cases in which no sexual abuse was found do not attract much attention in the public media.) But there are so many judges who believe these people that we have a national scandal.

At the time I write this (1995), I believe that judges are becoming increasingly aware of the perversity of what is going on in the sex-abuse scene and are less prone to believe some of the preposterous scenarios that are being presented to them in court. My hope is that this trend will continue, so that we will ultimately look back upon this period as one of the "crazy times" in our society, similar to that which occurred at the time of the Salem witch trials.

THE RELATIONSHIP BETWEEN THE TESTIFYING EXPERT AND THE JUDGE

I believe that the most important determinant as to whether a judge is going to take the expert's testimony seriously is the basic personal feelings the judge has about the expert who is testifying. No matter how brilliant, no matter how insightful and compelling one's testimony, if the judge dislikes the expert, little, if anything, the examiner says will have any effect on the judge's decision. In contrast, if the judge is impressed with the expert—whether justifiably or not—the most inane drivel will be viewed as pearls of wisdom and have a formidable influence on the judge's decision. Judges are no different, then, in this regard than the rest of us human beings. Accordingly, the evaluator does well to try to establish a good relationship with the judge. First and foremost, the testimony should be professional and hopefully impressive. In addition, the examiner should be aware that other things are going on that are going to affect the judge's receptivity, things that go beyond the "wisdom" of one's testimony.

What can one do then to enhance this relationship? In some situations, the experts testifying are so situated that they have an opportunity to look at the judge, even with side glances. Under such circumstances the examiner does well to use every opportunity to look at the judge in a manner similar to the way one speaks to another person in the course of a more relaxed conversation. Unfortunately, my experience has been that most courtrooms are so set up that such an opportunity is not present. Furthermore, when there is a jury trial, one is usually sitting between the judge and the jury, and when one is trying to speak to the judge, one is directing one's attention away from the jury. In jury trials, when one has a choice of whom to look at, it is better to choose the jury because it is the jury who has more power. (I will elaborate on this point below.)

Another way of enhancing one's relationship with the judge is to write a detailed report. As mentioned, some lawyers prefer a short report, some as short a report as possible. They do not want to "tip their hands" in advance and prefer to give the other side as little information as possible. As mentioned in Chapter Three, I believe the disadvantages of this practice far outweigh its advantages. And one of the advantages of the more comprehensive report is that it enables the examiner to provide the judge with all the details supporting one's most compelling arguments. Whether the examiner is serving as a court-appointed independent or as an expert representing one side, the report is generally introduced into evidence at the time of one's testimony. Testimony rarely allows for a full presentation of all the details. This is especially the case when an aggressive opposing attorney is frequently interrupting and objecting. And this is even more the case when the objections are sustained by the judge. Having a full report enables the judge to read one's complete opinion, even if only part of it has gotten through the filtration of adversarial proceedings. Accordingly, if one did not convince the judge on the witness stand, there is still the possibility that the judge may be convinced later while reading the examiner's report.

In the course of my testimony, I can generally get a sense of whether the judge is sympathetic to what I am saying. The best clue to this is his (her) reactions to the objections by the opposing attorney. When a high percentage of these objections are sustained, it indicates that the judge is not particularly interested in hearing what the expert has to say. In contrast, when a high percentage of these objections are overruled, it indicates that the judge is receptive to the expert and wants to hear more of what he (she) has to say. However, it is important for the examiner to appreciate that a high rate of sustained objections does not necessarily mean that the testimony is at fault, is deficient, or is in itself the turnoff. It may be that this is a reflection of the judge's general bias in the particular case and that every witness on the side supported by the expert is treated similarly.

Another indicator of the judge's receptivity is his (her) interest in directly questioning the expert. Courts vary with regard to the flexibility of such inquiries. My own experience has been that they are generally allowed. However, judges appreciate that too many such inquiries could subject them to criticism, especially the criticism of trying to take over the trial. They are supposed to be neutral referees rather than interrogators. Interrogation is the attorney's role. These considerations notwithstanding, my experience has been that in the majority of the cases in which I have been involved, the judge does conduct some direct inquiry with me. Under these circumstances, it is generally closer to a direct examination than a cross-examination in that few yes/no questions are posed. The attorneys cannot object to the judge's questions and generally sit silently during the course of his (her) inquiry. Most often, this inquiry occurs near the end of my testimony. Often it is the last inquiry before I leave the witness stand. I generally consider it a good sign because it indicates that the judge has respect for what I have to say, especially because such an inquiry indicates that the judge is willing to take the risk of being considered to be conducting himself (herself) improperly.

As mentioned, judges sit in an enormous position of power. There are some who are primarily attracted to this position because it provides them with so much power. As Lord Acton said: "Power corrupts and

198 THE JUDGE AND THE JURY

absolute power corrupts absolutely." I have encountered judges who epitomize this important observation. And one way they exhibit this power is to deprecate those who have the misfortune of testifying in their courtrooms. Examiners must not only have a thick skin with regard to subjecting themselves to the indignities of cross-examination but, on occasion, must subject themselves to the indignities of being treated shabbily by an arrogant judge. It is *crucial* that examiners not "lose their cool" under such circumstances. To do so could have profound consequences in the trial, especially if one is a central witness. And a court-appointed independent examiner is indeed a central witness. One way of protecting oneself from untoward emotional reactions to such denigration is to recognize that there is absolutely no good reason for subjecting a competent and dedicated professional to such "treatment." The problem, then, is not the examiner's but the judge's. It is a reflection of some psychological problems within him (her), often in the category of compensation for feelings of inadequacy and the use of others as scapegoats for his (her) own pent-up hostility—hostility stemming from other sources. Although one may, on rare occasions, respond to a put-down wisecrack by a cross-examining attorney with a retort in the same vein, it would be very risky and very injudicious to respond similarly to a judge.

I recall one situation in which the judge was particularly condescending to me. It was clear that he was extremely biased against the defense, whose position I was supporting. His bias was obvious because he was supporting just about every objection raised by the prosecutor (this was a criminal case) and overruling just about every objection raised by the defense. It was a sex-abuse case and it was clear that he hoped to enjoy significant notoriety by putting the alleged perpetrator in jail. It was also apparent to me from the outset that he was extremely unreceptive to my providing testimony and was overtly condescending to me throughout the course of my testimony. He took every opportunity to be provocative to me, and it took a significant degree of self-control for me to ignore his provocations and to go on testifying. I knew that the best (and really only) response was to say absolutely nothing in response to his provocations. In the course of all this, the reasoning that I found most useful was this:

These people have spent an enormous amount of money in this case. They view me as a central witness and I must not let them down. To "lose my cool," to rise to the challenge of responding to this man, might blow this case out the window. I must not let them down. I must not rise to his bait. In a sense they are also paying me to allow myself to be subjected to these indignities.

Ultimately, the jury found the defendant not guilty and I believe that my testimony played a role in this happy outcome.

At this point, I will elaborate on what I have said previously regarding my use of the term *play it cool*. The implication of this is that there is an artificial play-acting quality to one's calmness. Although this is sometimes the case, more often I *am* "cool" because I handle myself in such a way that I do not have significant feelings that may get out of control. Hard work, thorough command of the material, and the belief that my position is the valid, right, and ethical one is the best defense against "losing one's cool." One factor that is operative in losing one's cool is defensiveness and the underlying recognition that one is not strong in one's position.

I once had an experience in the courtroom that demonstrates this principle well. It also demonstrates other aspects of courtroom experience (especially judges' behavior) that may be useful for the reader. It was not long after I began testifying in the case that it became apparent to me that the judge exhibited two personality qualities, each of which is a serious deficiency. However, when they simultaneously exhibit themselves in the same individual, they represent a formidable personality defect, and individuals who possess this combination cause much grief in the world. I am referring to the qualities of arrogance and ignorance. This man exuded arrogance. He was condescending toward everyone in the courtroom: the attorneys, the clients, the court reporters, the security guard, and this examiner (last but certainly not least). Furthermore, I quickly appreciated that this man was ignorant. Whether he basically had a low IQ or whether he was essentially functioning at that level, I cannot know with certainty. Because he graduated from law school, I suspect that the latter explanation was more probable, but there are certainly attorneys who fit into the former category with regard to their intellectual endowment.

As I sat there listening to some of the drivel that oozed from his mouth, I could not but think of the old poem:

> He who knows not and knows not he knows not, he is a fool, shun him.
> He who knows not and knows he knows not, he is simple, teach him.
> He who knows and knows not he knows, he is asleep, wake him.
> He who knows and knows he knows, he is wise, follow him.

There was no question that this judge was in category *one*. In this case I had submitted not one but *three* reports. The first had been submitted one year previously, at the time of the completion of my original custody/visitation evaluation. However, there was a change in circumstances on the mother's side (which warranted an update), and then there was a change in circumstances on the father's side (which warranted a further update). Gradually it became apparent to me that the judge had not read any of these reports. At the time of my testimony the case had literally been going on for five years. Early in my testimony it became clear that he had little knowledge of the details of the case. His ignorance resulted in his frequently interrupting the lawyers' interrogations of me to ask questions. It was clear that had he read the reports, he would not have asked these questions. For example, at one point in my testimony I made reference to the mother's allegation of physical violence. At that point he interrupted the inquiry and, while snarling at me, said: "I don't know what you're talking about. What's all this about physical violence?" In response, I calmly stated, "In July 1986 Mrs. X claimed that her husband had physically abused her. In my report dated December 12, 1986, I discussed the results of my inquiry into this matter and stated therein my reasons for coming to the conclusion that there was no evidence that this allegation was valid. My main reasons for coming to this conclusion were . . ." At this point the judge grumbled incoherently and instructed the attorney to continue with his examination. My response was stated in a calm and methodical manner.

At another point, after I had elaborated on a question posed during direct examination, he interrupted, looked at me in an angry and condescending way, and said, "I don't have the faintest idea what you're talking about." I believe that my explanation was clear and straightforward and that everyone in the courtroom, including the security guard (who was listening intently), understood exactly what I had said. Accordingly, in a matter-of-fact way, I simply repeated—this time more clearly and slowly—exactly what I had previously said. I then said to him, "Your Honor, I would be pleased to elaborate on anything that I have just said that may not be clear to you." He said nothing and angrily instructed the attorney to continue with his interrogation.

His favorite expressions to me were, "You're being illogical," "What you're saying is not logical," and "You're being *extremely* illogical." Again, I was convinced that what I said was consistent, logical, and readily understood by everyone else in the courtroom. When I would ask him if he could please be more specific regarding what *was* illogical, so I could elaborate, he never took me up on the invitation. I was convinced, however, that he just did not understand what I was saying and protected himself from awareness of his ignorance by attributing the problem to me. Again, although I found his interruptions and condescending attitudes mildly irritating, I remained completely calm, methodical, and direct.

At one point, he interrupted the proceedings with a little speech to everyone in which he proudly and sanctimoniously stated that he was, above everything else, concerned with the best interests of the children. He said this in an extremely self-righteous manner, with the implication that everyone else in the courtroom was totally unconcerned with the children's welfare. He seemed not to appreciate that everyone waves that banner and that his little self-aggrandizing speech was a total waste of time. In the course of his self-serving diatribe about his concern for the children's welfare, he stated that I had lost sight of this fundamental point. Obviously, as a witness on the stand, I did not have the opportunity to ask him exactly how I was not serving their interests.

I was on the stand from 9:30 A.M. to 12:30 P.M., with only one short break. Throughout that time he exhibited nothing but the condescending attitude that did not succeed in hiding his abysmal ignorance. And, throughout that time, I handled myself with calm, never once letting on to the inner feelings that I had about this man. Not once did he "get to me." Not once did I exhibit any irritation. My main feelings were those of pity for these poor people who had been sitting in his court for five years and whose future lives depended upon his decisions. When I returned at 1:30 P.M. there was more of the same. However, at about 2:30 P.M. something happened that was quite dramatic. Suddenly, all arrogance stopped. He adopted a most respectful attitude toward me and began quoting my earlier comments as if they were gospel. It was as if someone had suddenly put a screwdriver in his head and turned a loose screw approximately 180 degrees. From then on, through him, my recommendations were implemented. I believe that this judge ultimately allowed himself to appreciate the judiciousness of what I was saying. However, I do not think that such receptivity would have occurred had I not handled myself with calm and dignity in spite of the numerous provocations, insults, and condescending remarks directed toward me. The experience is an excellent example of the "speak-softly-and-carry-a-big-stick" principle.

JUDGES WHO SHOULD NOT BE JUDGING

Judges, like members of any profession, range from those who are lazy and incompetent to those who are hardworking and extremely competent, and all points in between. Accordingly, over the 35 years during which I have been providing testimony, I have seen judges at all points along this continuum. Here I focus on those at the lower end of the scale. A common practice is for judges to be reading material while I am providing testimony. In some cases the documents being reviewed are related to the case under consideration. On some occasions, I was convinced that what the judge was reading had nothing to do with the case on which I was testifying. In both of these cases the judge was acting in a way that was not in the best interests of the proceedings. I do not believe that a human being can read a document and listen to another party at the same time. There are some people who claim that they can do this. I myself cannot and I have never personally seen someone who *really* can, professions of the ability notwithstanding.   In social situations I will generally say to a person who does this to me, "I'll wait until you finish reading and then I will continue talking."

If the person says, "I can do both," I generally respond that I cannot and I do not believe that he (she) can. Accordingly, I will wait and try to be polite until the person directs his (her) attention to me. Obviously, this cannot be done from the witness stand. Even if the judge is reading my own submitted report, I am dubious that he (she) can attend to both my testimony and what is being read. Yet, this is a common practice. I consider it a judicial compromise.

I have even seen judges reading a newspaper while the trial is going on. They are not doing this in such a manner that everyone in the courtroom can see the newspaper. Rather, the paper lies flat and can only be seen by someone on the witness stand if he (she) wishes to take notice.

I can recall three or four occasions when judges were actually sleeping while I was providing testimony. Yet, no one said a thing. The lawyers continued to conduct the trial as if he were awake, and no one had the guts to lightly tap him on the arm in order to regain his attention. And I certainly was not going to do this either. And so we all went on acting as if he were awake. On the first two occasions (in my earlier years), I acted no differently. During the last two occasions, I spoke very loudly and was successful in waking him up. This is the procedure I recommend. Of course, one must always consider the possibility that it was my testimony that was putting them to sleep! I believe that increasing utilization of television cameras in the courtroom will help solve this problem.

I have seen judges for whom everything must be a compromise. In this way, they cannot be strongly criticized by either side nor are they as likely to be considered biased by a court of appeals. However, their compromises cause disaster for both sides. I often compare this to two individuals, each standing on a cliff overlooking a chasm. The compromise involves both of them meeting each other halfway. Probably one of the most common such compromises seen in recent years is in sex-abuse cases. The mother claims that her ex-husband sexually abused the child. The father denies that it ever happened. After a lengthy trial, by which time the father may be financially wiped out, the judge does not see any evidence for sex abuse, but to "play it safe" orders ongoing supervision until the three-year-old child is in the teen period—when he or she can presumably then defend himself (herself) against the father's depravity. There is no evidence to support the allegation, yet the child's relationship with the father is so seriously compromised that it can never be healthy.

At the time of this writing I have testified in approximately 25 states all over the United States. I have testified in large cities, medium-sized cities, and small towns. My experience has been that the smaller the city, the greater the likelihood of contaminated trials. The fewer the number of lawyers, the greater the likelihood they know one another intimately, and the less the likelihood that they are going to be true adversaries. There is nothing unethical about two golf partners representing opposing clients. Yet, this intimacy is a serious compromise because they cannot zealously support their clients' positions if there is the risk that it might compromise the lawyers' social relationship. Similarly, there are judges who have relationships with important participants in the trial, relationships that clearly compromise the judges' objectivity. For example, I have seen judges who routinely appoint experts with whom they have a social relationship. These experts have been guardians-ad-litem or court-appointed independent examiners. Such individuals might be in the judge's own church or might even be a relative. It is rare for the judge to rule against the findings of that expert, no matter how biased and no matter how incompetent. One judge typically appointed his son-in-law as the guardian-ad-litem. One of the main reasons for his selection was that everybody else recognized this man's incompetence and no one else would voluntarily pay him any money.

I have found judges who have been unsympathetic to my testimony because of small-town prejudices against northeastern Ivy League schools. The general attitude has been: "What's the matter with us? Is there no one around here in this small town in middle America that we can use for this case? Is our only recourse to get some professor from an Ivy League school?" Under these circumstances, I have found significant unreceptivity to my testimony. There is little the examiner can do regarding the existence of regional prejudices, but one should be aware of them anyway when providing testimony in areas significantly distant from one's office.

A related situation is one in which the judge has a deep-seated loyalty to the local child protection service (CPS). The agency is viewed as his (her) "right hand." When someone comes in and argues that CPS may not have acted judiciously in this particular case, the judge is not going to accept that testimony lest he (she) compromise the relationship with the local people. Experts from afar come to town, testify, and go home. The judge does not have to have any contact with them afterward. The local people are there and must be catered to or protected from hurt feelings.

In the early 1970s, when I first began to do child-custody evaluations, I received a call from the chief judge of my local family court. He and other family court justices wanted to have lunch with me. I was pleased to meet with them. They told me that they were very impressed with my reports, but they did not wish me to send copies to the clients and attorneys, only to them directly. I asked them if it was not true that the clients were entitled to copies of their reports and that to withhold them not only would be unethical but illegal. They basically told me that *they* decide what is ethical and legal in *their* courts and that I should cease and desist from this practice. I responded that I myself consider it unethical and possibly illegal not to send a report to a person whom I had evaluated, and I was not going to comply with this request. They in turn told me that I could not expect to get any referrals from their courts. I told them that I thought I would somehow survive their loss of business, and we parted ways. Subsequently, when thinking about the whole situation, I realized what was going on. They indeed were impressed with my reports, so much so that they would include large segments of them in their rulings (with slightly modified terminology). Recognizing that this might show them up as being less knowledgeable than they wanted to appear, they wanted to be able to lift more chunks from my reports without my identity being known. As mentioned, that occurred many years ago. Now all agree that files must be open and that no mental health professional can refuse to provide a report to any patient under any circumstances.

As mentioned, I view our judicial system as having certain analogies to religion. Many religions subscribe to the same Bible. Each religion selects from the text those segments that support its particular beliefs and selectively ignores or reinterprets those segments that do not. Our body of law is similar. One decides what conclusion one wants to come to and then finds the legal justification, which is always there if one looks hard enough and long enough. The system basically "goes through the motions" of searching for "the truth" and providing people with "justice." This, I believe, is the external facade for the aforementioned basic process in which the conclusion comes first and the system provides the justifications. The system does, however, provide lawyers with money and judges with prestige and a predictable income. These things can be said with certainty.

Fain (1977), an attorney states:

> One must always bear in mind that the exercise of discretion by a judge is far less a product of his learning than of his personality and his temperament, his background and his interests, his biases and his prejudices, both conscious and unconscious.

JURIES

THE JURY AS A PRODUCT OF MARKET RESEARCH

In Chapter One I have commented on the evolution of the jury system. Its evolution dates back over 900 years and it is still evolving. Probably the most important recent development is the "science" of jury selection. We are now seeing a new breed of experts, experts who advise attorneys on jury selection. These are not people who are basing their selection on hunches, bias, or vague generalizations about which kind of juror might vote in which particular direction. No way. These people mean business. They do market research in every sense of the word. They do market surveys, breaking down people into categories of sex, race, gender, political orientation, profession, educational background, and a wide variety of other indices that help them predict, yes I say predict, exactly how a juror is going to vote. They recognize well that prejudices are the most important determinants as to how people are going to vote. At the time I write this, early 1995, the O. J. Simpson trial is attracting worldwide attention. Two-and-a-half months were spent on jury selection. Three-hundred-and-four people were screened at legal costs in the hundreds of thousands of dollars. Obviously, such an indulgence is not available to everyone. There are people who are saying that the decision has already been made, that each juror has strong opinions at the outset regarding how he (she) will vote, and that the jury selection basically represents the end of the trial. I believe that those who say this are probably right.

I myself have had encounters with such experts. They are brought in at great expense in high-profile trials. They actually had me testify before a mock jury, a jury composed of people similar to those whom they suspected would be selected for the actual trial. Following my "testimony," inquiries were made of the "jurors" regarding their reactions to my testimony. This information was then fed back to me in order for me to "improve" my testimony. Although the feedback was highly positive, I was given a bit of additional advice by the consultant (not the "jury"), namely, that I should buy a more expensive pen and that if any member of the jury saw that I was using a cheap plastic pen, it might compromise my testimony. Although the jury consultant might have been right, I did not submit to the belief (perhaps naive) that this was going to be the important determinant as to whether jury members would find my testimony convincing. If it is indeed true that jury selection experts are so skilled that the decision has already been made by the time the jury has been selected, then it would seem logical not to have the trial at all and just have the jury vote on the basis of their biases, which is probably what happens anyway.

THE RELATIONSHIP BETWEEN THE TESTIFYING EXPERT AND THE JURY

Just as I emphasized the importance of establishing a relationship with the judge, it is crucial that one try to establish a relationship with the jury. In fact, it is even more important because a jury has anywhere from six to twelve people, whereas a judge is only one person. Fortunately, people who provide testimony face the jury; most often they do not have the opportunity to look directly at the judge (at least for long periods). I try to make eye contact with members of the jury. I try to talk to them as if I were talking to a friend. I do not focus on any single person. I move randomly from one person to the next. If, during the course of my testimony, I have the opportunity to say something that might link me closer to one or more jury members, I will do so. For example, during my voir dire, I will make note of my military service. This fact, per se, belongs in my voir dire, if only to account for the years 1960–1962. However, it was during that period that I served as chief of child psychiatry at a U.S. Army Hospital at Frankfurt am Main Germany. Accordingly, there was further reason for including it in the voir dire. When I am testifying in a jury trial, it may have the fringe benefit of enhancing my relationship with another veteran and thereby contributing to his being more receptive to my testimony. Although this may appear to be a small point, I believe that these little things are often far more important than such issues as the power of my testimony and the need that "justice be done." Sometimes, I may have the opportunity to mention that I grew up in the southwest part of the Bronx, a now poverty-stricken section of New York City. This may link me closer to some jury member who grew up with similar privations. If I have the opportunity, I may mention that my father was an immigrant. There are bound to be some people in the jury whose parents were immigrants. If I have the opportunity to mention that I worked my way through college as a bus boy, I will do so. This obviously links me up with those who have endured similar low-prestige occupations. Obviously, some of this personal data may not be easily slipped in during the course of one's testimony.

One could argue that I am being somewhat artificial here and that I am pandering to the jury. My response is that experts who merely address themselves to "the facts" and the degree to which their arguments are compelling are only addressing themselves to part of what is going on. In fact, they may be focusing on the least important elements, the brilliance of their testimony notwithstanding. Pandering implies duplicity. I have never said anything on a witness stand that is not true and I do not select things from my personal life that are not valid. More importantly, I am doing everything possible to be of help to the patient, which is my main reason for testifying. I put such comments in the category of the traditional "bedside manner," which facilitates healing. Penicillin is more likely to kill germs when the doctor has a good bedside manner than a bad bedside manner. Medical treatment from a friend is far more effective than medical treatment from an enemy, even though it may be the same medical treatment.

SEVEN
RECOMMENDATIONS FOR THE FUTURE

INTRODUCTION

Throughout this book, I have periodically made reference to various criticisms of the adversary system. I have always worked on the principle that if one is going to criticize something, it behooves the criticizer to recommend improvements and changes. These changes in the adversary system, however, are not likely to be made without changes in the educational programs of the lawyers and mental health professionals who are directly involved in such disputes. Recommendations for changes in the training of people in both of these realms are therefore desirable. I believe that the implementation of the recommendations described herein provides us with an excellent opportunity for practicing preventive psychiatry. There are a wide variety of psychiatric disturbances caused by the embroilment of parents and children in child-custody and sex-abuse disputes. (Elsewhere [Gardner, 1986] I have described these other disorders in detail.) The implementation of the recommendations provided in this chapter would also reduce, I believe, the incidence of these disorders.

THE EDUCATION OF LAWYERS

If the recommendations made in this book are to be brought about, it is crucial that significant changes be made in the education of attorneys. If law schools continue to churn out graduates who are as committed to the adversary system as those of past years, then it is unlikely that many of my proposed reforms will be realized. At this time there is good evidence that many law schools are *beginning* to make such changes. Some schools have introduced courses in mediation and other alternative methods of dispute resolution. However, the schools still have a long way to go.

Law School Admissions Procedures

Most of the major law schools with which I am familiar do not interview students who are being screened for admission. Rather, the criteria upon which the decision is made are mainly class standing, grade-point average, the academic prestige of the institution(s) from which the student has graduated, letters of recommendation, and last (but certainly not least) the applicant's score on the Law School Aptitude Test (LSAT). Most often, this information is fed into a computer and a decision is often made without human intervention. A school will often grant an interview if an applicant requests it, but this aspect of the admissions procedure is not well publicized or encouraged. The faculty generally prefers to use the above criteria to determine suitability for admission rather than devoting significant time to interviewing the sea of applicants who apply to the best law schools. Some of these applicants have been discouraged from applying to medical school because of the glut of physicians in densely populated areas and because of the AIDS epidemic. Others have been discouraged by the paralysis that many physicians experience in association with the glut of paperwork required to practice medicine in recent years. Bureaucratic snags and failure of health insurance providers to fulfill their obligations have made medicine an onerous occupation for many physicians, some of whom have actually left medicine because of their frustration over these developments. More recently, the constraints of working in managed-care programs have further discouraged people from entering medicine. Some of these people, then, gravitate toward law, presumably because of the hope for significant financial remuneration.

I believe that the failure to interview applicants is an unfortunate practice. Medical schools also receive floods of applicants (recent discouragement factors notwithstanding) and yet routinely interview those among the highly qualified group under serious consideration for admission. Medical school admissions committees consider themselves to have an obligation to both the school and society to learn something about the morals, ethics, values, and psychological stability of potential candidates. Although law schools claim that such information will be found in the undergraduate school's letter of recommendation, there is no question that colleges try to portray graduate school applicants in the best possible terms. The more prestigious the schools their graduates enter, the more prestige the undergraduate school will enjoy. Under these circumstances, hyperbole is commonplace in the letters of recommendation because even a hint of impairment is likely to doom the candidate—*especially* at the more prestigious law schools.

Such an admissions policy contributes to the development and continuation of some of the problems described in this book. Specifically, those lawyers who perpetrate the evils described herein must have certain personality defects in order to operate in the way they do. They must have significant impairments in their sensitivity to the feelings of others and be capable of blinding themselves to the psychological damage they are inflicting on clients—both their own clients and those of their adversaries. They must be people with little sense of guilt concerning their actions. In extreme cases such individuals are justifiably labeled *psychopaths*. Psychopaths, by definition, are people who have little guilt or remorse over the pain and suffering they cause others. They have little capacity to place themselves in the position of those whom they are exploiting or traumatizing. The primary deterrent to their exploitive behavior is the immediate threat of punishment or retribution from external sources. They have little, if any, internal mechanisms to deter them from their heinous activities.

There is a continuum from the normal to the psychopathic type to the extreme psychopath—with varying gradations of impairment. When

I use the term *psychopath*, I am referring to the people at the upper end of the continuum. *Psychopathic types* are found lower down on the continuum, but they still exhibit occasional psychopathic traits. Individuals in both of these categories may very well gain acceptance into law school, especially if no interview is required. I am not claiming that interviewers would routinely detect such individuals, only that astute interviewers should be alerted to their existence. Interviewers who screen applicants for medical schools are generally concerned with such types. Although medical school interviewers may certainly be fooled by psychopaths, they are less likely to be duped than computers.

Psychopathic types can be very convincing and ingratiating; they are often master manipulators. They may do quite well for themselves at the undergraduate level, demonstrating their brilliance to professors and convincing school administrators and faculty that they are major contributors to their academic institutions. Such individuals often receive the most laudatory letters of recommendation to law schools and other graduate institutions. It is important for the reader to appreciate that I am not by any means claiming that all lawyers who engage themselves in adversarial proceedings are psychopaths or psychopathic types. I am only claiming that law school admissions procedures are not well designed to screen such people, and the legal educational process intensifies such tendencies when they exist.

It is important for the reader to appreciate that my negative comparison between medical school and law school admissions procedures is not a statement of my belief that we do not have psychopathic types in medicine. Rather, I believe that we have too many and that admissions screening procedures are not stringent enough and interviewers not astute enough always to detect such individuals at that point. I do believe, however, that there are fewer psychopaths in medicine than in law, partly due to admissions interviews. Furthermore, legal education is likely to enhance preexisting psychopathic behaviors, whereas medical education is far less likely to do so. In fact, medical education may very well bring about a reversal of psychopathic tendencies in some individuals. The adversary system (as will be elaborated on below) teaches deceit, professional denial of this notwithstanding. Medical education emphasizes honesty, both to oneself and one's patients. I fully appreciate that we in medicine have our own brands of psychopathology and personality disorder, as does every field. I am not whitewashing medicine here; I am only pointing out certain differences in admissions procedures relevant to the issues in this chapter.

Another category of psychopathology likely to be found among members of the legal profession is *paranoia*. A paranoid individual is generally defined as someone who has delusions of persecution. Specifically, paranoids believe that others are persecuting, plotting against, exploiting, and engaging in a variety of other harmful acts against them when there is no evidence for such. These individuals may be always on the defensive and may seize upon every opportunity to "fight back." *Paranoid types* are individuals who have paranoid tendencies but are not grossly paranoid. They are at a point along the continuum between normal and paranoid, but closer to the paranoid end. Paranoid tendencies and the practice of law go well together. These individuals may view legal education as a vehicle for providing themselves with ammunition for protection against their persecutors. Again, we certainly have our share of paranoids in medical school; however, because our admissions procedures lessen the likelihood that paranoids will gain admission, I believe that there is a higher percentage in the legal profession. Paranoids are very likely to encourage litigation, whether it be custody litigation or any other type.

Of particular pertinence to this book is the paranoid type or paranoid lawyer who does not appreciate that a mother who is inducing in her child the severe category of parental alienation syndrome (Gardner, 1992a) may be basically paranoid. Or such an attorney may not appreciate that a person who is promulgating a false sex-abuse accusation may be paranoid and that the belief that the accused has sexually abused the child is part of a paranoid delusional system. As mentioned elsewhere (Gardner, 1992b, 1995), such an attorney is more likely to support her delusions, much to the grief and detriment of all concerned. And if the judge as well has such tendencies (not a remote possibility considering that judges are generally drawn from the pool of lawyers), then the mother's paranoia may be even more harmful. In short, when a paranoid parent is supported by a paranoid lawyer and presents her (his) case before a paranoid judge, the likelihood of family devastation approaches the 100 percent level.

Then there is the plethora of lawyers graduating from law schools. As mentioned, the best estimates are that there is approximately one lawyer for every 302 people in the United States. The ratio in Japan is one to 10,000. Although we live in the most litigious society in the world, even we cannot use so many lawyers. In such a situation, there are many "hungry" lawyers willing to take on any clients who are simpleminded or sick enough to engage their services. The lawyer and client work together as a team. Both must commit themselves to the "cause." The client who is foolish and gullible enough to believe that adversary litigation is the best first step toward resolving a custody/visitation dispute then teams up with an attorney who is hungry enough to exploit such a client, and we have a "team."

One possible remedy for this problem, obviously, is to reduce the number of people entering law school. This is not going to be easily accomplished. Many schools (including law schools) are money-making propositions. There is no medical school in the United States that earns money on each medical student, regardless of how high the tuition. Hospitals, laboratories, faculties in more than 20 specialities, and extremely expensive equipment make the cost of medical education extremely high. By comparison, legal education is relatively inexpensive for a university. There are no laboratories and expensive equipment, as are necessary in departments of chemistry, psychology, physics, biology, engineering, and other scientific disciplines. Of course, a law library is necessary; otherwise, all that are required are classroom facilities. Legal training, then, may be a "money-making proposition" and may help to offset the costs of the more expensive departments within a university (such as medical schools). So there is little likelihood that universities are going to curb law school admissions.

Imposing restrictions on the number of people entering the legal profession would generally be viewed as undemocratic. In this "land of opportunity" we believe that everybody should have the chance to pursue any reasonable goal. The vast majority of disciplines and trades have restrictions on membership. Certainly the maintenance of standards of competence is a factor. Also, many disciplines restrict the number of trainees because they want to maintain high earning power for those who have gained admission. Unions do this routinely; in fact, nepotism is the rule among many trade unions. Although considered undemocratic, the practice is widespread. As long as there is a sea of lawyers, many of whom are hungry, there will be many attorneys available to perpetuate the kinds of exploitation of people described in this book.

Teaching Law Students about the Deficiencies of the Adversary System

Prevention is best accomplished by attending to the earliest manifestations of the processes that bring about a disorder. With regard to the prevention of psychiatric disorders and the personal grief that result from protracted adversarial proceedings, one does well to start at the law school level—where lawyers first learn the system. Although all law schools teach that the adversary system is not perfect, most professors teach their students that it is the best we have for ascertaining the truth when such determination is crucial to resolve a dispute. Law students are taught that the system has evolved over centuries and that it is the best method yet devised for determining whether a defendant has indeed committed an alleged crime. It is based on the assumption that the best way of finding out who is telling the truth in such conflicts is for the accused and the accuser each to present to an impartial body (a judge or jury) his (her) argument, in accordance with certain rules and guidelines of presentation. More specifically, each side is permitted to present any information that supports its position and to withhold (within certain guidelines) information that would weaken its arguments. Out of this conflict of opposing positions, the impartial body is presumably in the best position to ascertain the truth.

Many in the legal profession have never given serious consideration to the system's weaknesses and hence blindly adhere to its tenets. Essential to the system is the principle that the impartial body attempts to rule on and/or require settlement of the dispute through the application of some general rule of law. Although this system certainly serves to protect individuals from misguided justice, it produces in many legal professionals what I consider to be an exaggerated deference to "the law." This may result in a blind adherence to legal precedents, statutes, and laws—often with little consideration to whether they are just, honorable, or fair. I focus in this section on what I consider to be some of the grievous weaknesses of the adversary system, weaknesses that directly contribute to psychiatric disturbances and misery in those unfortunate enough to have become victims of the system.

Lies of Omission and Lies of Commission Lies can be divided into two categories: lies of omission and lies of commission. A merchant who sells a piece of glass while claiming it is a diamond is lying by commission (a lie has been committed). A pregnant woman who does not tell her husband that he is not the father of the child she is carrying is lying by omission (she has omitted telling him the truth). In both cases someone is being deceived. The adversary system basically encourages lies of omission. It encourages withholding information that might compromise a client's position. This is lying. The same attorneys who routinely justify such omissions in their own work would not hesitate suing a physician for malpractice for the omission of information that could be detrimental to a patient. Many lawyers get defensive when one tries to point out that lies of omission are still lies and that teaching law students to utilize them is to teach deceit. The argument that this is how the adversary system works is not a justifiable one. It is a rationalization. Psychiatrists, and physicians in general, work on the principle that all pertinent information must be brought to their attention if they are to make the most judicious decisions regarding diagnosis and treatment. The same principle holds with regard to the solution of other problems in life. The more information one has, the better is one's capacity to deal with a problem. The adversary system encourages the withholding and covering up of information.

The argument that the other side is very likely to bring out what is withheld by the first is not a valid one. The other side may not be aware that such information exists. Furthermore, the procedure encourages nitpicking and other time-wasting maneuvers, delays, and investigative procedures that usually impede rather than foster the divulgence of information. These time-wasting elements in the system often so becloud an issue that important facts get lost or are not given proper attention. Furthermore, only the wealthiest can afford a trial that attempts to ensure that all the pertinent information will ultimately be brought forth. But even then, a significant amount of the client's money is used in the service of withholding the information that the other side may want to bring to court.

It is unreasonable to expect that one can teach law students how to lie in one area and not to do so in others. These practices tend to become generalized. Attorneys have been known to say to clients, "Don't tell me. It's better that I don't know." The next step, after a client has unwittingly provided the compromising information, is for the attorney to say, "Forget you told me that" or "Never tell anyone you said that to me." And the next step is for the attorney to say, "You know it and I know it, but that is very different from their *proving* it." This "deal" is, by legal definition, collusion: an agreement between the lawyer and the client that they will work together to deceive the other side. Like chess, it is a game whose object is to trick and entrap the opponent.

Professors at many law schools may respond that such criticism does not give proper credit to or demonstrate respect for the "higher" principles taught at their institutions. They claim that their students are imbued with the highest ethical and moral values known to humankind. Although they may actually believe what they are saying, my experience has been that the graduates of these same institutions are still prone to involve themselves in the aforementioned deceitful maneuvers with their clients. Moreover, even these institutions teach the adversary system. When one begins with a system that is intrinsically deceitful, one cannot expect those who implement it to use it in an honest manner. To use it is to deceive and to risk an expansion of deceit into other areas. If one teaches a child to steal pennies and only pennies, one should not be surprised when the child starts stealing nickels. To say I only taught the youngster how to steal pennies is no defense. If one teaches a child to lie to the butcher but not to the baker, one should not be surprised when the child lies to the baker as well. After years of involvement with adversarial deceit in the professional realm, many attorneys no longer appreciate how deep-seated their tendency to fabricate has become. Cover-ups and lies of omission become incorporated into their personality and lifestyle. Many reach the point where they no longer appreciate that they have been corrupted by the system within which they earn their livelihood.

The Encouragement of Unethical Practices Strict adherence to adversarial proceedings frequently results in the lawyer's being unethical. Let us take, for example, acting in what is the best interests of children. Everybody waves that banner: the parents, their attorneys, the guardian ad litem, and the judge. Merely embroiling children in adversarial litigation, even without requiring direct testimony, is not likely to be in their best interests. But subscribing strictly to the adversarial principle that the lawyer must zealously argue and support the client's position often results in a situation in which children are being harmed. There are many custody disputes in which it is obvious to just about everybody as to which parent would better serve the children, obvious also to the attorney of the defective parent. Yet that attorney zealously supports his (her) client's position, even though prevailing in the lawsuit may be devastating for the children. There are many situations in which it is obvious to all concerned that a sex-abuse accusation is false and even a product of psychotic delusion or conscious fabrication. And this too is obvious to the accuser's attorney; but this does not stop him (her) from zealously supporting the client. Again, the children suffer. Support of such defective clients is basically immoral, yet the adversary system encourages such representation (or more correctly, misrepresentation). Attorneys often blind themselves to the immorality of what they are doing. If they were to allow themselves to see clearly the immorality of what they were doing, they might have to suffer guilt and, if they were moral enough, remove themselves from the case and suffer the financial privations attendant to such withdrawal or refusal. There are, of course, attorneys whose morality will work along these lines, but this is inversely proportional to the amount of money that the client has available for the litigation. The conflict between morality and adherence to the principles of the adversary system is well demonstrated with the following composite of many conversations I have had over the last 35 years:

I receive a telephone call from an attorney in which he begins: "Doctor Gardner, my name is Mr. So-and-So. I'm an attorney and was referred to you by Dr. So-and-So." The introduction is innocuous enough. It is with the next sentence that the trouble begins. It is usually a run-on sentence, with the second half being stated much more rapidly than the first: "I would like to know whether I can engage your services in testifying on behalf of my client who is involved in a custody conflict with her husband (the pace quickens here); however, Doctor, I want you to know that the best interests of the children are paramount."

To this I generally respond, "Suppose, after seeing your client, I were to conclude that I cannot support with conviction her position and I decide that it would be in the best interests of the children for them to live with their father. Would you still use my testimony in court?"

The attorney then often answers in a confused and irritated manner: "Doctor, you can't be serious, suggesting that I use your testimony to support my adversary's client. Are you suggesting that I put you on the stand to testify on behalf of the other side?"

My response: "But I understood you to have said before that the best interests of the children were paramount. If that were truly the case, I would think you would welcome my testimony in order to do what is best for them. What you're telling me now suggests to me that supporting your client is *really* paramount!"

At this point the attorney may tell me (directly or indirectly) that it is clear that he has made a mistake in calling me and that the person who referred him to me wasn't aware of how ignorant I was of legal matters.

This attorney is essentially doing what he was taught in law school, namely, to support his client's position. He knows that psychiatrists are concerned with children's best interests and that the best way to ingratiate himself to such people is to profess a similar commitment. However, the basic inconsistency in his comments quickly becomes apparent. One cannot automatically commit oneself to support a client's claim for custody and *at the same time* state that the children's interests are paramount. At times it is in the children's best interests to live with the client whom the attorney is representing; at other times it is not. When the latter is the case, the attorney must make a choice. Almost invariably that choice will be to support the client's claim, not the children's needs.

In addition, the attorney who is deeply committed to the adversary system may see nothing inappropriate in asking me to testify on behalf of his client *before I have even seen her*. I cannot be too critical of him here, because there are mental health professionals who will promise to provide such support before anyone has been seen. Such "hired-gun" examiners are a disgrace to our profession. The attorney here is only a product of his system—a system based on respect for the adversarial process as a way of solving human problems. He is committed to the idea that "truth" emerges from conflict. And I am a product

of my system—a system based on the premise that free and open inquiry is the best way to gather data for settling human conflicts.

Another example of the immorality of the adversary system:

Two clients (having no relationship with one another) have appointments to see an attorney. The first is a man. He is currently married
to a woman who has been divorced and who has two children. This is his
first marriage. She has custody of the two children. He comes to the
lawyer to ask the attorney's advice regarding the advisability of adopting his stepchildren, whose biological father has no interest in them and
is receptive to the adoption. The attorney strongly discourages him from
doing so, informing him that if this marriage were to end in a divorce,
and if he were to have adopted the children, then he would have the
obligation to provide for their financial support. However, if he does not
adopt them, he would have no obligation for their support after a divorce, but their natural father might. Accordingly, the attorney strongly
dissuades his client from going ahead with the plans for adoption. The
man leaves and may be very grateful that he has had the good fortune to
engage the services of such a clever lawyer.

The next client to see the *same* attorney is a woman. She has been
divorced, has two children, and is now married for the second time to a
man who has never been married before. She has custody of the two
children. She has come to the attorney to ask his advice about her new
husband adopting the children. Her former husband is receptive to the
adoption. The lawyer advises her to proceed as rapidly as possible with
the adoption plans. He tells her that once her new husband has adopted
the children, he will be obligated to support them financially, even if
this marriage ends in divorce. Furthermore, he warns her that if her
new husband were not to adopt the children, he would have no obligation at all to provide for their support if there were to be a divorce. The
woman leaves and may be very grateful that she has had the good fortune to engage the services of such a clever lawyer.

In each case the attorney is seemingly protecting his client's best
interests—especially if one considers monetary considerations to be paramount. At no point in his advice to these clients is there any consideration
for the welfare of the children. His primary concern is the pocketbook
of his clients. The decision whether or not to adopt should be based on
a variety of considerations including the financial and the psychological

effects on the parties concerned. Parenting is far more a psychological than a monetary phenomenon. The feelings and attitudes of the adoptive father, the reactions of the children (especially their feelings about being adopted and how this will affect their relationships with their natural father and their stepfather), and the reactions of the mother should all be taken into consideration. Although this lawyer may get an A+ from his law school professor, he would get an F- from this psychiatry professor.

The Failure to Allow Direct Confrontation Between the Accused and the Accuser It amazes me that after centuries of utilization, adherents of the adversary system do not appreciate that they are depriving themselves of one of the most valuable and predictable ways of learning the truth. I am referring here to the placing of the accused and the accuser together in the same room in direct confrontation. Proponents of the system will immediately take issue with me on this point. They will claim that one of the reasons for the development of the adversary system was the appreciation that the system's predecessor, the inquisitorial system, left accused parties feeling helpless, especially with regard to this issue. During the early use of the inquisitorial system, accused individuals were not permitted direct confrontation with their accusers and frequently did not even know who they were. This insistence upon the right of accused individuals to face their accusers is considered to be one of the cornerstones for the adversary system and one of the strongest arguments for perpetuating it.

Unfortunately, many of the system's proponents fail to appreciate that the confrontations insisted upon are not as free and open as they would like to believe. When referring to this practice, the general assumption is that the confrontation will take place in an open courtroom. This too is considered an advance over inquisitorial procedures, in which the proceedings were often held in secret. On the one hand, this is an advance because there are many witnesses to the confrontation: a judge, a jury, and often observers in the audience. On the other hand, the confrontation is extremely constrained by rites of courtroom procedure, and both parties are required to work under very confining circumstances. They are rarely allowed direct communication with one another;

rather, communication is usually through their attorneys. These elements significantly compromise the benefits that are presumably obtained from the confrontation. In short, the principle of direct confrontation between accused and accuser is certainly a noble one, but its implementation in the adversary system has reduced its efficacy enormously.

The central problem with the adversarial courtroom confrontation is that the two individuals are not permitted to speak directly to one another. The argument that in more volatile situations they might cause one another physical harm is no justification for such formidable constraints. Litigants for whom such a risk exists could, if necessary, be provided with some kind of physical barrier such as a perforated steel screen (through which they could still converse). The argument that the accused and the accuser are still better off having representatives is, I believe, a residuum of the medieval practice of trial by champion. No matter how brilliant the lawyer and the judge, no matter how obsessive they are with regard to getting the details of the alleged incident, no matter how devoted they are to the collection of their data, the fact is that *they were not present as observers of the alleged incident.* The accused and the accuser know better than anyone else whether the events actually occurred. Similarly, with rare exception they know each other better than any of the other parties involved in the litigation. If the system were to allow the two to talk directly to each other, and confront each other with their opinions of each other's statements, much more "truth" would emerge. Of course, less money would be made by the "middle men," the alleged facilitators of communication and confrontation. In some cases their "services" could be dispensed with entirely and the confrontation facilitated and moderated by a third party who has the power to conduct a civilized proceeding. This is certainly what happens when conflicts are mediated and arbitrated. In other cases attorneys would still be necessary because of their knowledge of the law and other genuine services that they could provide their clients. It would be an error for the reader to conclude that I am suggesting that we dispense entirely with traditional courtroom procedures and that lawyers never be used. I am only suggesting that there be some place in the legal system for truly direct confrontation between the accused and the accuser.

These factors are especially valid for custody litigation and sex-abuse accusations arising in the context of such disputes. The litigants know one another "inside out." Each knows better than anyone else when the other party is fabricating. Each knows the signs and symptoms of the other's lying: stuttering, the hesitations, the embarrassed facial expressions, and the wide variety of other manifestations of duplicity. The adversary system does not give individuals the opportunity for an "eyeball-to-eyeball" confrontation. I am convinced that this is one of the best ways of finding out who is telling the truth, and I am astounded that after all these years, the system still deprives itself of using this valuable source of information. Perhaps I should not be so amazed. Perhaps it is more a statement of public gullibility that people allow themselves to be convinced that adversarial procedures of confrontation are superior to the traditional face-to-face.

It is for this reason that I make joint sessions mandatory in my custody evaluations (Gardner, 1986, 1989). In addition, I do not preclude them entirely in my sex-abuse evaluations (Gardner, 1992b, 1995) but do conduct them in certain selected situations. In such meetings the parties can immediately "smoke out" one another's lies in a way far superior to the procedures used in the courtroom. Furthermore, in joint interviews the examiner has the opportunity to telephone immediately other individuals who might be able to provide important information regarding which person is telling the truth. The judge cannot do this; an impartial evaluator can do so readily. It might take weeks or months to bring in a third party to provide testimony in a courtroom, and even then one might not be successful in doing so because of the reluctance of the person to "get involved." However, a telephone call made by one of the spouses is much more likely to elicit the third party's comments during a brief conversation over the telephone. Such participation is very different from appearing on a witness stand in a courtroom. And the person who is lying and risks being exposed by such a call is not likely to resist strongly because of the knowledge that such resistance implies guilt, shame, or some kind of cover-up that will compromise the resister's position in the custody evaluation. There is no lawyer involved to "protect" the client's rights and to justify thereby cover-ups and the perpetuation of the fabrication. There is no time lag to allow the individual to "prepare a response" and thereby selectively withhold information or even introduce fabrications.

Accordingly, when I conduct custody and sex-abuse evaluations under the aegis of the court, I do so with the proviso that I be free to bring the involved parties together in the same room at the same time, at my discretion. Here, again, I am surprised that the tradition is for the courts to send a child to examiners such as myself and ask us to evaluate the child alone to find out whether there has been sex abuse. Or I may be asked to evaluate a man with regard to the question of whether he sexually abused a particular child, but I am not permitted to interview the child. In fact, it is extremely rare in criminal proceedings for the same evaluator to interview both the accused and the alleged victim, even in situations when both would be willing to participate in an evaluation by the same party. There is nothing illegal about such an interview. The Fifth Amendment of the United States Constitution protects the accused from being forced to speak not only in the courtroom but to anyone at all, including mental health professionals on either side. However, the Fifth Amendment *does not preclude* such conversations, and many accused parties are quite willing to speak to any mental health professional, regardless of which side proposes the evaluator. But even in civil cases, where there are traditionally fewer constraints allegedly justifying such a separation of evaluations, I have found it extremely difficult to accomplish this goal when I have asked for the opportunity to bring the alleged abuser and the child into the same room at the same time (at my discretion). As mentioned, I routinely do this in custody/ visitation disputes and reserve the right to do this in selected cases of sex-abuse accusations. I am often met with an incredulous response. Certainly, there are situations in which one might not want to do this. However, there are other situations in which it would be highly desirable. Admittedly, there are extra complicating factors in such situations, such as the child's fear of the confrontation and the repercussions of the disclosures. However, these drawbacks notwithstanding (there is no situation in which there are no drawbacks), routinely precluding such joint interviews seriously compromises the evaluation.

The Issue of Conviction for the Client's Position Most lawyers believe that they can be as successful helping a client whose cause they may not be particularly in sympathy with as they can with one whose position they strongly support. From their early days in law school, they are imbued with the idea that their obligations as lawyers are to serve the client and work as zealously as possible in support of his (her) position. They are taught that they must do this even though they may not be in sympathy with the client's position and even though they might prefer to be on the opponent's side. This is another weakness of the adversary system. It assumes that attorneys can argue just as effectively when they have no commitment to the client's position as when they do.

In most law schools students are required to involve themselves in "moot court" experiences in which they are assigned a position in a case. The assignment is generally made on a random basis and is independent of the student's own conviction on the particular issue. In fact, it is often considered preferable that the assignment be made in such a way that students must argue in support of the position for which they have less or even no conviction. On other occasions, the student may be asked to present arguments for both sides. Obviously, such experiences can be educationally beneficial. We can all learn from and become more flexible by being required to view a situation from the opposite vantage point. However, I believe that attorneys are naive who hold that one can argue just as effectively without conviction as one can if one has conviction. Noncommitted attorneys are going to serve less effectively in most cases. Accordingly, before they enter the courtroom, their clients are in a weakened position. Most (but not all) attorneys are not likely to turn away a client whose position they secretly do not support. (One doesn't turn away a paying customer so quickly.) Accordingly, it would be very difficult for a client to find a lawyer who is going to admit openly to a lack of conviction for the client's position.

I recall a situation in which I had good reason to believe that an attorney was basically not supporting his client, the father in a custody case, and that his lack of conviction contributed to his poor performance in the courtroom. In this particular case I served as an impartial examiner and concluded that the mother's position warranted my support. However, once in the courtroom, I was treated as an advocate of the mother (the usual situation). Early in the trial, the guardian ad litem suggested that I, as the impartial examiner, be invited into the courtroom to observe the testimony of a psychiatrist who had been brought in as an advocate for the father's side. The father's attorney agreed to this, which surprised me because I did not see what he had to gain by my having direct opportunity to observe (and potentially criticize) his client's expert. I thought that this attorney had much to lose and nothing to gain by my observing his expert's testimony because the evaluator would be likely to provide me with more "ammunition" for the mother.

While the advocate expert testified, I took notes and, as was expected, the father's attorney provided him ample time to elaborate on his various points. When I took the stand, I was first questioned by the mother's attorney, the attorney whose position I supported. He gave me great flexibility with regard to my opportunities for answering his questions. Then the father's attorney began to question me. To my amazement, he allowed me to elaborate on points on which I disagreed with him. At no time did he confine me to the traditional yes/no answers that are designed to weaken and distort testimony. He persistently gave me opportunities for elaboration, and naturally I took advantage of every one of them.

During a break in the proceedings, when the judge and attorneys were conferring at the bench, I heard the judge ask the father's lawyer, "Why are you letting Gardner talk so much?" I suspect this was an inappropriate statement for the judge to make, but it confirmed how atypical and seemingly inexplicable was the attorney's cross-examination of me. The lawyer shrugged his shoulders, said nothing, and on my return to the stand continued to allow me great flexibility in my answers. I had every reason to believe that he was a bright man and "knew better." I had no doubt that he did not routinely proceed in this way. To me, this attorney's apparently inexplicable behavior was most likely motivated by the desire (either conscious or unconscious) that his own client lose custody because of his recognition that the mother was the preferable parent. He "went through the motions" of supporting his client, but did so in such a way that he basically helped the other side win the case.

In recent years I have seen the same phenomenon operate—with devastating consequences—in sex-abuse cases. Here, the defendant's attorney, professions of support for his client's position notwithstanding, clearly believes that his (her) client is guilty of the accusation. Such attorneys have been swept up in the hysteria of our times and work under the assumption that "children never lie" and that "there must be something to it or why would the child make such a statement?" In criminal trials they may quickly encourage their clients to plea-bargain when they might have gone to court, where only one of 12 jurors need be dubious in order to exonerate the defendant. Or they might take the approach that the child was abused but not by their client. There are many people in jail now because of this misguided stratagem. To me, this maneuver is tantamount to giving away 95 percent of the case before even going to trial. One is basically admitting that the child was abused and it is now just a question of pointing the finger at someone else, often someone who warrants even less suspicion, and possibly even someone who is unknown. Or such attorneys may accept the conclusions of such "experts" as "validators," obvious zealots, and incompetents. They do not consider the approach of trying to discredit these people. It would have been far better for these clients if their attorneys had been taught in law school that it is unethical to support the position of a client for whom they have little or no conviction.

Competent and sensitive therapists, in contrast, generally work in accordance with the principle that if they have no conviction for what they are doing with their patients, the chances of success in the treatment are likely to be reduced significantly—even to the point of there being no chance of success at all. If, for example, the therapist's feelings for the patient are not strong, if there is no basic sympathy for the patient's situation, if the relationship is not a good one, or if the therapist is not convinced that the patient's goals in therapy are valid, the likelihood of the patient's being helped is small if not nil. Without such conviction the therapy becomes boring and sterile—with little chance of any constructive results.

Watson (1969), an attorney, encourages lawyers to refuse to support a client's attempts to gain custody when the attorney does not consider the client to be the preferable parent. He considers such support to be basically unethical because one is likely to be less successful with a client for whose position one does not have conviction. This is a noble attitude on this attorney's part. Unfortunately, far too few lawyers subscribe to this advice, and most succumb to the more practical consideration that if they do not support their client's position, they will lose that client and the attendant fee.

The Issue of Emotions and Objectivity Attorneys are taught in law school that emotions compromise objectivity. They use the word *objectivity* to refer to the ability to "stay cool," think clearly, and thereby handle a situation in the most judicious and "clear-headed" way. Emotions are viewed as contaminants to such clear thinking, i.e., they are *subjective*. Objectivity is equated with the ability to deal with a situation in the most judicious way. And this is the concept of the word that I will utilize here. Accordingly, they are taught that if one gets emotional in a legal situation, one's clients may suffer. This polarization between emotions and objectivity is an oversimplification and compromises many attorneys' capacity to represent their clients optimally.

I consider there to be a continuum between objectivity and emotions. To set up a dichotomy is not consistent with the realities of the world. An emotion in fact *exists*. That one cannot measure it or weigh it does not negate its existence. To say that a thought is objective and a feeling is not is to make an artificial distinction between two types of mental processes. Emotions have many more concomitant physiological responses outside the brain than do thoughts, but this does not mean that emotions are thereby "not real" (the implication of the word *subjective*). At one end of the continuum are thoughts with little if any emotional concomitants. At the other end are emotions with little if any associated thoughts. As one moves from the cognitive (thoughts) end toward the affective (emotional) end, the percentage of thoughts decreases and the percentage of emotions increases. At some point along this continuum, closer to the cognitive end, are *mild* emotions. As I will discuss in detail below, I believe that extremely strong emotions generally will compromise objectivity, but mild ones are likely to *increase* objectivity—if used judiciously. Again, I use the word *objectivity* here to refer to the capacity to handle a situation in the most effective way.

Attorneys generally do not differentiate between strong and mild emotions; they simply view all emotions as potentially contaminating one's attempts to learn the truth. *Both mild and strong emotions are sources of information.* When a psychotherapist, while working with a patient, exhibits emotions, he (she) does well to determine whether they are in the mild or strong category. The therapist has to differentiate between emotions that will compromise objectivity and those that will enhance it. If a therapist experiences mild emotions—which are engendered by the patient's behavior and are similar to emotions that the vast majority of individuals are likely to have in that situation—then the expression of such emotions to the patient can prove therapeutic. For example, if a therapist becomes irritated because the patient is not fulfilling financial obligations, the therapist does well not only to confront the patient with the default but also to express the frustration and irritation thereby engendered. After all, if a psychotherapist is not going to be open and honest with the patient about his (her) *own* emotional reactions, how can the therapist expect the patient to do so? Therapists should serve as healthy models for their patients, and expressing proper and appropriate emotions judiciously is in the service of this goal. Also, one of the services for which the patient is paying is the therapist's honest responses. Accordingly, such expression of feelings by the therapist enhances the efficacy of the treatment. I am therefore in sharp disagreement with those who consider the presence of such emotions in the therapist to be necessarily inappropriate, injudicious, psychopathological, or a manifestation of a lack of objectivity.

As to the issue of very strong emotions, these may be useful or not useful, therapeutic or antitherapeutic, in the treatment process. Because the therapeutic process is another "slice of life" in which the same general principles of living are applicable, my comments on the roles of emotions in treatment apply to their role in handling situations elsewhere. An example of a severe emotion in the therapeutic process is: If a patient threatens to kill a psychotherapist, the therapist is likely to be frightened and/or extremely angry. And such feelings may be very powerful. If these feelings are used judiciously, the therapist may save his (her) life and may even protect the lives of others. We see here how a strong emotion may be useful and not necessarily becloud objectivity. If the therapist, however, fears for his (her) life when there is no actual threat, then he (she) is likely to be delusional and is clearly compromised in his (her) capacity to help the patient. Here inappropriate, strong emotions are operative in reducing the therapist's objectivity.

Consider a more common situation: If a therapist overreacts because of psychopathological reactions to what the patient is saying, he (she) becomes compromised as a therapist, e.g., getting angry at a patient for leaving treatment, or having sex with a patient. Such overreaction results in injudicious, antitherapeutic, or unethical handling of the matter—again reducing the therapist's objectivity. In short, emotions per se do not compromise objectivity; they may or they may not. When mild they are less likely to; when very strong they are more likely to. Even strong emotions, used judiciously, can enhance one's efficacy (and thereby objectivity) in dealing with a situation.

Accordingly, lawyers have to appreciate that the traditional advice that they should be unemotional is misguided. They should try to be sensitive to their emotions and make the kinds of discriminations I have just described. They should recognize that emotional reactions are not necessarily a hindrance to their work, nor do they interfere with objectivity. They should view their own emotions as a potentially valuable source of information about what may be going on with their clients. Lawyers should use their emotions to help their clients; they should not deny their emotions and conclude that their expression will be a disservice to their clients. We fight harder when we are angry to a reasonable degree. We lose our efficiency in fighting when our anger deranges us and we enter into states of rage and fury. We flee faster when we are frightened. However, if the fear becomes overwhelming, it may paralyze us.

The failure of attorneys to appreciate these principles relating to emotions and objectivity has caused me difficulty on a few occasions in the course of courtroom testimony. By the time of my courtroom appearance I generally feel a deep conviction for a particular client's position. This is an outgrowth of my having committed myself strongly to the evaluation, worked assiduously at the task, and come to the point where I can firmly present my conclusions on the witness stand. In the course of my testimony, I have *on occasion* expressed feelings—sympathy, irritation, frustration, and a variety of other emotions. Some lawyers have seized upon my admission of such feelings as a justification for discrediting me as being compromised in my objectivity. My attempts to explain that these emotions were engendered by the reality of the situation, and that I was reacting like any other human being, often proved futile. My efforts to impress upon the attorneys that such emotions have an objectivity of their own and could enhance my understanding of the case were met with incredulity and distrust. And even presiding judges usually agreed with the attorneys that it was inappropriate of me to have these emotions. Because of this prevailing notion among members of the legal profession, I came to consider it injudicious to express my emotions and I was much more cautious about revealing them—so as not to compromise the position of the party whose position I was supporting.

This is an unfortunate situation. On the one hand, I would prefer to state, with a reasonable degree of emotion, the position I hold and then explain that these attendant emotions do not necessarily compromise my objectivity. I would prefer to describe how they are not only an important source of information for me, but enhance my efficiency. On the other hand, to do so just invites refutations that may compromise me on the witness stand. It would give an adversary attorney "ammunition," even if unjustifiable. Accordingly, I generally follow the judicious course of not revealing the emotional factors that have played a role in the decision-making process. My hope is that attorneys will become more sophisticated regarding this issue so that evaluators might ultimately be able to provide more complete and honest testimony.

Other Changes in Law School Education That Would Benefit Attorneys and Their Clients

Medical schools require that certain courses be taken at the premedical level, courses that serve as foundations for medical education. It is generally recognized that certain science courses at the undergraduate level, especially chemistry, biology, and physics, are so useful in medical school that a candidate who has not proven significant efficiency in them would not be considered for admission. Law schools generally do not have any prescribed prelaw curriculum. Most require only three or four years of college. It matters not whether one studied engineering, political science, anthropology, biology, psychology, or any other subject. This is unfortunate. I believe more serious attention should be given to this issue. Obviously, if one is going into patent law, one does well to acquire some training in the sciences and engineering. If one is going to use the law as a route to politics, then one should have some background in political science, sociology, and psychology. If one is going to go into family law and involve oneself in divorce litigation, then one should certainly have some background in normal and abnormal psychology as well as child development. And students who are not sure which aspect of the law they wish to enter should be required to take appropriate prelaw courses before applying to law school. Just as people who belatedly decide they want to go to medical school are required to first pass their premed courses, those who belatedly decide they want to go to law school should be required to first pass the aforementioned prelaw courses. And those who have made no decision prior to entering law school should be required to lengthen their legal education in order to accommodate the inclusion of the appropriate foundational courses.

It is unfortunate (to say the least) that attorneys have been so slow to recognize the importance of postgraduate specialization. Most lawyers are viewed by the public as "jacks of all trades" and even "masters of all trades" within the law. People go to "a lawyer," whether the problem be divorce, preparation of a will, or getting a mortgage on a house. The assumption is that good lawyers are trained in all of these areas. Actually, they are trained in very few of them. Most attorneys learn from their experiences over the years. These same individuals will, however, go to an orthopedist, gynecologist, surgeon, or other specialist. Most people recognize that the general medical practitioner is a "jack of all trades, but a master of *none.*" The arguments given by attorneys for not setting up rigorous programs of specialization are not, in my opinion, valid. They will argue that it is very difficult to decide what the criteria should be for certifying someone in a particular legal specialty and they question who should be doing the examining. Medicine seems to have worked out these problems. No one is claiming that the specialization system is perfect, but most physicians agree that it is better than having no system at all for specialty training and certification. The real reason, I believe, relates to money. "Jacks of all trades" need not turn away anyone. Specialists are generally required to do so.

Some of the damage done to clients in the course of custody and sex-abuse litigation would be reduced if prelaw students planning to go into family law were required to include courses in clinical psychology (normal and abnormal) in their undergraduate training. Furthermore, there should be a postgraduate discipline, involving one or two years of further study, in which there would be specific preparation and experience in family law. During such training many of the issues raised here would be taught—issues such as the drawbacks of the adversary system in general, the disadvantages of the adversary system as it applies to custody litigation, and psychopathological disorders that result from protracted custody litigation. Considering the sex-abuse hysteria that we have witnessed in recent years (Gardner, 1991c), it would be crucial that there be courses in normal and abnormal sexual behavior. Moreover, I would include such topics as ethics and values in the law, sensitivity to the feelings of clients, and psychopathy and paranoia among lawyers and how these disorders harm clients. Again, I recognize fully that we in medicine are not free from our share of psychopaths, paranoids, and incompetents, but we in medicine do much more than lawyers to screen such individuals at every level of training.

Concluding Comments

Riskin (1982), a law professor who is very critical of the adversary system and legal educational programs that promulgate it, states:

> Nearly all courses at most law schools are presented from the viewpoint of the practicing attorney who is working in an adversary system. . . . There is, to be sure, scattered attention to the lawyer as planner, policy maker, and public servant, but 90 percent of what goes on in law school is based on a model of the lawyer working in or against a background of litigation of disputes that can be resolved by the application of a rule by a third party. The teachers were trained with this model in mind. The students get a rough image with them; it gets sharpened quickly. This model defines and limits the likely career possibilities envisioned by most law students.

In further criticism of the narrowness of the adversary system he states:

> When one party wins, in this vision, usually the other party loses, and, most often, the victory is reduced to a money judgment. This "reduction" of nonmaterial values—such as honor, respect, dignity, security, and love—to amount of money, can have one of two effects. In some cases, these values are excluded from the decision makers' considerations, and thus the consciousness of the lawyers, as irrel-

evant. In others, they are present by transmutation into something else—a justification for money damages.

These "irrelevant" issues—"honor, respect, dignity, security, and love"—are certainly professed by attorneys involved in custody litigation, especially when they wave the banner of the best-interests-of-the-child philosophy. In reality the children are often merely the objects that are "won." Often there may be a trade-off of the children for monetary awards. Children become chattel, objects, or booty—with only lip service paid to the emotional consequences of the litigation. Due to the adversary system and the legal education that promulgates the method, attorneys are programmed in their earliest phases of development to ignore these crucial elements in their work.

THE EDUCATION AND TRAINING OF NONLEGAL PROFESSIONALS

Introduction

On a few occasions I have been asked, when presenting my credentials to testify in court, what my formal training has been in custody and sex-abuse litigation. My answer simply has been "none." The questioning attorney has generally been quite aware that I had no formal training in this area because there was no such training in the late 1950s when I received my residency training. The attempt here was to compromise my credibility by attempting to demonstrate to the court that I was not qualified to testify on child-custody and sex-abuse issues. Asking me that question is the same as asking an internist, who like myself attended medical school in the mid-1950s, to state what education he had at that time on the subject of AIDS. (Obviously, this question was not asked by the attorney whose position I supported.) Unfortunately, there are young people today who are asked the same question and must also provide the same answer. Considering the widespread epidemic of sex-abuse and custody litigation that now prevails, the failure to provide training in these areas at the present time represents a significant deficiency in the education and training of professionals doing such evaluations. Most people, like myself, have "learned from experience." Some have learned well and some have not. Accordingly, I would consider it mandatory that all child-therapy programs in psychology, psychiatry, social work, and related disciplines require training and experience in custody and sex-abuse litigation. In such programs particular attention should be given to procedures for differentiating between true and false sex-abuse accusations (Gardner, 1992b, 1995).

Serving as a Hired Gun
Should Be Unethical

In such programs I would emphasize the point that having professionals automatically serving as advocates ("hired guns") in litigation is a reprehensible practice and a terrible disservice to the family, the legal profession, and the mental health professions as well. The attempt here would be to bring about a situation in which attorneys looking for hired guns would not be able to find any mental health professional who would allow themselves to be so utilized. Although I believe that this is an ideal that will never be reached, we would still do well to have the principle promulgated at the earliest levels of education and training. It is my hope that this principle would be incorporated into the ethical standards of the various professional societies. A strong statement that such advocacy is unethical would certainly help protect and discourage mental health professionals from this type of prostitution of their talents and skills. Such refusal could be considered to be a kind of preventive psychiatry in that it would remove us from contributing to legal maneuvers that play a role in bringing about the parental alienation syndrome and other disorders that result from protracted divorce/custody litigation.

Mediation

Such training would also involve impressing upon the trainees the importance of their doing everything possible to discourage their patients from involving themselves in such litigation and to point out the variety of psychopathological reactions that can result. Elsewhere

(Gardner, 1986), I have described many of these in detail. In addition, trainees should be advised to encourage their patients to involve themselves in mediation as a first step toward resolving divorce/custody disputes. They should be helped to appreciate that adversary litigation should be the parents' very last resort, after all civilized attempts at resolution have failed.

Currently, mediation is very much a "growth industry." Lawyers and mental health specialists are the primary professionals attracted to the field (Coogler, 1978; Fisher and Ury, 1981; Haynes, 1981; Folberg and Taylor, 1984). However, there are many others with little if any training or experience who have gravitated to the field. Currently, there are no nationally recognized standards with regard to training requirements. These will inevitably have to be set up, and I believe that they should be set up soon. Mediation has been popular since the early 1980s. This might be considered too short a period to give us enough information to decide what the standards should be. Still, I think sufficient time has elapsed to enable us to propose guidelines for a training program. My own view is that it should take place at the graduate level. I would consider two years of course work and a year of practical work under the supervision of experienced mediators to be optimum. During the first two years the program should provide courses in both law and psychology. There should be courses in basic law as well as marriage and divorce law. Courses in finance should cover the kinds of financial problems that divorcing people are likely to encounter. In the mental health area there should be basic courses in child development, child psychopathology, sexual development, family psychodynamics, and interviewing techniques. Furthermore, there should be courses in mediation techniques and conflict resolution. This academic material would serve as a foundation for the clinical work in the third year.

At this time universities in the United States do not appear to be particularly enthusiastic about setting up such programs, although some have been started. My hope is that they will become more appreciative of the need for these in the near future. In addition, I believe that graduate programs in psychology, social work, and residency training programs would also do well to incorporate mediation training as part of their general curricula. However, training at these levels cannot provide the same kind of in-depth experience that one gets from a full two- or three-year program of the aforementioned type.

RESOLVING CHILD-CUSTODY DISPUTES WITHOUT ADVERSARIAL PROCEEDINGS

Unfortunately, alternative methods of dispute resolution are not likely to be utilized in a widespread fashion. The main reason for this is that changes in the adversarial system must generally come from state legislators, many (if not most) of whom are lawyers themselves. Frequently, they have left law firms at the time they have assumed public office. Many still continue active involvement in their law firms while serving simultaneously in the state legislature. Many hope to return to law firms if they are not reelected or possibly at the time of retirement from the legislature. Many have brothers, sisters, fathers, mothers, and children who are lawyers. When one considers this, the likelihood of such legislators passing laws that are going to constrain the adversary system is extremely small, if not impossible to imagine. When one adds to this factor the billions of dollars (I have no hesitation using that number) earned by lawyers via their utilization of this system and the billions that would be lost if it were to be dismantled and replaced, there is even less of a likelihood that anything significant is going to happen to it in the foreseeable future. It is my hope that what I have said in this chapter will play a role (admittedly small) in bringing about some changes.

My repeated observations, over many years, of the devastating effects of adversarial proceedings on families has led me to consider nonadversarial methods of child-custody dispute resolution—methods that go beyond mediation—methods that would preclude entirely the utilization of adversarial proceedings. The proposal presented here describes such a system. I will first discuss briefly the way in which I have continued to serve as a mediator, and then I will elaborate upon an alternative proposal for resolving child-custody disputes.

Mediation

Over the years I have served as a mediator, and I continue to do so. I have been a "pure" mediator (in which I have facilitated the parents' own resolution of the custody conflict); and I have conducted thorough custody evaluations, the findings of which were used as a point of departure to reach a mediated settlement. Generally, the parents are referred by lawyers who seek to remove the custody conflict from other areas of contention and recommend that I mediate the custody dispute.

As a mediator I use the same principles of evaluation that I employ when I serve as a court-appointed impartial examiner. I evaluate the parents and children in varying combinations, review records that have been submitted to me, come up with a recommendation, and present it to the parents as a point of departure for the mediation process. However, before agreeing to mediate a custody dispute, I require the parents to sign a statement in which they pledge that under no circumstances will I be involved in their litigation. No report is prepared because it might ultimately find its way into the courtroom. There is no contact with lawyers, but I do agree to review legal papers. My conclusions and recommendations are given verbally and can be transmitted to the parents' attorneys and subsequently incorporated into the proper legal document.

An Alternative System

I am currently promulgating (through lectures and writing) a three-stage system for the resolution of custody disputes. This method, although utilizing attorneys, would remove custody disputes entirely from adversarial proceedings.

Mediation In my procedure, mediation would be required as the first step toward resolution of the child-custody dispute. This is the situation in California, where the conciliation courts routinely attempt to mediate all custody disputes at the outset. In recent years many other states have introduced mandatory mediation before parents are permitted to embark upon adversarial litigation.

In the system I propose, parents could choose to mediate their dispute within or outside the court system. They could avail themselves of the services of psychiatrists, psychologists, social workers, lawyers, mediators, arbitrators, pastoral counselors, clergymen, and others qualified to conduct such evaluations either privately or in clinics. Obviously, training programs and standards would have to be set up in order to ensure that only qualified mediators could be utilized at this stage. Parents involved in a custody dispute would also be free to avail themselves of similar services under the aegis of the court or of court-designated mental health clinics. These would provide mediation services at a fee appropriate to the parents' financial situation. In the course of the mediation each party would be free to consult with an attorney who represents that party's interests. Such attorneys, however, would not be people who would be committed to the adversarial method of resolving custody disputes; rather, they would be people who are not only committed to mediation but who might very well serve as mediators for other clients. These attorneys would be available to communicate with the mediator, either singly or together, in order to help resolve inequities or disputes. If the mediation is successful, then a formal parenting plan is drawn up and this is given to the attorney(ies) preparing the separation agreement. Because divorce is still a legal matter (and no doubt will be for the foreseeable future), the services of an attorney remain necessary. However, my hope is that other disputes related to the divorce (in addition to custody disputes) could also be resolved by mediation. Whether or not the parents are successful in accomplishing this, the custody dispute would not be dealt with by proceedings within the adversarial system.

Arbitration Mediation has its drawbacks. The most skilled mediator can make mistakes. Mediation may break down for a variety of reasons, one of the most common of which is the refusal by one or both parties to make full disclosure of finances. Or each spouse may be so convinced of the other's ineptitude as a parent that the necessary compromises may not be possible. The mediator's own psychiatric problems may interfere with the parents' ability to make the needed compromises. When mediation breaks down, most people today have no choice but to involve themselves in custody litigation. In the system I propose, when mediation fails, the parents would be required to submit their dispute to an arbitration panel within the court structure.

I believe that the best panel to deal with such a dispute would be one consisting of two mental health professionals and one attorney. The panel members would be selected by the parents from a list of properly qualified individuals provided by the court. (The training and experience requirements for such certification have yet to be determined.) The mental health professionals on the panel would be expected to conduct the kind of custody evaluation described elsewhere (Gardner, 1989). The lawyer would be involved in the legal aspects of the dispute and would draw up the panel's final decision in proper legal form.

There are many advantages to this system. Like a judge, the panel (especially the lawyer) would have the power to subpoena medical records, request financial documents, etc. This power is particularly necessary when there is reluctance or refusal by one or both parties to disclose pertinent information. Most important, the parents would meet directly with the panel members. Although the discussion would be free and open, the panel would still have the authority to prevent the proceedings from degenerating into a free-for-all. By having three panel members there could be no tie vote; the majority would prevail. Obviously, a panel of three is less likely to be biased than an individual mediator or judge.

Perhaps a more compelling reason to use the panel is the panel's data-collection process. Whereas a judge is confined by the constraints of the adversarial method of data collection (i.e., gathering of "evidence"), the proposed arbitration panel would be free to avail itself of the more flexible and far more appropriate procedures used by mental health professionals.

The panel would be free to bring in any parties who might be helpful, and such parties could include attorneys to provide independent representation. However, such attorneys would be required (like all other participants) to involve themselves in free and open discussion. They would not be permitted to impose upon the proceedings courtroom procedures of inquiry, which constrain open discussion and can obscure or hide important information. This would be a crucial difference between the panel's method of inquiry and that of the courtroom. Such independent representation might be especially useful, for example, for a passive wife who might not be able to hold her own against an overbearing husband. The panel could serve to protect such a person from being squelched and possibly exploited.

Appeals Panel The crucial question remains as to whether the findings and recommendations of the arbitration panel should be binding. On the one hand, three people can make a mistake, and it can be argued that the parents should be free to enter into adversarial proceedings in order to appeal to a higher authority. On the other hand, one could argue that the process has to end somewhere and that an arbitration panel, as the next step after mediation, is a good enough place to make final decisions in matters such as custody disputes.

At this point, I am in favor of a plan (again removed from adversarial proceedings) in which there would be the possibility of appeal to another panel of three individuals (again an attorney and two mental health professionals) who have significant experience in child-custody mediation and arbitration. This panel would have the power to make a final decision. Like the arbitration panel, the appeals panel members would be selected by the clients from a roster provided by the court. Many would be people with experience on arbitration panels.

The appeals panel would involve itself in a two-step process of review. The first step would be similar to that of traditional courts of appeal, wherein the members review documents from the lower-court level. At this stage the appeals panel would have the power to refuse to consider the case further, in which case the findings of the arbitration panel would be final. The appeals panel might direct the arbitration panel to collect further data or reconsider its decision because of certain factors. Or, after reviewing the arbitration panel's documents, the appeals panel might conclude that another hearing is warranted and could then hear the parties directly and conduct whatever evaluations were necessary.

The hearing could involve interviews as well as other forms of data collection similar to those used by the original arbitration panel. The appeals panel might even meet with the arbitration panel and the parents all together. The appeals panel, as well, might choose to hear parties brought in by the parents, and such parties might include attorneys serving as advocates. However, once again, traditional courtroom procedures of examination would be replaced by open and free discussion (moderated by the panel to prevent deterioration of the proceedings). Whereas traditional courts of appeal allow only lawyers to provide testimony, the appeals panel would have the power to interview directly those parties it considered useful to hear. And the decision of this appeals panel would be final.

In order to discourage frivolous use of the appeals process, panels would have to be quite stringent with regard to changing the recommendations of the arbitration panels. In addition, litigious individuals in the appeals process would be at risk of losing what they had previously won.

One possible deterrent to the "reflex appeal" would be the appeals panel's practice of reviewing the arbitration panel's records for the presence of perjury, slander, and libel. In all the years that I had been involved in divorce and custody litigation, there was hardly a case in which I did not see blatant examples of all of these practices. Yet not once was anyone ever prosecuted for these crimes. And not once was such behavior even brought to the attention of the litigants by the court. If the appeals panel were to establish for itself the reputation of reviewing the arbitration panel's records for such behavior, this too could serve as a deterrent to groundless appeals by disgruntled parties.

It should be noted that the three-step procedure I have outlined above (mediation, arbitration panel, and appeals panel) does not involve adversarial proceedings at any level. The system would protect clients from the polarization and spiraling of animosity that frequently accompany the utilization of adversarial procedures and contribute to the development and perpetuation of psychopathology. My proposal would replace the cumbersome and inefficient method of evidence gathering used by the courts with the more flexible and efficient data-collection process used by mental health professionals. The parents would be given the opportunity to choose their own panel, protecting them from the sense of impotence felt by parents who are "stuck" with a judge who all recognize to be ill equipped to deal appropriately with custody conflicts. In short, under my proposal parents choose their own judges. By requiring decisions to be made by the majority of a three-member panel, the likelihood of bias is reduced. Last, and most important, the system I propose precludes any possibility of adversarial proceedings for people involved in a custody dispute. The law would thereby protect them from involvement in a system that was never designed to deal with the question of who would serve as a better parent for children of divorce.

Due Process and Constitutional Rights

The system I propose does not deprive the parents of any of their constitutional rights of due process. They retain the right to representation by counsel at all three levels. The constitutional right of the accused to confront an accuser is protected. Even better, in this system the accuser is given the opportunity for direct confrontation of the accused, without the utilization of intermediaries (lawyers) and the restrictions of courtroom procedures. Although individuals now have the opportunity for such direct confrontations in the courtroom (if they act as their own attorneys), this is not commonly done. In the system I propose, the parents are essentially operating as their own attorneys. But even when they choose to bring in attorneys to represent them, the discussion will still be far freer than that found in the courtroom. Nowhere in the Constitution is anyone (including lawyers) given the right to subject another individual to the frustrations and indignities of yes/no questions. (I have sometimes wondered whether yes/no questions deprive witnesses of their right to freedom of speech.) The Constitution requires that such confrontations take place in the court of law. The whole system proposed here could very well be applied under the aegis of the court. The arbitration and appeals panels would either convene within the courthouse or in a location under its jurisdiction.

The constitutional right to a hearing before an impartial judge is protected in my proposed system. Here, the parents have not one but three "judges" (serving in a sense as a tribunal). And protection against bias is enhanced by the requirement that the majority vote will prevail. The requirement that two of the "judges" be mental health professionals is not only desirable for the purposes of the custody evaluation, but is in no way unconstitutional. Nowhere in the Constitution is anything said about educational or professional requirements to serve as a judge. In addition, the Constitution presumably guarantees a speedy trial. It requires a morbid expansion of the meaning of the word *"speedy"* to believe that this is true for the vast majority of litigants in custody disputes. My proposal is more likely to provide such speed, primarily because of the advantages of its method of data collection over that of traditional adversarial courtroom proceedings.

It is important that the reader of my proposal appreciate that it is just that: a proposal. It outlines what I consider to be a reasonable approach to the resolution of custody disputes. I am not claiming that it is perfect, and I suspect that if implemented it would probably require modification. Although the three-step procedure may appear cumbersome, there is no question that it would prove to be far more efficient and less expensive than adversarial proceedings. And although the plan is designed to protect disputing parents from injudicious judicial decisions, I suspect that the professionals involved in making the custody decisions, being human, will certainly make their share of mistakes.

However, I believe that the number of people harmed will be far less than the number inevitably traumatized by traditional adversarial litigation. Although the three-step procedure is most relevant to custody disputes, I believe that (with proper modifications) the model lends itself to application in other kinds of disputes as well, especially custody disputes in which there is a sex-abuse accusation.

ADDENDUM I

OUTLINE OF SEX ABUSE / CUSTODY
PROVISIONS DOCUMENT

Whenever possible, I make every reasonable attempt to serve as a court-appointed impartial examiner, rather than as an advocate, in sex-abuse litigation. I recognize that this is more easily accomplished in civil, as opposed to criminal, litigation. Furthermore, I make no promise beforehand to support the position of the inviting party.

Sex-abuse evaluations are of greatest use to the court when the examiner has the opportunity to interview the accuser, the accused, and the alleged child victim—individually and in combination, as warranted. This does not mean that the examiner will automatically place the alleged child victim and the accused in the room together, but should be given the opportunity to do so if he (she) considers such interviews warranted. The greater the number of compromises made with regard to this ideal, the less valuable will be the evaluator's services to the court.

Before accepting an invitation for involvement, I ask that the following steps be taken:

1) (The inviting party will do everything that is reasonably possible to have me appointed the court's impartial examiner. I recognize that this is much more easily accomplished in civil than criminal cases. The order will require the accuser, the accused, and the alleged child victim to participate in the evaluation. Because joint interviews are crucial to my evaluation,) the order shall specifically require all participants to cooperate in such interviews to the degree that I see fit. I will not necessarily interview together the child and the alleged abuser; rather, I must have the freedom to do so if I wish to. If a restraining order is in force, an order that prohibits one party from having any direct contact with the other, a specific waiver shall be included that will allow me to conduct such interviews.

2) If step #1 is not successfully accomplished, then the inviting parties will ask the court to order the unreceptive side to participate in the evaluation. Such order should require the evaluation of the accuser, the accused, and the alleged child victim(s). Although recognized in such circumstances as the expert of the inviting parties, I will still conduct the evaluation as if I were serving as an impartial examiner and therefore make no promise beforehand that I will support the position of the inviting parties, even though deemed by the court to be their advocate.

3) If step #2 is not successfully accomplished, my evaluation will be seriously compromised because I will not be given the opportunity to evaluate all involved parties. Under such circumstances, I will be willing to review materials and conduct whatever interviews I can in order to make a decision about whether or not I can support the inviting parties' position. If I can do so with conviction, I will be willing to testify in court on behalf of that side, with the full recognition that answers to some of my questions will have to be considered hypothetical.

My fee for conducting a sex-abuse evaluation is $250 per full hour of my time. Time spent in interviewing, as well as time expended in report preparation, dictation, telephone conversations, court preparation, and any other time involved in association with the evaluation will be billed at the $250 per hour rate. My fee for court appearances in the Greater New York City area is $500 per hour while in court, and $200 per hour travel time to and from my office. During the data-collection phase of the evaluation, payment shall be made at the time services are rendered. Payment for court appearances shall be made in advance—in accordance with estimates provided prior to the rendering of these services. My fee schedule for providing legal services beyond the Greater New York City area is available on request.

I also request at the outset an advance security deposit of $2500. This will not serve as an advance retainer, in that the aforementioned fees will not be drawn against it—unless there has been a failure to pay my fees. Of course, when my services are no longer warranted, this deposit (with proper adjustments) will be returned to the payer(s).

Please know that if you do wish to enlist my services, I will do my utmost to provide a thorough and fair evaluation.

Richard A. Gardner, M.D.
Clinical Professor of
Child Psychiatry
Columbia University
College of Physicians
and Surgeons

ADDENDUM II

**PROVISIONS FOR ACCEPTING AN
INVITATION TO SERVE AS AN IMPARTIAL
EXAMINER IN SEX-ABUSE/CUSTODY LITIGATION**

Whenever possible, I make every reasonable attempt to serve as a court-appointed impartial examiner, rather than as an advocate, in custody litigation in which there has been a sex-abuse accusation. In order to serve optimally in this capacity I must be free to avail myself of any and all information, from any source, that I consider pertinent and reasonable to have. In this way, I believe I can serve best the interests of children, parents, and other parties who may be involved in such litigation. Accordingly, before agreeing to serve in this capacity, the following conditions must be agreed upon by both litigants (the accuser and the accused):

1) The presiding judge will agree to appoint me impartial examiner to conduct an evaluation of the concerned parties. Because joint interviews are crucial to my evaluation, the order shall specifically require all participants to cooperate in such interviews to the degree that I see fit. I will not necessarily interview together the child and the alleged abuser; rather, I must have the freedom to do so if I wish to. If a restraining order is in force, an order that prohibits one party from having any direct contact with the other, a specific waiver shall be included that will allow me to conduct such interviews.

2) I will have available to interview *all* concerned parties for as many interviews (individual and in any combination) as I consider warranted. Generally, these would include such persons as the allegedly abused child, the alleged abuser, the accuser, and any other members of the child's family who are potential sources of information for me. I do not automatically place the alleged perpetrator and the alleged child victim in joint interview, but I must have the right to do so if I consider such an interview warranted. I do, however, consider joint interviews between the accuser and the accused to be crucial to my evaluation, so crucial that I will refuse to accept an invitation to conduct an evaluation if I am not permitted to conduct such joint interviews. In addition, I will have the freedom to invite any and all other parties whom I would consider possible sources of useful information. The decision to inter-

view such additional parties will be based solely on the potential value of their contributions to the data-collection process and not on whether one party is represented by more such people than the other.

3) Information will be gathered primarily from the aforementioned clinical interviews. Although I do not routinely use formal psychological tests, in some evaluations I have found certain psychological tests to be useful. Accordingly, the involved parties shall agree to take any and all psychological tests that I would consider helpful. In addition, they will agree to have the child take such tests if I consider them warranted. Some of these tests will be administered by me, but others by a psychologist of my choosing if I do not consider myself qualified to administer a particular psychological test.

4) In order to allow me the freedom of inquiry necessary for serving optimally parties involved in sex-abuse/custody litigation, the parties shall agree to a modification of the traditional rules of confidentiality. Specifically, I must be given the freedom to reveal to one party what has been told to me by the other (at my discretion) so that I will have full opportunity to explore all pertinent points with both parties. This does not mean that I will not respect certain privacies or that I will automatically reveal all information provided me—only that I reserve the right to make such revelations if I consider them warranted for the purpose of collecting the most meaningful data.

5) The parties shall agree to sign any and all releases necessary for me to obtain reports from others, e.g., psychiatrists, psychologists, social workers, teachers, school officials, pediatricians, hospitals (general and psychiatric), etc. This includes past records as well as reports from professionals who may be involved with any of the parties at the time of the litigation. Although I may choose not to request a particular report, I must have the freedom to request any and all such reports, if I consider them useful sources of information.

6) My fee for conducting a sex-abuse/custody evaluation is $250 per full hour of my time. Time spent in interviewing as well as time expended in report preparation, dictation, telephone conversations, court preparation, and any other time invested in association with the evaluation will also be billed at the $250 per hour fee. My fee for court and

deposition appearances is $500 per hour while in court and at the deposition site, and $200 per hour travel time to and from my office. During the data-collection phase of the evaluation, payments shall be made at the time services are rendered. Payments for the final conference at which my findings and recommendations are presented (item #9 below), the court report, and my court appearance shall be made in advance—in accordance with estimates provided prior to the rendering of these services.

Prior to the initial interview the payer(s) will deposit with me a check (in my name) for $2,500. This shall be deposited in the Northern Valley-Englewood Savings and Loan Association branch in Cresskill, New Jersey, in my name, in a day-to-day interest bearing account. This money, with accrued interest (taxable to the payer), shall be returned *after* a final decision has been made by the court and after I have received a letter from *both* of the attorneys that my services are no longer being enlisted.

This payment is a security deposit. It will not serve as an advance retainer, in that the aforementioned fees will not be drawn against it, unless there has been a failure to pay my fees. It also serves to reassure a nonpayer that my objectivity will not be compromised by the fear that if I do not support the paying party, my fee will not be paid.

The average total cost for an evaluation is generally in the $5000-$7,000 range. Although this figure may initially appear high, it is generally far less costly than protracted litigation. If as a result of the evaluation the litigation is shortened (often the case) or the parties decide not to litigate further over custody and/or the sex-abuse allegation, then the net savings may be significant. It is very difficult, if not impossible, to predict the cost of a particular evaluation, because I cannot know beforehand how many interviews will be warranted and whether or not I will be asked to testify in court.

On occasion, I am invited to conduct evaluations in cities at varying distances from Cresskill, New Jersey. This generally entails situations in which there is a choice between my traveling to the family's location and all interviewees traveling to New Jersey and acquiring temporary accommodations in the area of my office. Although I prefer that the evaluation take place in my office, I have on occasion agreed to conduct the evaluation elsewhere. However, my fees for such evaluations are higher than for those conducted in my office and are determined by the distance I have to travel and the time I am being asked to be away from my office. My fee schedule for such distant evaluations is available on request.

7) Both attorneys are invited to send to me any material that they consider useful to me. I am particularly interested in reviewing videotapes of interviews conducted by previous examiners with allegedly sexually abused child(ren).

8) After receiving 1) the court order signed by the presiding judge, 2) the signed statements (page 8) from both parties signifying agreement to these provisions for my conducting the evaluation, and 3) the $2,500 deposit, I will notify both parties that I am available to proceed with the evaluation as rapidly as is feasible. I generally cannot promise to meet a specific deadline because I cannot know in advance how many interviews will be required, nor can I predict how flexible the parties will be regarding availability for appointments I offer.

9) Upon completion of my evaluation—and *prior to* the preparation of my final report—I generally meet with both parents together and present them my findings and recommendations. This gives them the opportunity to correct any distortions they believe I may have and/or alter my opinion before it becomes finalized in my report. In addition, it saves the parties from the unnecessary and prolonged tension associated with wondering what my findings are.

Both attorneys are invited to attend this conference. However, this invitation should be considered withdrawn if only one attorney wishes to attend because the presence of only one attorney would obviously place the nonrepresented parent in a compromised position. When a guardian ad litem has been appointed by the court, he or she will also be invited to attend this conference. Before accepting this invitation attorneys should appreciate that the discussion will be completely free and open. Accordingly, during this conference it would be improper for an attorney in any way whatsoever to restrict or discourage the client from answering questions or participating in the discussion. On occasion, the litigants have used this conference as a forum for resolving their dispute and avoiding thereby the formidable expense and psychological trauma of courtroom litigation. After this conference the final report is prepared and sent simultaneously to the court, attorneys, and parents.

10) After this conference I strictly refrain from any further communication with either parent or any other party involved in the evaluation. However, I am willing to discuss any aspect of the case with *both* attorneys at the same time, either personally or by conference telephone call. Such communication may occur at any time from the end of the aforementioned conference to the end of the trial. This practice enables me to continue to provide input to the attorneys regarding what I consider to be in the child's best interests. And this may be especially important during the trial. However, in order to preserve my status as impartial, any information I provide either attorney is only given under circumstances in which the other is invited to participate.

11) When there has been a significant passage of time between the submission of my report and the trial date, I will generally invite the primary participating parties for an interview update prior to my court appearance. This conference enables me to acquaint myself with developments that succeeded my report and ensures that my presentation in court will include the most recent information. All significant adult participants will be invited to this meeting and on occasion one or more of the children (especially teenagers). This conference will be held as long as at least one party wishes to attend.

My experience has been that conducting the evaluation in the manner described above provides me with the optimum conditions for providing the court with a thorough and objective recommendation.

SERVING AS AN ADVOCATE

12) Often one party will invite my services as an impartial examiner and the other will refuse to participate voluntarily. On occasion, the inviting party has then requested that the court appoint me impartial examiner and order the reluctant side to participate. Generally, there are three ways in which courts respond to this request:

A. The court responds affirmatively and appoints me the impartial examiner. In such cases I then proceed in accordance with the above provisions (#1-#11).

B. The court is not willing to formally designate me its appointed impartial examiner, but rather orders the reluctant side to cooperate in interviews with me as if I were the advocate of the initiator. (This usually occurs when the presiding judge orders both parents to be evaluated by each one's selected adversary examiner.) In such cases, I still do not view myself to be serving automatically as the advocate of the initiating party. Rather, I make it understood to all concerned that I will proceed as closely as possible with the type of evaluation I conduct when serving as impartial examiner—*even to the point of testifying in court as an advocate of the initially reluctant party.* The party who initially invited me, however, will still have the obligation to pay for my report as well as my court testimony, whether or not it supports that party's position. I believe that this plan ensures my input to the court regarding what I consider to be in the child's best interests and precludes my serving merely as a hired advocate.

C. The court refuses to order my participation but recognizes the right of the inviting party to enlist my involvement as an advocate. In such cases I proceed in accordance with provision 13.

13) A. On occasion, I am willing to *consider* serving as an advocate in custody/visitation litigation. However, such participation will only be considered after evidence has been submitted to me that: 1) the nonparticipating side has been invited to participate and has refused and 2) the court has refused to order such involvement. If I do then suspect that the inviting party's position merits my consideration, I would be willing to interview that party with no promise beforehand that I will support his (her) position. On occasion I have seen fit to support the participating party's position, because it was obvious to me that the children's needs would be served best by my advocacy and/or not to do so would have deprived them of sorely needed assistance. On other occasions I have concluded that I could not serve with conviction as an advocate of the requesting party and so have refused further services to the client.

B. If I do decide to serve as an advocate, I ask for the standard $2,500 security deposit, which is dealt with as described in item #6. Furthermore, if in the course of my evaluation in which I am serving as an advocate, the nonparticipating party decides belatedly to participate I will, at that point, no longer consider myself automatically committed to serve as an advocate for the original party. Rather, I will conduct the evaluation, as far as possible, in accordance with the provisions for my serving as an impartial examiner—even to the point of testifying in court in support of the belated participant. Before interviewing the belated participant, however, all parties will have to agree upon any possible modifications of the fee-paying arrangement that may be warranted

Richard A. Gardner, M.D.

I have read the above, discussed the provisions with my attorney, and agree to participate in the evaluation procedures delineated above. I agree to pay __% of the $2,500 advance security deposit and __% of the fees in accordance with the aforementioned payment schedules. I recognize the possibility that Dr. Gardner may *not* ultimately support my position in the litigation. Nevertheless, I will still fulfill my obligation to pay __% of his fees. I appreciate that this may entail the payment of fees associated with his preparing reports that do not support my position and even testifying in court in support of my adversary.

Date: _____   _____
Parent's Signature

ADDENDUM III

OPTIMAL ARRANGEMENTS FOR INTERVIEWING CHILDREN ALLEGED TO HAVE BEEN SEXUALLY ABUSED AT SITES BEYOND THE GREATER NEW YORK CITY AREA

When I interview children who are alleged to have been sexually abused, at sites requiring travel from my office, I generally prefer that my interviews be videotaped and that attorneys, parents, and other appropriate parties view the interview in a nearby room via a video monitor connected to the camera in the interviewing room. For children under seven or eight, it is important for parents to bring along a babysitter to watch the child during those segments of the evaluation in which I interview the parents. The children and babysitter must be situated in a third room in that it would be inappropriate for them to be viewing the adult's interviews via video monitor, especially because sexual issues may be focused on.

Obviously, the video camera and operator must be in the same room in which I conduct interviews. My experience has been that a video camera and operator in the room is generally not a distraction after the first few minutes. Preferably, the video camera should be operated by a professional person. Please be sure that the video camera enables recording of the hour and minute and, if possible, the date. Obviously, if such timing is not present on the videotape display, it is much more difficult to pinpoint particular segments, especially in the courtroom. Also, please be sure that the video camera is so positioned that it can include three or four people simultaneously in that it is important that all people involved in the conversation be within the camera's range during recording. I generally sit at a table (3' x 6' or a comparable size) so that I can comfortably take notes, and the parties being interviewed sit with me at the same table.

I prefer that attorneys—representing both sides—be present throughout the whole course of the interview. If a guardian ad litem is involved, I would also appreciate his (her) being present throughout the course of the interview. Such involvement may prove useful for resolving difficulties that may arise during the course of the evaluation. And this may make the difference between my continuing the interview or having to interrupt it and possibly coming back for its continuation at another time, obviously at great inconvenience and expense for interviews conducted at significant distances from my office. I welcome the opportunity to interview parents because it gives them the opportunity for input, especially after they have viewed the first segment of the child's interview. In addition, if the child wants the parent to accompany him (her) for any reason, they would then be readily available for such participation. The child's knowledge that the parents are viewing from another room can also be reassuring and lessen interview anxieties.

In some cases, a restraining order is in place that prohibits the sex-abuse suspect from having any contact at all with the children. Although I do not routinely conduct joint interviews with alleged perpetrators and their alleged victims, there are certain situations in which I have found such interviews useful, especially in family situations in which the children are quite familiar with the suspect. Because joint interviews are extremely useful in all evaluations, it is important that I have the *option* to conduct a joint interview between the suspect and the child, with or without other parties present, as warranted, Accordingly, when such restraining orders are in place, it is most important that everything be done to obtain a court order lifting that restriction for the purposes of my evaluation.

Most often, I accomplish my evaluation in one day in which I typically begin interviewing at around 8:30 or 9:00 in the morning and by 2:30 or 3:00 P.M. have enough data to come up with preliminary conclusions. Generally, this could be accomplished if we take only ten to fifteen-minute breaks and send out for sandwiches. I then meet with the attorneys from mid- to late afternoon and then leave. However, in some situations, especially when there is more than one child to evaluate, this cannot be accomplished in one day and I may require one-and-a-half or even two days. In such circumstances, the conference with the attorneys and clients is conducted at the end of the second day. These conferences give clients and attorneys opportunity for input before preparing my final report. In some cases (such as lawsuits in which damages are being demanded), such interviews are generally not conducted. In either case, a decision regarding such a conference is generally made prior to my departure from New Jersey.

On occasion, a one-way mirror set-up is available. Under these circumstances the same procedures are generally followed, with the exception that the camera operator is behind the one-way mirror with the observers, rather than in front of it.

ADDENDUM IV

OPTIMAL ARRANGEMENTS FOR INTERVIEWNG CHILDREN ALLEGED TO HAVE BEEN SEXUALLY ABUSED

(Office Interview in Cresskill, New Jersey)

When I interview in my office patients who have alleged to have been sexually abused, patients who are also involved in lawsuits, I stipulate that the interviews be videotaped. Courts are becoming increasingly appreciative of the value of such videotapes, to the point where in some jurisdictions such videotaping is required. I generally invite the patient's attorney and selected third parties (such as the patient's parents and the opposing attorney) to view the interview via a video monitor in another room. All substantive aspects of the interview are videotaped.

I welcome the opportunity to interview parents because it gives them the opportunity for input, especially after they have viewed the first segment of the child's interview. In addition, if the child wants the parents to accompany him (her) for any reason, they would then be readily available for such participation. For children under seven or eight, it is important for parents to bring along a babysitter to watch the child during those segments of the evaluation in which I interview the parents.

My equipment enables me to simultaneously make three copies of the master videotape. When the interview is over, one copy of the tape(s) will be given to the child's attorney, one copy to the attorney who represents the opposing side, and one copy will be kept in my office (along with the master).

ADDENDUM V

**SUGGESTED QUESTIONS FOR
DR. RICHARD A. GARDNER'S VOIR DIRE**

I suggest you use these questions regarding your inquiry about my professional background. I believe my answers will provide a healthy balance between "underkill" and "overkill."

Dr. Gardner, I'd like to ask you some questions about your professional background:

Where did you receive your undergraduate education and what was your date of graduation?

Where did you attend medical school and what was your date of graduation?

Where did you intern and what were your dates of internship?

Would you please tell the court about your subsequent training in general psychiatry?

Would you please tell the court about your subsequent training in child psychiatry?

Did you receive any distinctions when you trained in child psychiatry? If so, what were they?

Would you please tell the court about your training in psychoanalysis?

Are you board certified in psychiatry?

In what year were you certified?

Are you board certified in child psychiatry?

In what year were you certified?

Did you receive any distinctions when you took your board certifying examinations in child psychiatry? If so, what were they?

Do you have any hospital appointments? If so, please describe them.

Do you have any medical school faculty appointments? If so, please describe them.

Do you have any past teaching or medical school appointments? If so, describe them.

Are you in private practice?

Since when have you been in private practice?

What is the breakdown between your therapeutic work and your forensic work?

Have you written any books?

How many books have you written?

Who were the publishers?

You mentioned that Creative Therapeutics is your own publishing company. How did it come about that you have published some of your books through your own company?

Do you still publish books through other companies, other than Creative Therapeutics?

When was the last time you published a book with another publisher, other than Creative Therapeutics?

Please name those books that are particularly pertinent to these proceedings, especially those related to your expertise.

Have you written any articles?

Approximately how many professional articles have you written?

Dr. Gardner, can you tell us what is meant by peer-reviewed articles?

How many of your articles have been peer reviewed?

What are the other categories of articles you have written?

Can you please describe some of these, especially those pertinent to these proceedings.

Have you provided lectures to professional groups?

When did you first begin lecturing professionally?

How many professional lectures would you say you have given over the years?

Can you name some of the professional groups to whom you have lectured?

In how many states have you provided professional lectures?

Have you lectured abroad?

Can you name some of the cities and countries in which you have provided professional lectures abroad?

Have you ever testified in court previously?

When did you first begin providing psychiatric testimony in courtrooms and under what circumstances?

Will you trace briefly your subsequent experiences which involved court testimony, especially testimony related to issues involved in this case?

To the best of your recollection, about how many times do you recall having testified in court?

To the best of your recollection, in how many states have you provided testimony?

Have you ever testified in any foreign countries? If so, in which countries and cities?

Has a court ever ruled that you are not qualified to provide expert testimony?

Your honor, I submit that Dr. Gardner is qualified to provide testimony in these proceedings.

Please do not let the opposing attorney interrupt or shorten this presentation by claiming that he (she) recognizes me as an expert. If that happens, I would suggest comments along these lines:

Your honor, I believe it is extremely important for the court to have a complete appreciation of Dr. Gardner's expertise before he provides his testimony. This is especially the case because I have good reason to believe that comments about Dr. Gardner's qualifications will be made by subsequent witnesses at a time when he will not be present for me to question him again on redirect examinations.

REFERENCES

Alexander, G. J. (1984), Trial by champion. *Santa Clara Law Review*,34(3):545–564.

American Bar Association (1994), Membership Report, February 1995. Chicago: American Bar Association.

Bazelon, D. L. (1974), The perils of wizardry. *The American Journal of Psychiatry,* 131:1317–1322.

Coogler, O. J. (1978), *Structured Mediation in Divorce Settlement.*Lexington, Massachusetts: Lexington Books (D.C. Heath and Company).

Daubert v. Merrell Dow Pharmaceuticals, Inc. 113 SCt 2786, 1993.*Encyclopedia Britannica, Macropedia* (1982), Laws of Evidence, 7:1–6.

Encyclopedia Brittanica, Macropedia (1982), Legal Profession,10:779–784.

Fain, H. M. (1977), Family Law—"whither now?" *Journal of Divorce*, 1(1):31–42.

Fisher, R. and Ury, W. (1981), *Getting to Yes*. Boston: Houghton Mifflin Co.

Folberg, J. and Taylor, A. (1984), *Mediation: A Comprehensive Guide to Resolving Conflicts Without Litigation*. San Francisco: Jossey-Bass Publishers.

Frye v. United States 54 App. D.C. 46, 47 293F 1013, 1014 (1923).

Gardner, R. A. (1970), *The Boys and Girls Book About Divorce*. New York: Jason Aronson, Inc.

———— (1971), *The Boys and Girls Book About Divorce* (paperback edition). New York: Bantam Books.

———— (1976), *Psychotherapy of Children of Divorce*. New York:Jason Aronson, Inc.

_____ (1977), *The Parents Book About Divorce.* New York: Doubleday and Co., Inc.

_____ (1978), *The Boys and Girls Book About One-Parent Families.* New York: G. P. Putnam's Sons.

_____ (1979), *The Parents Book About Divorce* (paperback edition). New York: Bantam Books.

_____ (1981), *The Boys and Girls Book About Stepfamilies.* New York: Bantam Books.

_____ (1982), *Family Evaluation in Child Custody Litigation.* Cresskill, New Jersey: Creative Therapeutics, Inc.

_____ (1983), *The Boys and Girls Book About One-Parent Families* (paperback edition). New York: Bantam Books.

_____ (1986), *Child Custody Litigation: A Guide for Parents and Mental Health Professionals.* Cresskill, New Jersey: Creative Therapeutics, Inc.

_____ (1987), *The Parental Alienation Syndrome and the Differentiation Between Fabricated and Genuine Sex Abuse Allegations.* Cresskill, New Jersey: Creative Therapeutics, Inc.

_____ (1988), *Psychotherapy with Adolescents.* Cresskill, New Jersey: Creative Therapeutics, Inc.

_____ (1989), *Family Evaluation in Child Custody Mediation, Arbitration, and Litigation.* Cresskill, New Jersey: Creative Therapeutics, Inc.

_____ (1991a), *The Parents Book About Divorce, Second Edition.* Cresskill, New Jersey: Creative Therapeutics, Inc.

_____ (1991b), *The Parents Book About Divorce, Second Edition* (paperback edition). New York: Bantam Books.

_____ (1991c), *Sex Abuse Hysteria: Salem Witch Trials Revisited.* Cresskill, New Jersey: Creative Therapeutics, Inc.

_____ (1992a), *The Parental Alienation Syndrome: A Guide for Mental Health and Legal Professionals.* Cresskill, New Jersey: Creative Therapeutics, Inc.

_____ (1992b), *True and False Accusations of Child Sex Abuse: A Guide for Legal and Mental Health Professionals.* Cresskill, New Jersey: Creative Therapeutics, Inc.

_____ (1992c), *The Psychotherapeutic Techniques of Richard A. Gardner.* Cresskill, New Jersey: Creative Therapeutics, Inc.

_____ (1995), *Protocols for the Sex-Abuse Evaluation.* Cresskill, New

Jersey: Creative Therapeutics, Inc.

Hathaway, S. R. and McKinley, J. C. (1989), *Minnesota Multiphasic Personality Inventory-2*. Minneapolis, Minnesota: University of Minnesota Press.

Haynes, J. M. (1981), *Divorce Mediation: A Practical Guide for Therapists*. New York: Springer Publishing Co.

Lambuth, D. (1923), *The Golden Book on Writing*. Hanover, New Hampshire: Dartmouth College Press.

Landsman, S. (1983), A brief survey of the adversary system. *Ohio State Law Journal*, 44(3):713–739.

Lieberman, J. K. (1983), *The Litigious Society*. New York: Basic Books.

Millon, T. (1987), *Millon Clinical Multiaxial Inventory-II (MCMI-II)*. Minneapolis, Minnesota: National Computer Systems.

Murray, H. (1936), *The Thematic Apperception Test*. New York: The Psychological Corp.

Neef, M. and Nagel, S. (1974), The adversary nature of the American legal system from a historical perspective. *New York Law Forum*, 20:123–164.

Riskin, L. L. (1982), Mediation and lawyers. *Ohio State Law Journal*, 43:29–60.

Rorschach, H. (1921), *The Rorschach Test*. New York: The Psychological Corp.

Saxe, D. B. (1975), Some reflections on the interface of law and psychiatry in child custody cases. *Journal of Psychiatry and Law*, 3(4):501–514.

Summit, R. C. (1983), The child sexual abuse accommodation syndrome. *Child Abuse and Neglect*, 7:177–193.

Underwager, R. and Wakefield, H. (1993), A paradigm shift for expert witnesses. *Issues in Child Abuse Accusations*, 5(3):156–167.

United States Census Bureau, *Current Population Reports*, Series P-25-1104. Population Projections of the United States by Age, Sex, Race, and Hispanic Origin: 1993–2050. Washington, D.C.: U.S. Census Bureau.

Watson, A. S. (1969), The children of Armageddon: problems of custody following divorce. *Syracuse Law Review*, 21:55–86.

AUTHOR INDEX

SUBJECT INDEX